A RAINBOW
IN THE NIGHT

By Dominique Lapierre

Once upon a Time in The Soviet Union

A Thousand Suns

Beyond Love

The City of Joy

By Dominique Lapierre and Xavier Moro

Five Past Midnight in Bhopal

By Dominique Lapierre and Larry Collins

Is New York Burning?

The Fifth Horseman

Freedom at Midnight

O Jerusalem

. . . Or I'll Dress You in Mourning

Is Paris Burning?

A RAINBOW IN THE NIGHT

THE TUMULTUOUS BIRTH OF

SOUTH AFRICA

DOMINIQUE LAPIERRE

New York Times Bestselling Author of *The City of Joy*
and Coauthor of *Is Paris Burning?*

TRANSLATED FROM FRENCH BY KATHRYN SPINK
WITH RESEARCH ASSISTANCE FROM XAVIER MORO

DA CAPO PRESS
A Member of the Perseus Books Group

Designed by Pauline Brown
Set in 12 point Fairfield Light by the Perseus Books Group

Cataloging-in-Publication data for this book are available from the Library of Congress.

First Da Capo Press edition 2009
Originally published in French as *Un arc-en-ciel dans la nuit*
by Editions Robert Laffont
Hardcover ISBN: 978-0-306-81847-9
International Paperback ISBN: 978-0-306-81882-0

Published by Da Capo Press
A Member of the Perseus Books Group
www.dacapopress.com

Da Capo Press books are available at special discounts for bulk purchases in the
United States by corporations, institutions, and other organizations. For more information, please contact the Special Markets Department at the Perseus Books Group,
2300 Chestnut Street, Suite 200, Philadelphia, PA 19103, or call (800) 810-4145,
ext. 5000, or e-mail special.markets@perseusbooks.com.

10 9 8 7 6 5 4 3 2 1

*To Helen Lieberman
and to all those—whites, blacks, and coloreds—
who put an end to apartheid oppression and
brought about the triumph of freedom,
unity, truth, and reconciliation*

CONTENTS

AUTHOR'S NOTE

WHEN I WROTE *A Rainbow in the Night*, I did not set out to compile an exhaustive history of South Africa. Rather, I wanted to recount, as accurately as possible, a powerful human epic. Much of the information contained in this book is the product of extensive personal research and has not been published previously. I would like to point out, however, that to make the account more vivid, I have chosen to dramatize the proceedings of a secret meeting among the architects of apartheid. This reconstruction is nevertheless based on the historical record and grounded in careful research. For additional information on my sources and a list of selected readings on South Africa, please refer to the bibliography at the end of the book.

—D. L.

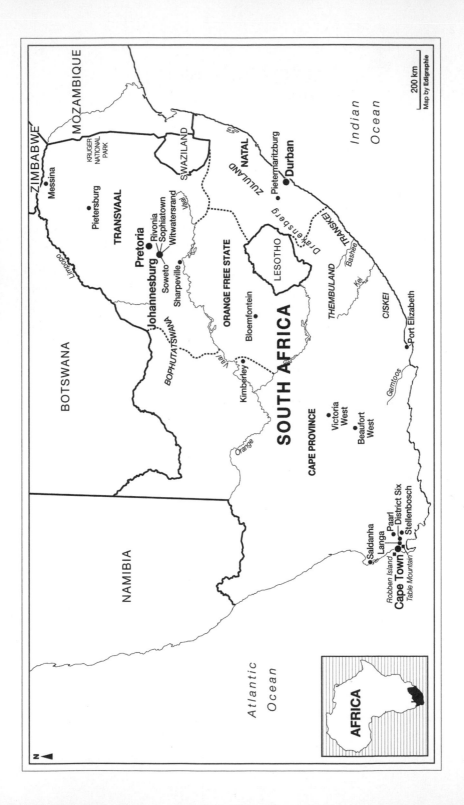

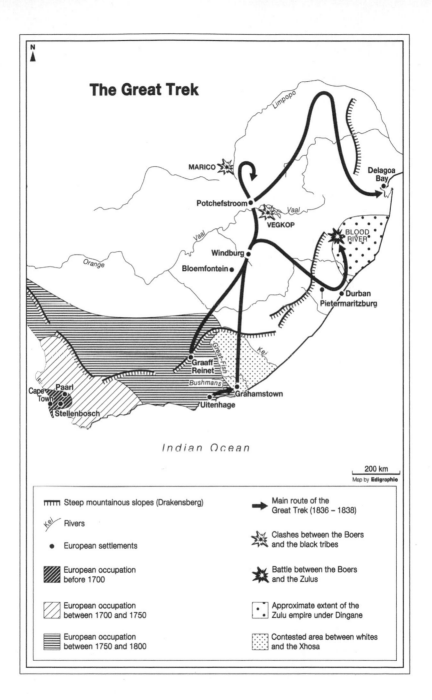

The Great Trek

N

MARICO

Potchefstroom

VEGKOP

Vaal

Vaal

BLOOD RIVER

Orange

Windburg

Bloemfontein

Delagoa Bay

Durban
Pietermaritzburg

Great Fish

Kei

Graaff Reinet

Bushmans

Grahamstown

Uitenhage

Cape Town

Paarl

Stellenbosch

Indian Ocean

Limpopo

200 km

Map by **Edigraphie**

⊤⊤⊤ Steep mountainous slopes (Drakensberg)		➤ Main route of the Great Trek (1836 – 1838)	
Kei Rivers		✺ Clashes between the Boers and the black tribes	
● European settlements		✸ Battle between the Boers and the Zulus	
▨ European occupation before 1700		⬚ Approximate extent of the Zulu empire under Dingane	
⬜ European occupation between 1700 and 1750		⬚ Contested area between whites and the Xhosa	
☰ European occupation between 1750 and 1800			

Each one of us is as intimately attached
to the soil of this beautiful country
as are the famous jacaranda trees of Pretoria
and the mimosa trees of the bushweld . . .
—a rainbow nation at peace with itself and
the world.

—NELSON MANDELA

One

In Search of
a New Promised Land

PILLAGE, RAPE, MURDER: it was a sixteenth-century crusade against heresy so violent it was almost unique in history. Holland's northern provinces were engulfed in flames and blood, occupied by savage troops sent from pious Spain. Day and night, the stakes burned thousands who followed the new religion preached by the monk Martin Luther, who had just made his stand against Rome and its avaricious pope. Luther's revolt was swiftly followed by another, spread by an austere, long-nosed Picardian with a goatee and a tight fur collar. From his refuge in Geneva, the theologian John Calvin sent out hundreds of thousands of copies of his manifesto seeking to make the Bible recognized as the unique source of faith and as revealing that God had expressly chosen certain people to have dominion over the whole of creation.

The Bible! For men and women in the Dutch lowlands trying to wrest their freedom from the papist legions, it was already their beacon. And now came messengers from Geneva informing them that they were the new children of Israel, chosen by God to liberate their land, as the Hebrews had once won the land of Canaan. Nothing could have strengthened their will to survive more than this affirmation that they belonged to a chosen people. "For you are a people holy unto the Lord! Thou shalt not be affrighted for the Lord thy God is among you . . . His angel is fighting at your side!" recited the bearded iconoclast's emissaries in the churches that had been hastily turned into Protestant places of worship. Citing the Holy Scriptures, they told the rebels that after their subjection to the Spanish crown and the papal tiara, they were now ready, like the patriarchs of the twelve tribes of Israel, to conquer their promised land. "If Yahweh has chosen you," they proclaimed, "it is not because you are the most populous race on earth, but because you are the smallest." Then, quoting Deuteronomy, they exclaimed, "Every place whereon the soles of your feet shall tread shall be yours, and there shall be your frontier."

Twenty centuries earlier God had sent the emperor Cyrus to release the Jews from captivity in Babylon. Now God sent William of Orange to liberate his captive people in the Dutch provinces. In half the time it took Joshua to seize the promised land, the Calvinist William rid his new homeland of its Spanish tyrants, transforming seven modest provinces into a vibrant republic and one of the world's most modern and powerful states. The prophet Calvin had not been mistaken. God had indeed chosen little Holland for a privileged destiny. The Batavian people would remember this grace for centuries until the day when their descendants, condemned to survive amid other people, would commit one of the greatest crimes in history. But in the early 1600s that fateful moment was still far off. "Blessed is he whose transgression is forgiven," the psalm reassured the new Dutch Reformed Church congregations. Along the North Sea coast, in the lowlands and towns of Zeeland and Frisia, a golden age was about to dawn, and Amsterdam was its New Jerusalem. In less than twenty years Holland's capital would become the cultural, artistic, and financial center of Europe. Stimulated by the spiritual and intellectual energy drawn from biblical texts and Calvin's writings, it was open to all cultures, all trades, and all religions. Masterpieces (and what masterpieces!) soon evoked this era of vibrant optimism, reflected in the powerful canvases of Rembrandt, Frans Hals, Vermeer, and Bruegel. Life in Dutch society may have continued to bear the stamp of Calvinist Puritanism, but the austere facades of the new patrician dwellings concealed unequalled luxury. The somber clothing seemed to exclude all frivolity but was belied by the sumptuous silk and satin fabrics worn by the notables of the capital.

The small republic's economic prosperity became evident as large companies were established through the issuing of stock. The Dutch East India Company, founded in 1602, secured a monopoly on trade throughout Asia, especially in spices—cloves, cinnamon, and pepper in particular. It was granted the right to open trading posts, deal with local rulers, and install armed forces wherever it wished to establish itself. Soon amassing 150 merchant vessels and some 40 warships, the Company became a state within the state that had absolute control over the greatest trading enterprise of its day. Its directors were a council of seventeen lords in black satin doublets and white silk collarettes, the Heeren XVII. Their headquarters was an imposing patrician-style building on the banks of the Kloveniers Burgwal canal. In the year 1653 alone, the value of the cargo they traded exceeded the budget for Louis XIV's France.

This commercial supremacy allowed Holland to enrich itself through colonial conquest. In 1651 the maps on the walls of the Council of Seventeen's chamber showed no shortage of territory to colonize, whether in Africa, America, or even Asia. A people reminded every Sunday of their God-given exceptional destiny did not question setting off to occupy some other corner of the globe, as they did when they seized the island of Manhattan and founded the city of New Amsterdam. To what new destination and on what mission would the Heeren XVII's caravels be headed at the end of that year 1651?

An energetic fellow, over six feet two, dressed in a sober black woolen doublet with an embroidered white collar, was about to find out. With a thick shock of brown curls falling onto his shoulders and a determined look under a wide forehead and bushy eyebrows, thirty-three-year-old Jan van Riebeeck exemplified the kind of adventurer Frans Hals liked to paint. The son of a renowned Amsterdam surgeon and a qualified surgeon himself, he had put down his forceps and scalpels to travel the world with his wife, Maria, and their children in the service of the Company. The Seventeen had just recalled him from his post as chief administrator in the Indonesian city of Batavia, which he had helped to found. They had new ambitious plans for their protégé. Jan van Riebeeck was thrilled to be setting off on another adventure. Having read the Bible and listened to Calvin's prophecies with patriotic fervor, he was ready to serve his country's grand designs. "Ask of me and I will make the nations your heritage," the psalmist assured. The young Dutchman had no doubt that cold morning in December 1651: the Council of Lords would send him on a mission of conquest.

★

POOR VAN RIEBEECK! Farming lettuce! That was his mission on the southern tip of the African continent. The Company explained that its crews aboard the spice ships were being decimated by scurvy, a scourge even more murderous than pirates, corsairs, and rival countries. If unchecked, this blight would paralyze the world's premier naval fleet and Holland would be ruined. Van Riebeeck knew from experience what terror a serious outbreak of scurvy could cause on ship decks and in their sleeping quarters. The specter of poor wretches bleeding and feverish with their gums swollen and spongy, their limbs rigid as iron bars, still haunted him. He knew that a diet rich in vegetables, fruit, and fresh meat would prevent the fatal illness.

Still, the young Dutchman was keenly disappointed. From Calvin's teaching, he knew God had chosen his native people for great work. Now he was being told that this would not be his vocation. The five caravels under his command would not be carrying cannons or powder kegs or soldiers, but only a few muskets for self-defense. Their cargo would be spades and picks, lettuce seeds, rice, and wheat for planting, and butcher's knives to cut up locally raised sheep and goats. The men in black satin doublets and white collarettes did not dream of colonial conquest. To console their frustrated protégé, they told him what the sixty shipwrecked people off the *Nieuw Haarlem*, one of the Company's three-masters, found during their enforced stop near his African destination: an abundance of fresh water, fish, wild antelope, domestic cattle, and even, at certain times of the year, herds of seals and whales. In short, it was a kind of earthly paradise. This idyllic description did little to satisfy Van Riebeeck. What stance would he take toward the local population? The response was emphatic: he was to avoid any contact with the indigenous people beyond offering them gifts and trinkets to barter for fresh meat. No other relations, no attempt to educate, convert, or subjugate. Above all, no fraternization. The native people were "foreigners" and should remain so. Holland's only objective was to gain a foothold on a small piece of supposedly uninhabited southern Africa and supply its ships sailing to the Indies with fresh produce. He should carry out this mission "with his back to the rest of the continent." There was nothing heroic about it. The disappointed young Dutchman setting out to plant lettuce could never have imagined he was about to write the first chapter in the history of a country, which did not yet exist: South Africa.

★

"TABLE MOUNTAIN ONE MILE TO PORT!" The lookout's cry from the observation mast of the *Drommedaris* caused a commotion on deck. Jan van Riebeeck's caravel had sailed from Amsterdam 105 days previously in the company of four other four-hundred-ton ships. On the morning of April 6, 1652, a miraculous calm prevailed around the African peninsula, which the Portuguese, who had lost so many men on its rocks, had named the Cape of Storms and later the Cape of Good Hope. Even the "Southeastern," the brutal wind that darkened the sun with black clouds and sent the Indian Ocean's swell crashing against swells of the Atlantic in gigantic peaks of foam, was surprisingly calm. The new arrivals dropped anchor beneath the majestic table-shaped mountain whose sides plunge into the transparent turquoise waters of the bay and were struck at once by the beauty of the natural world that greeted them. This narrow peninsula was a pristine realm of forest and flowers, ferns, and aloe bushes. Inhabiting this tropical paradise were hordes of exotic multicolored birds.

Even more astonishing were the animals they encountered. "This morning we chanced upon a family of lions in the process of devouring an antelope," Van Riebeeck wrote in one of his first letters.

For the first few weeks, the Khoikhoi herdsmen they saw tending their animals at the foot of the flowering escarpments of Table Mountain eluded the Dutchmen. Van Riebeeck was eager to exchange the baubles and ornaments brought from Europe for cattle, but the natives shied away. Their suspicions would not be overcome with feather and metal fripperies. The Heeren XVII sent Van Riebeeck an order from Amsterdam to build a fort and surrounding wall to protect the settlement. They also sent a high-level engineer named Rykloff van Goens to assess the possibility of digging a canal across the Cape Peninsula to separate it from the rest of the continent and make it a piece of Holland, geographically independent of Africa. This extravagant project was greeted with enthusiasm by the Dutch settlers. Soon, however, they saw its impracticality. How could a hundred or so poor men with picks and spades divide Africa in two? The idea was pure madness! Unless, of course, thousands of Khoikhoi would give them a hand. Van Riebeeck could see no solution but to countermand his superiors' orders. Once more he sent emissaries to the black herdsmen sighted around Table Mountain. The jewelry, mirrors, and finery he had brought from Europe must finally dispel their mistrust. But none of the natives would agree to serve the white men who had come into their land like thieves. The Calvinists' tentative incursion on African soil had made an inauspicious beginning.

Refusing to be discouraged, Van Riebeeck consulted the small Bible he always carried in his pocket. He chose a verse from Deuteronomy to reassure his companions. "And I will give their kings into your hand and you shall make their name perish under the heaven," he exhorted them and reminded them how, according to the psalmist, the God of Israel brought his people out of darkness: "For he shatters the doors of bronze and cuts in two the bars of iron." He then came up with an idea for separating his companions from hostile blacks whom he believed destined by God for damnation. Unable to excavate a canal, he planted a double row of wild almond trees across the narrow peninsula. Four centuries later, the scent of honey and camphor issuing from the long bluish flowers of the offshoots of those trees still perfumes the countryside south of Cape Town, a distant echo of the first act of racial segregation perpetrated by whites against blacks in South Africa.

★

WITH THEIR SMALL FORT and their few dry stone dwellings set amid fields of carrots, cabbages, and lettuce, in a few months Van Riebeeck and the settlers succeeded in establishing a modest refreshment station. The tiny European enclave had no relation to the African people or the land surrounding them and was devoted solely to fattening up goats and chickens and supplying passing ships with vegetables. In Amsterdam the company notaries swiftly ratified the ownership of this African settlement with an official deed, with no one venturing to raise an objection about its legitimacy. How could a few sandy lettuce patches be regarded as a territorial conquest? The Heeren were euphoric. This tentative venture at the tip of Africa promised to achieve their goals precisely. Spice ships were already heading for the small base to load up with the fresh produce to protect their sailors from scurvy.

Van Riebeeck was keen to convince his backers that this small settlement should be expanded. If they would grant him permission to have a few slaves brought from West Africa, the Indies, or Indonesia, he would do his best to multiply its undertakings tenfold. Their response fell like an ax. The Heeren rejected their representative's dreams of expansion. They absolutely did not wish to expand their small African base. It was to remain limited and self-sufficient and, above all, cost the Company nothing. But aid came to Van Riebeeck unexpectedly. The Southeastern, the African wind unknown in the canals of Amsterdam, brought him the additional workforce he needed when the Dutch ship *Amersfoort*, which had earlier captured a Portuguese three-master and taken 250 of its Angolan slaves on board, shipwrecked off the coast. Many perished, but more than 150 managed to reach shore. Their owner was among the survivors, and Van Riebeeck immediately bought them from him. At a stroke his numbers doubled and thus his capacity to increase the acreage for his crops and the extent of his poultry and sheep farming. Good-bye to scurvy! Lettuce, carrots, and fresh meat would be permanently available on the tip of the Cape.

Trouble arose when young slave women attracted the attention of the colony's bachelors. Though Van Riebeeck banned his companions from having sexual relations with the shipwrecked girls, the community soon buzzed with the murmurings of illicit love. Called after their places of origin—Mary of Bengal, Catharina of Batavia, or Suzanna of Mozambique—unless they had biblical names like Rachel, Ruth, or Eve, many ended up sharing impetuous Dutchmen's straw mats. The Heeren XVII were beside themselves with indignation when they heard about it. Instead of recalling the guilty parties, however, they used a trading initiative to punish them. Holland had just set up a second mercantile company, the Dutch West India Company, and gave it a monopoly on trade with America and exclusive rights to the African slave trade throughout the world. The new company ordered that all the women from the *Amersfoort* be handed over, dealing a severe blow to the men sharing their lives with them. Especially since preparations were under way for a remarkable event: the official wedding of a thirty-five-year-old Dutch citizen to a twenty-four-year-old slave woman from Equatorial Guinea, Catharina Antonis. She spoke a few words of Dutch and knew the rudiments of the Christian faith. These marriage plans scandalized the Company administrators in Amsterdam. It was contrary to their business ethics. By marrying one of their employees, the young African woman was actually acquiring the right to her freedom. For the Heeren, always mindful of their profits, the sacrifice of two hundred guilders for the liberation of a slave was intolerable. Happily for them, this was to be an almost unique case. Most of Van Riebeeck's companions maintained pitiless master-servant relations with slaves of either sex. They called them kaffirs, a term that would become akin to "niggers," and assigned them the hardest and most menial agricultural and domestic work. Van Riebeeck subjected them to draconian rules. Any slave out after ten o'clock at night must signal his presence by carrying a lantern, unless accompanied by his owner, and present a pass if his work required him to travel beyond a certain distance. To prevent thoughts of escape, no black could have contact with another black working for a different white. Simple offenses such as theft, disobedience, or running away were punishable by flogging, branding, or even hanging. The mere act of raising a hand, armed or not, to a superior could bring a slave agony on the wheel, an instrument of torture that would break his bones and dislocate his limbs without necessarily causing immediate death. A woman who had accidentally set fire to her employer's house was impaled in the smoldering building and burned alive. Corpses of slaves were left exposed on the site where they had been put to death, to be devoured by vultures in plain sight of everyone. A servant girl guilty of letting her baby die was condemned to have both breasts torn off with white-hot tongs. In an upsurge of Christian charity, Van Riebeeck issued a reprieve. The poor girl was then tied in a sack and thrown into the open sea off Table Mountain.

★

IN MAY 1657 THE GOATEED FATHER of the doctrine of predestination must have been turning for joy in his Genevan grave. His beloved little Holland had once again confirmed its preeminence among men. "The Lord be praised!" wrote Jan van Riebeeck to his superiors in Amsterdam. "For the first time wine has just been pressed from the grapes we planted on African soil." This was an unexpected development after the lettuce, chickens, and goats. "Send me farmers who know how to grow vines," he implored. "The land is admirably suited to this undertaking. We could make a killing selling our wine to passing ships." Despite this appeal to their commercial appetites, the Heeren XVII held faithful to their policy of restricted settlement and refused to send more workers to their little outpost in Africa.

But the king of France Louis XIV suddenly forced their hand when he revoked his grandfather Henri IV's Edict of Nantes, which gave Protestants freedom to practice their faith and sent several thousand Huguenots, French Protestants, into exile. These men and women sought refuge in Holland, Germany, and Switzerland. For Van Riebeeck it was a miracle. The Company agreed to give some fifty families their passage to the Cape, granting each a few hectares of land and providing them with the necessary tools. In return they had to swear fidelity to the Company and to remain on the land for at least five years.

In April 1688, 175 Huguenots landed on the tip of the Cape. Twenty had perished during the crossing. They came from the French provinces of Provence, Aquitaine, Bourgogne, and Dauphiné. Their names were Villiers, du Plessis, Labuscaigne, and Dubuisson. For the most part they were farmers and vine growers, but there were also among them a few craftsmen, three doctors, and even a clergyman, Pastor Pierre Simon. Company agents saw to it that they were immediately integrated with the settlers of Dutch descent, known locally as Boers, or "farmers." As a result the appearance of the French language and culture at the extreme tip of Africa was only fleeting.

Yet the arrival of this small wave of Europeans radically changed the character of the agricultural refreshment station the Heeren XVII had conceived in their misty Holland. The simple base providing spice ships with fresh supplies of lettuce, dairy products, and meat turned into a full-fledged trading establishment. But a local development was to trap Holland into the colonial venture it had always rejected. After several seasons of quietly growing their vegetables, one day nine of Van Riebeeck's companions expressed the desire to break officially with the Company and farm their land and raise livestock for themselves. To the Dutchman's surprise, Amsterdam agreed to the request. Maintaining a hundred settlers at the bottom of the world was extremely expensive, and the Company was not sorry to reduce its costs and increase its profits in this way. So it agreed to let these nine Boer families have their freedom, on condition that they would sell the Company all their agricultural produce at a price fixed by the Company. Van Riebeeck carved off nine six-hectare plots at the edge of his trading post and distributed them to the people who from then on would be known as free burghers, "free farmers." He loaned each of them a few animals, some tools, seed, and materials to set up a small farm, hardly cause for them to reach for the stars and dream of becoming conquerors. And yet without realizing it, distant Holland had just opened to a handful of its children the doors of a continent on whose soil they would soon, by dint of sacrifice and willpower, write the most grandiose and ferocious of colonial epics.

★

IT WAS AN EPIC BORN OF A FIT OF ANGER. The land they had been given was too poor for the free Boers to make a decent living for their families. What was more, the price set by the Company for their produce was too low to make it worthwhile for them to keep up their experiment as independent farmers. Some preferred to pack their bags and leave on the next ship passing on its way to Amsterdam. Others looked to the Bible for reasons to persevere. And there, sure enough, in the book of Joshua, was Moses's successor calling out to them. "Have I not commanded thee be strong and of good courage?" asked the prophet. "You shall go in to possess the land, which the Lord your God giveth you to possess it." God's land? Was it the steppe they could make out on the horizon, yellowed by the austral winter? That empty, arid landscape stretching away to the north? Were pastures for their herds somewhere out in that vast, torrid expanse?

Certain of being the elect of God's new covenant, the Dutch farmers loaded their wives, children, slaves, and meager possessions onto narrow, big-wheeled, ox-drawn wagons and headed north. Despite the heat and the dust, the women wore their embroidered headdresses and ankle-length cotton skirts. The men walked alongside their teams, singing battle songs of their native Holland, their round hats with turned-up brims shielding them from the relentless sun. At any moment they were ready to grab muskets and powder horns from the wagon lockers. There was danger everywhere in these hostile expanses. When night fell over the great plains that the Boers called the veld, and when heaven and earth merged in lightning-streaked blackness that swallowed up the savannah, the caravans came to a halt. They formed *laagers*, wagons positioned in tight circles for protection against raiding tribesmen or wild animals. Then, beneath the brightest night sky on earth, began the day's only meal: flanks of grilled antelope or wild boar, washed down with swigs of *mampoer*, a rotgut liquor made from fermented berries. Afterward, in a silence broken only by the trumpeting of elephants or the roar of a prowling jungle animal, Africa's first white tribe listened to commentary on the Bible from the oldest father among them, whom they called their patriarch because of his long, square-trimmed beard. For these Dutch people, most of whom were illiterate, the Bible was the only source of culture, the only book their hands had ever touched. Deciphering its pages under the direction of the patriarch was how their children learned to read. By listening to the Bible each day, these Trekboers (nomad farmers), as they came to be called, strengthened both their native courage and endurance and their thirst for freedom. "For if ye shall diligently keep my commandments, I will give you the rain of your land in due season . . . and I will send grass in thy fields for thy cattle, that thou mayest eat and be full. . . . For ye shall pass over Jordan to go in to possess the land which the Lord your God giveth you, and ye shall possess it and dwell therein."

At the banks of the Gourits River, the Dutch caravans finally stopped. This—they were sure of it—was where their new homeland promised by the Scriptures began. Here they would stay to raise their animals and cultivate the land. They ratified this covenant with a solemn declaration that was both a farewell to the Holland of their birth and a tribute to the Africa opening its embrace. To the Company envoy who came to claim payment of their taxes, young Hendrik Bidault replied fiercely, "Be off with you! We are no longer Dutch but Afrikaners!" That day the white tribe severed its ties with its mother country, as one might tear up a ticket home, and consciously became African.

"Afrikaner." The word exploded like a bomb from the sun-drenched shores of the Cape to the somber quays of Amsterdam. How could several hundred European immigrants decide to espouse a nonexistent country at the other end of the world? That question did not trouble the first Afrikaners, convinced from then on that they had no duty but to God. But their marriage to Africa began with the inconvenient discovery they were not the only ones who had breached the wildernesses of the continent they had just adopted. Indigenous people from the same ethnic group of Khoikhoi as the natives Van Riebeeck had first sighted around Table Mountain were already in the region, driving their herds from grazing land to pastures. In their language *khoikhoi*— literally "men above men"—was an affirmation of their superiority. Driven from the north by the Bantu over the centuries, they were the first Africans to arrive in the southern part of the continent. Clans had settled and started families along the bay of the Cape where they had built their round huts of branches and cow dung. After a difficult start, Van Riebeeck had succeeded in establishing profitable commercial relations with some of the inhabitants of these villages, exchanging trinkets, ornaments, and tobacco for meat. He had even taken a young Khoi orphan into his home, christening her Eva and bringing her up as his own daughter according to the strict precepts of his revered master,

John Calvin. Such acts of fraternization were strictly prohibited by the Heeren, but they were extremely rare and occurred only with the Khoi who inhabited the shores of the peninsula and were used to foreign incursions. In the vast expanses to the north where whites were unknown before the first Afrikaner wagons began to arrive, the situation was very different.

The Khoi nomads in their animal skins and bird feathers perceived the white people in bonnets and round hats as a threat. The thinness of the stranger's livestock betrayed their true intentions: they had come to take over the region's grassland. The history of South Africa does not record the exact date in June, July, or August of 1658 when the first confrontation resulted from this realization. But that date marked the beginning of a three-and-a-half-century conflict that would only subside when white Afrikaners and black Africans were forced to reconcile and chose Nelson Mandela to lead their country.

As so often in history, the conflict began with a minor incident. A few stray cows captured, a rain of arrows poisoned with cobra venom falling on the settlers; with this the blacks of South Africa launched their first revolt against white oppression. So fierce was this attack that the Dutch retreated, some as far back as the little fort on the Cape. The withdrawal was temporary. Fortified by their Bible reading, they set off northward again. "Show us thy strength, Lord, and grant us courage in our suffering," they prayed. This time the Lord did them even better by sending them a few specimens of one of the noblest animals in creation. A ship from Batavia had just unloaded some fifty horses. With the reinforcement of this unexpected cavalry the Afrikaners were able to regain the advantage. As a result, Africa's blacks came under the sway of a new law, the right of whites to seize their lands. Thus began the long process of dispossession that, along with slavery and the condemnation of native people to work for miserable wages, would one day form the basis for the institution of apartheid.

In the end, their pastures, herds, and villages taken from them, the Khoi capitulated. But were they not "men above men"? Acting in the greatest possible secrecy, one of them organized a revolt. His name was Doman. A slender, thirty-five-year-old athlete, he was a legend in Khoi society because he had worked in the Dutch administration in Indonesia. During that time, he had made a crucial discovery that he thought would enable his brothers to avenge their honor and erase their defeat. Since moisture made musket powder unusable, they would act when it was raining. The D-day Doman chose was near freezing and damp. He had managed to recruit Eva, the long-haired Khoi girl living in Van Riebeeck's household. Convinced that the true chosen people of God were not her white benefactors but her black ancestors, she set fire to her adoptive parents' house while they slept. They managed to escape but dozens of other fires decimated the whites' settlements and crops.

The uprising failed and was harshly punished. From then on the Khoi had no choice but submission to the white men. When Jan van Riebeeck returned to Holland, leaving a commemorative statue of himself on a granite pedestal facing Table Mountain, he could be satisfied with the results of his bold African mission. With his vegetables, lettuce, and fresh meat, the Company's ships had been rid of scurvy. By encouraging its settlement, he had turned his humble refreshment station into a real colony. New waves of immigrants—Germans and French Huguenots for the most part—and the regular importation of slaves hugely increased its population. The band of 100 expatriates was now a colony of 25,000. Whether the Heeren in Amsterdam cared or not, the white conquest of South Africa was definitively under way.

★

AND OF COURSE THEY DID CARE; they were in a state of panic. By the final years of the seventeenth century, the colonists in search of more fertile land had driven their wagons more than

150 kilometers north of the Cape. It seemed nothing could stop them from occupying their new promised land: neither ambush by the few surviving Khoi lurking in the forests, nor the desolate province of the Karoo they had to cross. Despite the Company's efforts to bring them back inside its frontiers, the call of those virgin territories drew them on.

Desperate to contain this exodus, the Company began to expand the settlement. Giving new immigrants fertile land, raising the prices paid to farmers for crops, lowering duties and taxes, importing slaves—they did everything they could to lure the Boers back within the confines of the colony. Before long a miniature capital grew up between the dry stone fort built by Van Riebeeck and the slopes of the majestic Table Bay: Cape Town. With a Protestant church like those in distant Zeeland, the official governor's residence and administrative buildings perfectly aligned on either side of a central street, and its living quarters with pretty ochre-colored facades, Cape Town from its inception promised to be a gem of tropical urbanization. Other small settlements sprang up among the lush, verdant environs, such as Stellenbosch, where the Huguenots of French extraction made the wine that would one day grace the tables of the world's gourmets.

★

HISTORY SHOULD NEVER have preserved the name of the obscure commissioner who landed on the Cape on the afternoon of Tuesday, February 13, 1713. Forty-seven-year-old Johannes van Steeland, curly-haired with a short mustache, disembarked from the *Amstel*, a caravel from Amsterdam, accompanied by a few sailors and passengers. Who would have suspected that this distant successor to Van Riebeeck carried death in his suitcase? His wife and four children, as well as many crew members and several passengers, had died, struck down by a sudden epidemic characterized by the eruption of purulent lesions all over the body. By surviving, he put the colony in jeopardy. How could the governor know that the dirty linen he gave the laundresses at his official residence carried the lethal smallpox virus?

In three days, half the slaves working in the laundry had died, and whites fell ill less than a week later. There were not enough coffins so bodies were wrapped in sheets before being incinerated in common graves. Soon the number of victims in the Cape region reached in the hundreds. Prayer vigils were hastily organized in improvised places of worship. Only the farmers moving between grazing grounds with their herds more than fifty kilometers to the north escaped the tragedy. In Cape Town, in Stellenbosch, in Paarl, terrified people maintained that this epidemic was a punishment inflicted by God on his people. But for what sin? Moral laxity perhaps? After all, there were several hundred free unions between whites and slaves in the colony. On May 9 two pigeons plummeted for no apparent reason from the roof of the governor's residence, and witnesses predicted an even worse catastrophe. This time, it affected the Khoi families still living on the peninsula. Lacking any resistance to the disease, they died like flies, their corpses littering the trails. Convinced they were the object of some malediction from heaven, the survivors fled, making for the interior with their meager possessions and livestock. Posses of white colonists caught up with them and slaughtered them in the hope of stopping the spread of the epidemic. A few families and their animals made it to the banks of the Fish River, 150 kilometers east of Cape Town. There Afrikaner stock farmers mounted on swift horses waited to seize their animals. There were fierce clashes. The Khoi sacrificed themselves in defense of their livestock, but they were doomed. Better armed and more mobile, the Afrikaners wiped out the last survivors of the heroic little tribe. It was a victory with immediate repercussions.

The victors lost no time. In a solemn assembly, people believing themselves predestined to heavenly redemption formally declared the superiority of their race. Belief in this predestination was to play a fundamental role in the formation of the country that would one day call itself South Africa. As they methodically took over the northern plains, Afrikaners agreed unanimously that they would never cohabit with the natives. This separation would lead to a political system that the world would one day come to look upon with horror.

But this was still far in the future.

★

GERRIT CLOETE, PIETER WILLEM, JAN VLOCK . . . their names would be soon forgotten. But at the turn of the eighteenth century these pioneers of the tribe of white men had just discovered God's paradise in the blinding heat of the South African veld. It proved to be a region of incredible richness. The Afrikaners cultivated wheat and maize and multiplied their herds. Their geographical distance from the Cape did not stop them from selling their produce to the Company's brokers. But soon, between the Kei and Fish rivers, these prospering farmers were met by herdsmen of another indigenous people. Like the Khoi, the Xhosa had been driven south by the Bantu tribes in the north. The two worlds had no hope of understanding each other. The white farmers subscribed to the values of work, family, and the Bible. Their branded cows and cultivated fields were synonymous with private ownership. The Xhosa, by contrast, practiced a form of radical democracy in which everything belonged to everybody. These differences resulted in a succession of frontier wars often with as little provocation as stealing a few cows or seizing patches of farmland for cultivation or pasture. But the defining events of that century for the Dutch farmers would not be their clashes with the descendants of Ham over the theft of a few horned beasts. Rather, there was first the decline and death, after 192 fruitful years, of the venerable dowager who had inspired and then supported Holland's African adventure. Deprived by the British and the French of her European markets, on April 15, 1794, the Dutch East India Company passed away, and with her the last white-collared Heeren, whose dreams of vegetable gardens 140 years earlier had banished scurvy from the ships of the world's premier merchant fleet.

On July 9, 1795, a squadron of galleons under full sail suddenly appeared off Table Mountain, putting the Dutch settlers on notice that the "old lady" had been supplanted. The ships were British and they carried several thousand soldiers. The recent conquest of Holland by French revolutionary armies had put London on alert. The strategic base at the Cape on the route to the Indies could not be allowed to fall into hostile hands. The landing of His Majesty's scarlet-uniformed regiments quickly dispelled this concern. But this sudden incursion by another white tribe struck fear into the Afrikaners facing the Xhosa at the northern frontier. And with good reason. Britain's desire to couple economic revitalization with changes to the colony's statutes angered the Dutch farmers. First came a decree abolishing slavery. This generous idea put forward by London Missionary Society activists condemned a whole generation of Boers to work themselves to exhaustion for lack of farm labor. It was followed by an ordinance granting freed slaves the right to choose their employers and even to become owners of the land they had worked. Finally, the new power allowed blacks to bring charges against their employers before a tribunal in the event of maltreatment. This court, known as the Black Circuit Court, sat in different places across the territory. One of its judgments narrowly avoided sparking off a civil war between the Boers and the British.

The affair began as a minor incident. A Boer farmer accused of maltreating one of his Khoi servants resisted arrest by black policemen in the pay of the British authorities. He was killed, and his brother and sixty colonists set off after the murderers. The brother was killed and six of his companions were arrested. They were tried, condemned to death, and hanged. The drama shook the colony. The Dutch farmers now had martyrs.

Friction between the Boers and the British grew as the British asserted their power in every domain, including the enforced

Anglicization of the entire white population, Boers included. In schools, public administration, trade, and the courts English became the official language. Ministers from Scotland ordered their colleagues in the Dutch Reformed Church to preach in the language of George III. The Dutch farmers who had espoused Africa to the point of calling themselves Afrikaners responded to this linguistic tyranny with surprising defiance. They looked for comfort to the book of Revelation, where Saint John speaks of "a new heaven and a new earth," a people of God without foreign languages or idols speaking the language of their ancestors. Like the Hebrews before them, the Boers would speak an African language. Cursed be the English of the governors in the Cape, the Dutch of their origins, the French and German of the other immigrants. The Boers would ever after speak their own language. It would come to be called Afrikaans. This extraordinary mix of Dutch, Portuguese Creole, French, and even Khoi and Malay became the cement of their African identity and the symbol of their cultural independence. Two centuries later the leaders of a sovereign South Africa would use it to harangue the entire world from the tribune of the United Nations. But for the time being its inventors had more serious concerns than linguistic oppression. The colonists from London were becoming a serious threat. Soon there were five thousand of them. They had to have land and pastures. Some had headed north and were already in the vicinity of the Afrikaner farms along the Fish River. Threatened by this white invasion on the one hand and the promise of yet another frontier war with their unpredictable Xhosa neighbors on the other, the Dutch farmers were apprehensive. Every evening after reciting psalms, they gathered at the center of their *laagers*. Should they hang on at all costs to the scorching expanses they had cleared even though others, greater in numbers and strength, now wanted to seize them? Or should they climb back on their wagons and set off again into the unknown to search for another promised land? Their response would be an epic of blood and suffering that became known as the Great Trek.

★

SCOUTS RETURNING FROM THE NORTH and east revealed that the continent's interior was largely uninhabited. So the adventurers of the Great Trek headed northeast at the beginning of March 1835, looking for free land where they could raise their children according to the principles of their ancestors. Before they left, one of their leaders, a descendant of French Huguenots named Piet Retief, sent a message addressed to the British Crown to a newspaper in the Cape: "We leave the colony with the full assurance that the British Government expects nothing of us, and that in future it will allow us to govern ourselves without interference." It was a farewell to the British sovereign and his dominion in the Cape, from a people burning with the desire to find their own Canaan, and there to proclaim the republic of their dreams, one that could bring the light of Christian revelation to Africa.

The trek wagons were given a new, sophisticated revamping. Fitted with a double roof against the heat and elements, with larger lockers to hold the family clothes, bedding, utensils, provisions, and weapons, they were remarkably well adapted to the terrible adventure ahead. Easily dismantled, they could be carried on men's backs across the deepest rivers and sheerest passes. Branches replacing the rear wheels acted as brakes when descending the steepest slopes. Christened "freedom wagons" by the Voortrekker adventurers, for weeks, months, years, they were indispensable aids on the march to the promised land.

At dawn on March 15, 1835, two caravans of about a hundred wagons each set out. Information provided by an ivory trafficker confirmed the region was virtually unpopulated. What the travelers did not know was the reason for this apparent emptiness. No one had heard about the genocide the Zulu king Shaka had inflicted a few years earlier on the tribes living in the eastern part of the country. This bloodthirsty monarch had his victims disemboweled to free their souls, which he thought were imprisoned in their entrails. Everywhere he went he exterminated his adversaries by impaling, stoning, drowning, strangling, or throwing them into crocodile-infested water.

After each raid he had withdrawn with his spoils to his kingdom in the Natal area beside the Indian Ocean. Terrified at the thought that Shaka might return to finish them off, the survivors of the decimated tribes had fled to the four corners of the country, which explained why certain regions appeared uninhabited. It was an illusion, however, and a welcoming committee awaited the Boers. To the north, between the Vaal and Orange rivers, were the Griqua, a mixed-race people of Khoi origin, armed with guns. Even farther north on the high plateaus of the Transvaal, the rebel Mzilikazi, who had broken away from the Zulus, controlled several thousand square kilometers with 20,000 warriors. The land to the south, behind the rocky escarpments of the Maluti, was occupied by the Basotho tribe and its king. Finally, far to the east was the domain of Dingane, who succeeded the ferocious Shaka after he was assassinated, and his Zulu warriors who had become more powerful than ever.

Nature in Africa presented dangers apart from wild beasts, crocodiles, and snakes. Swarms of tsetse flies and malaria-carrying mosquitoes descended upon the Voortrekkers. Their bites claimed the first victims of the Great Trek. To escape them the survivors turned toward the massif of the Drakensberg, the great mountainous barrier beyond which they hoped to reach the lush plains bordering the Indian Ocean. Climbing the rocky escarpments was a nightmare. Often screams rang out, signaling that a wagon along with its team and occupants had just hurtled to the bottom of a precipice. The vehicles continually had to be taken apart and reassembled, and their loads carried on foot.

Wagon trains that had left from different starting points joined together. Soon their leaders became figures of Afrikaner legend. Except for the Huguenot Piet Retief, author of the farewell message to Britain, they were simple farmers. Their names were Andries Pretorius, Gert Maritz, and Andries Potgieter. An attack on the wagon train under Potgieter's command heralded the black war against this Afrikaner invasion. On October 15,

1836, 10,000 Ndebele warriors fell upon Potgieter's column. He immediately retreated to a hill and formed his wagons into a tight *laager*. Every adult male had three guns at his disposal that the women and children reloaded. The gunfire claimed four hundred victims among the Africans while the Boers lost only two.

That evening, Piet Retief was elected president of the future Afrikaner Republic, and the leaders of the seven wagon trains were made members of the Volksraad, the first council of that same republic, which they all swore to proclaim at the first possible opportunity. The wagons set off again. In October 1837 the first ones reached a trading post for British merchants and adventurers on the shores of the Indian Ocean, called Durban. The location was magnificent, but settling in the area was out of the question without first negotiating the acquisition of land with the Zulu king Dingane. He demanded a large quantity of cattle in exchange for the requisite land. On February 6, 1838, Piet Retief presented himself at the royal kraal, together with 60 men and a herd of 250 horned cattle. As custom required and as a mark of good faith, the small troop let themselves be disarmed. It was a serious mistake. To cries of *Bulalani abatageti!* "Kill the white sorcerers!" the delegation was massacred, impaled, and left for the vultures.

The savagery of this crime undermined the Afrikaners' hope of living in peace with those whom God had placed along their way to the promised land. It was their duty to avenge Piet Retief. Their new leader, the farmer Andries Pretorius, brandishing his beige top hat, clambered onto the locker of a wagon to address his troops. "If God permits us to punish the Zulus, we shall make the date of this victory one that future generations will celebrate forever to the greater glory of God!" he exclaimed to a chorus of cheers. That date, December 16, would one day become one of South Africa's national holidays. But at the time all thoughts were on revenge and crushing the Zulu king.

Scouts reported that several thousand Zulu warriors were close to a wagon train that had stopped on the banks of a tributary of the Buffalo River. Pretorius immediately ordered his sixty-four

wagons to form themselves into a *laager*. As a precaution he had
the vehicles tied together. Then he placed several dozen horsemen in ambush on either side of the river. Hymns rose into the
night, punctuated by the voice of the minister reciting verses
from the Bible. "The Zulus will rise up to kill us," sang the defending Voortrekkers, "but the word of God is there to stop them." At
dawn, as the mist rose over the river, the Boers were still singing.
For the fierce king Dingane and his impatient hordes, the time
had come to attack. A first wave, followed by a second and then a
third, hurled themselves at the caravan. For four hours Zulu
corpses piled up in front of the wagon wheels. "The women
barely had time to reload our guns with a little powder and a car-
tridge before we had to be ready to kill a new assailant," one
combatant recounted. Pretorius ordered a sortie on horseback
and crushed the Zulu forces, leaving over three thousand dead.
The river turned red with the blood of survivors trying to escape
by swimming across it. For the Afrikaner nation, the Buffalo River
became the "Blood River," the river of the blood of vengeance.

Six thousand Boers came rushing from all over the center of
the country to support the victors of Blood River, who immediately announced the annexation of the region and proclaimed the
advent of a free and independent state, the Republic of Natalia.
At the center of a vast plain, they founded its capital, naming it
for the two heroes in their short history, Piet Retief and Gert
Maritz. With their republic and its thatch-roofed capital, Pietermaritzburg, the Afrikaners were sure they had finally reached
their promised land and won their place in the sun. It was a
short-lived illusion. The autonomy of this white tribe displeased
the rigid British bureaucrats governing the Cape. The Boers discovered they had been gravely mistaken in hoping the Crown
would stay out of their affairs once they had headed north. The
British immediately sent a military force to annex neighboring
Natal and prevent the Afrikaners from using the maritime facili-
ties in the port of Durban. In command was one of the most celebrated officers in their army, Captain Thomas Charlton Smith,
who had lost an arm at Waterloo.

This time the Afrikaners' main enemies were not black tribesmen but the British, who stepped up their provocation of Andries Pretorius, president of the Republic of Natalia, and those who had bought land and settled there. They attacked their villages, seized their herds, and set fire to their wagons. The ensuing skirmishes prefigured the great Anglo-Boer War that was to break out at the end of the century. Above all, the British meant to impose their humanist philosophy that was in total contradiction to Afrikaner thinking. Whether the question was slavery or racial discrimination, British and Afrikaner mentalities were poles apart. In the end, rather than take up arms in response to British harassment, Andries Pretorius and his friends preferred to pack up and leave. The Boer people's first free republic had lasted but a single season. Again the freedom wagons set off, now in the opposite direction, back over the terrible Drakensberg mountain range toward the two rivers that divide the center of southern Africa, the Orange and the Vaal. Boer communities who had settled among peaceful black populations along their route welcomed the travelers warmly. Soon the idea was born to expunge the failure of the ill-starred Republic of Natalia by founding a new state. Upon reaching the banks of the raging river that a missionary had named after the princes of Holland, Andres Pretorius did not hesitate. The Boers' new sovereign state would be called the Orange Free State.

The indefatigable planter's aspirations did not stop there. The Orange Republic with its executive council of twenty-four had scarcely been established when he launched his wagons northward through the bush as far as another river, the Vaal. In that powerful watercourse he saw a natural boundary for a second independent Boer State. Pretorius already had a name for this new territory: the South African Republic of the Transvaal. In gratitude for this unexpected gift, enthusiastic citizens built a church and dedicated it to their leader. Around this sanctuary a capital would soon grow up named Pretoria.

With the establishment of the Orange Free State and the South African Republic of the Transvaal, the heroes of the Great

Trek epic won their formidable gamble for independence and freedom. The region's black tribes would never dare contest the Boers' ownership of the expanses they had abandoned when they fled from King Shaka's massacring Zulu army. Never again would the British government dare to claim that because the Boers had once been citizens of the Cape Colony, they were still British subjects. The Afrikaner nation was now free and sovereign. This victory would define its collective memory, its behavior, its economic and mental structures, and above all else its politics of survival.

★

UNTIL 1852 THIS VICTORY went unrecognized in official London, which continued to maintain that Africa was so perilous that it was better to have those damned Boers with you than against you. On January 17, 1852, in a reception room adorned with stuffed lions' heads, at an inn on the banks of the Sand River, Her Majesty's government finally made the historic gesture Pretorius and the Boer nation had been calling for: it recognized the independence of the territories north of the Vaal River gathered into the South African Republic of the Transvaal. Two years later another Anglo-Boer convention sanctioned the existence of the Orange Free State. For the Afrikaners this was the culmination, the ultimate ratification of their Great Trek. Exactly two hundred years after Jan van Riebeeck and his band of gardeners had landed on the tip of the Cape there were two sovereign Boer republics on the African continent. Together they formed a landmass as large and as populous as Britain's Cape and Natal colonies.

The contrasts were immediately apparent. On the British side, a wind of political liberty blew across the Cape of Good Hope. Great Britain actually gave its Cape colony a representative government, a parliament, and a constitution proclaiming that all inhabitants over the age of twenty-one automatically enjoyed the right to vote, regardless of race, color, or religion, pro-

vided they earned at least £50 a year. Blacks could therefore run
for office. On the Boer side, the perspective was totally different.
The Afrikaner nation could not forget its painful experiences
with the Zulu, the Khoi, and the Xhosa, and the price it had paid
for the right to live in its African promised land. Now that it was
in a position of strength and its neighbors of color were peace-
able, it had to define what kind of relations it wished to entertain
with them. During the Great Trek, the Boer patriarchs had
thought unceasingly about the conditions of their future coexistence with the surrounding peoples. Motivated by a desire to
preserve their identity and by their Calvinist conviction that God
destined every people to a particular place where they would
thrive, in the end they reached a decision. The Afrikaner nation
would live *alongside* the continent's other races, colors, and cultures. The patriarchs had found the theological justification for
this separation in the Bible. In Genesis it is said of the people
who had one language and were building a city and a tower together: "So the Lord scattered them abroad from thence upon
the face of all the earth." Not that Afrikaners denied other races,
colors, and cultures the right to develop. But that right could be
exercised only in the place ordained by God, which must necessarily be different from the place reserved for his chosen people.
The first article of the founding text of the new Orange Free
State stipulated "only whites are citizens of the Republic." The
constitution for the Transvaal Republic showed itself to be even
more intractable by declaring "the nation recognizes no equality
between whites and natives." From the banks of the River Orange to the rich northern plains the lineaments of the racist system were being formed, and within a century it became, under
the Afrikaners, the face of southern Africa.

★

THE TWO CHILDREN PLAYING near their parents' small farm on the
afternoon of May 28, 1867, did not know Saint Matthew's direc-
tive: "Seek and ye shall find." They were not looking for anything

in particular. The pebble that eleven-year-old Erasmus and his nine-year-old sister Louisa spotted in the dust was just a fragment of stone like thousands of others lying on the arid ground along the border between British-controlled Griqua country and the Orange valley belonging to the Boers. With a deft kick young Erasmus dispatched the piece of mineral into a hopscotch square. Then he went home with his sister. Next morning, when the two children returned, the stone was still there. In the morning sunlight, the small stone glinted in a way that intrigued the boy. He picked it up and put it in his pocket. That evening he showed it to a passing hawker. The man seemed skeptical but took the little stone away and showed it to some traders in his village. Their reaction was unanimous: it was just an ordinary pebble. The hawker persisted. He wanted another opinion. In the nearby town of Colesberg he knew a doctor who had a friend who was a jeweler. After examining it closely the jeweler unequivocally pronounced it a diamond—a sumptuous twenty-one and a half carat diamond. When the jewel reached the hands of the British governor of the colony, he proclaimed, "This diamond is the rock on which the future success of South Africa will be built." The image was bold but inspired. Especially as it was not long before a Griqua herdsman tending his sheep in the same locality found another pebble, this one a bauble of eighty-three and a half carats. A marvel soon to be dubbed "the Star of South Africa," it brought the young black five hundred sheep, eleven heifers, a horse, and a gun—a fortune—though it was actually worth a thousand, ten thousand times more. This double discovery was to transform South Africa's rural and lackluster image in the world. In a stroke, a territory in a remote corner of the British Empire became an El Dorado that would affect millions of lives.

Prospectors came rushing by the hundreds and then thousands, undeterred by the blazing heat, the hard ground, or the malaria-carrying mosquitoes. They came from California and even Australia. And then a miracle happened: a huge seam was discovered buried in a lava chimney close to a farm belonging to two poor peasants, Johannes and Diederik de Beer, a name that would soon blaze like a comet in the firmament of the world diamond market. Hordes of prospectors began gnawing away like ants at the entrails of the De Beers's farm. Soon they had created the deepest hole ever dug by man. The immense crater held so many treasures that the prospectors called it Kimberley, in tribute to the Earl of Kimberley, the British secretary of state of the colonies who lost no time in annexing this El Dorado for Great Britain. Then the prospectors formed a trade union and founded the Diggers' Republic of Kimberley. The Boers in the neighboring Orange Free State protested vigorously. According to the maps appended to the peace treaty signed with London, the plot of land on which the De Beer brothers' farm was located was well within the boundaries of their republic. The Griqua tribal chiefs who had been living as nomads in the same area for seventy years also claimed ownership of the land. As for the British, they insisted the region had always been within their sphere of influence in central Africa.

There were persistent rumblings of war. Would a child's discovery of a diamond in the dust of the veld trigger a war between the Boers and the British? It would do more than that. It would bring onto South Africa's political and economic scene a protagonist who was to increase Great Britain's imperial claims tenfold.

This wunderkind with a frail constitution was Cecil John Rhodes. The son of an Anglican clergyman in the county of Hertfordshire, he was only seventeen when he debarked at the port of Durban to recover from tuberculosis on his brother's cotton plantation. The mild Natal climate did him so much good that after a few months he was able to begin the venture he had really come for: making his fortune. He headed for Kimberley and began selling sinking equipment and food supplies to the prospectors, earning enough money to purchase several mining concessions. His influence soon extended as far as the Cape, where he was able to induce parliament to vote him funds to build a railway line from the Cape to Kimberley. In 1880 the diamond capital was thus linked to the political and administrative capital of the British colony. Six years later, Rhodes returned to England with bulging pockets to finish his undergraduate studies at Oxford. In his meditations sitting on the benches of Trinity College, he outlined a vast imperial dream based on his deep conviction that the British had a duty to humanity to conquer the world. Like the Boers, but without subscribing to Calvinist doctrine, Rhodes believed in the predestination of all peoples. First among these, of course, was the *Homo Britannicus*, whose mission was world domination. When he returned to Africa with his university degree at the age of twenty-seven, Rhodes set to work acquiring the means of realizing his all-consuming goals. He won a seat in parliament representing the Cape, joined forces with the De Beer brothers to buy up all the southern African diamond mines, and soon controlled 90 percent of the country's production. Rhodes was thus positioned to become a key player in British politics in South Africa. He set up a private company, the British South-Africa Company, which he turned into a sort of state within a state with the rights to police, trade, mine, and build railways across a vast expanse of land between Angola and Mozambique. In time that territory would bear the name of the barrel-chested little man who, legend had it, came to Africa carrying nothing but a shovel and a Greek dictionary. It would be called Rhodesia. The construction of railway lines linking the regions under British influence; the beginnings of a grand plan for a railway unifying Africa under the Union Jack from the Cape to Cairo; the systematic crushing of tribes who resisted the hegemonic designs of the masters in the Cape . . . Cecil John Rhodes was the living embodiment of the dream of absolute imperial control of southern Africa.

Circumstances were miraculously favorable to him. After the diamond epic, Africa spat up another treasure. One morning in March 1881, a peasant named George Harrison, turning over the soil on his small farm in the eastern Transvaal, discovered gold. The place was called the Witwatersrand, the Ridge of White

Waters. Unlike the Kimberley diamonds, the precious metal appeared in the form of small, low-density crystals spread through beds of quartz. Prospectors rushed there with picks and shovels but these tools quickly proved inadequate to dislodge nuggets buried deep in the earth. The extraction of gold required advanced technology backed by huge sums of money and an equally sizable workforce. Rhodes would not watch from the sidelines as this venture went forward, but the great beneficiaries of the gold saga were primarily the Boers in the Transvaal.

In fifteen years, their republic's modest revenues would increase twenty times over. Next to their capital Pretoria, a new city sprang up, Johannesburg. Ten years after the construction of the first prospectors' huts, this cosmopolitan city already had over 80,000 inhabitants, for the most part European immigrants whom the Afrikaners contemptuously called Uitlanders, "foreigners." This white wave was joined by a tide of blacks seeking jobs as miners or laborers in the goldfields. The Boers were afraid of being submerged. Their traditional, rural, patriarchal, archaic civilization, founded on family values and Bible study, organized around home production and self-sufficiency, was now faced with an urban, industrialized world that threatened to engulf it.

But Calvin's disciples knew that come what may, God would vouchsafe the survival of his people. And sure enough, God placed an obstacle to block the all-encompassing ambitions of the British millionaire who had become prime minister of the Cape Colony. It was the bulky figure of a man who had spent his childhood in the wagons of the Great Trek. There would be a clash of giants at the southern extreme of the African continent, between two characters who embodied the virtues of courage and patriotism. Short, stocky, with bulging eyes, chin and cheeks framed by a carefully groomed beard, and a head of thick oiled black hair invariably covered by a top hat, sixty-two-year-old Paul Kruger, known as Oom Paul (Uncle Paul), was an icon in the Afrikaner nation. A Nbedele warrior attack on a Great Trek wagon train was his baptism by fire at age eleven. Three years later he killed his first lion with a spear and lost his left thumb shooting a rhinoceros with a rifle. At sixteen, armed this time with an antique musket, he routed a troop of Zulus that had infiltrated his family's *laager*. He married at seventeen and settled down to farming and big cat hunting in the virgin expanses of the Little Karoo. Widowed at twenty-one, he then married his late wife's cousin, who gave him sixteen children. Fanatical in his support of the Afrikaner cause, at thirty-nine he was elected commander in chief of the Transvaal Commandos, the lightning-quick cavalry that spearheaded the fledgling republic's small army. Deeply religious, Kruger was an ardent member of one of the most fundamentalist branches of the Dutch Reformed Church, the "Doppers," who refused to sing hymns because the words did not appear in the Scriptures. As an upright Boer, respectful of Calvin's message, he was sure that God had made a covenant with the Voortrekkers and sent them on their great journey to the Transvaal. He was a white supremacist who held the blacks in contempt. One of his first political interventions was to restrict migrants working in the mines from moving freely about the republic. He forced them to carry a domestic passport and confined them to ghettos near their workplaces, foreshadowing the concentration camp townships that were created a century later. But Great Britain was the particular target of his relentless energy—Britain, which had brought ruin to his humble farmer parents by freeing the three slaves on whom they depended to cultivate their strip of land; Britain, bent on taking control of the Boer republics and forming them, along with its Cape and Natal colonies, into a British confederation that would dominate the heartland of southern Africa; the same Britain now irritated by the sight of so much gold falling into the coffers of Transvaal and the Orange Free State.

At noon on April 12, 1877, in front of Pretoria's cathedral, an envoy of the Cape government proclaimed to 10,000 assembled Transvaal citizens that Great Britain had decided to annex their republic. The announcement sent a shockwave throughout the country. There were immediate calls to resist. At Kruger's instigation the population—men, women, and children—rallied in a surge of patriotism and national unity. In places of worship, in schools, and at demonstrations, orators reminded the Boer people that their patrimony could not be pried from them. God had given them a language and a land and had chosen them to bring civilization to South Africa. Blessed Afrikaner nation! Forty years after a heroic Great Trek had sealed its unity, this strike from a foreign enemy cemented anew its existence and its identity. Paul Kruger sent his mounted commandos to attack the British farms. From the very first confrontations the Afrikaans newspapers, including those in the British Cape Colony, published reports extolling the heroism of the defenders of the Transvaal. In an article taking up the entire front page, the influential *Die Patriot* declared in April 1878, "The hearts of all true Afrikaners beat as one with yours." The other Boer nation, the Orange Free State, proclaimed its support for its sister republic. So keenly did the descendants of Africa's first colonizers make their unity felt that the British began to fear a general Afrikaner uprising. There was no room for the lukewarm. Soon bodies were floating on the waters of the Vaal. Now whites were fighting whites. Commanded by a self-taught farmer, Piet Joubert, the descendant of a French Huguenot who had come from Vaucluse in 1688, the Afrikaner forces won a first victory against the British units on a hill near Pretoria. Kruger's cavalry was a marvel everywhere. One by one, the British garrisons occupying the Transvaal were surrounded and reduced to silence. Neither Cecil Rhodes, principal instigator of the annexation, nor the directors of operations in the London Colonial Office had expected such a reaction. Intoxicated with their military success, the Boers raised Kruger to the country's presidency. Before five thousand enthusiastic patriots, the elderly leader had the Transvaal colors hoisted over the town hall in the small town of Paardekraal, where he had made his headquarters. Then he agreed to meet envoys of the British government in Pretoria. In two days of heated discussion the stocky Boer had the annexation of his country annulled. The Afrikaners regained ownership of the Transvaal.

Cecil Rhodes immediately made the Boers pay for their success. He blocked them from building a strategic railway line between the Transvaal and the Indian Ocean. Then he forced them to allow the free passage of thousands of black workers from Mozambique hired by the British sugarcane planters of Natal. He did the same with workers recruited in Central Africa by the British owners of the Kimberley diamond mines. These decrees were all meant to anger Kruger and his government, who were anxious to limit the movement of blacks within their national territory. What poisoned relations between the Transvaal Boers and Britain above all, however, was the question of the status of the Uitlanders, the white foreigners working in the gold mines near Johannesburg. They had flowed in en masse from Europe and the United States after the great gold discoveries of 1881, and they demanded to be treated as immigrants. The Boers refused to accord them South African nationality or the civil rights associated with it. "These visitors can leave if they are not satisfied with their living conditions," Kruger declared. The British, with Cecil Rhodes at their head, did not appreciate his remark. "This arrogant little people," as Rhodes described the Boers, must be "brought to heel."

Secretly they planned a coup d'état to overthrow the Boer government in the Transvaal. It relied on an Uitlander uprising within the Transvaal, supported by a British army expedition from outside. The affair was carefully planned. Weapons were smuggled to the conspirators in Johannesburg. Once the operation had succeeded, the British High Commissioner would arrive in Pretoria from Cape Town and call for the election of an assembly to decide the territory's fate. The Uitlanders, who were in the majority, would then prevail, making the Transvaal an autonomous state under the British protectorate, swearing allegiance to the Federation of South African Countries dreamed of by Cecil Rhodes. But the British column never reached Johannesburg. It was intercepted and obliterated by Kruger's mounted commandos before it could join the insurgent Uitlanders, who were captured and imprisoned. Broken, Cecil Rhodes resigned as prime minister of the Cape Colony and returned to his foggy England.

★

DESPITE THIS RESOUNDING SUCCESS, Kruger and his people suspected that Britain would redouble the effort to achieve its ultimate goal: to seize the Transvaal gold deposits, even at the price of outright war with the "arrogant little people." Kruger decided to take precautions against such intentions. His privileged relations with Wilhelm II of Germany enabled him to purchase 20,000 Mauser repeating rifles to replace his obsolete Martini single shot rifles. He imported small artillery from France, including four 155mm Schneider cannons left over from the Crimean War, capable of firing forty-three kilo shells over ten kilometers. The British, for their part, unloaded several batteries from warships anchored in the ports of Cape Town and Durban and transported them to the Transvaal border.

But the two countries had not yet reached the point of war. Joseph Chamberlain, Britain's prudent colonial minister, wanted to buy time. He could wait to see the Union Jack hoisted over the Witwatersrand mines. The British army was not ready for a war. Reinforcements from various garrisons in the empire had not yet arrived. Chamberlain therefore invited the president of the Transvaal to London to explore ways of settling the differences between their two countries peaceably. The Afrikaner, seemingly eager to win favor with his host, suggested substantially lowering the taxes his country levied on profits from the gold industry. Then he offered to reduce from fifteen to five the number of years' residence in the Transvaal Uitlanders had to prove before they could become citizens of the Boer Republic. In his view, these two concessions ought to more than satisfy the principal British demands. Poor Kruger! His proposals met with such indifference that his bulging eyes flashed. He waved his cane about. Would he lose his composure altogether and leave, slamming the door behind him? Doubtless his interlocutors hoped so. For if war did break out, the British wanted history to record that the Boers had declared it.

The uncompromising Afrikaner was not slow to fulfill Britain's hopes. Two days after he returned to Pretoria, on Monday, October 9, 1899, at 5:00 PM, he gave Her Majesty's government an ultimatum: withdraw its forces from the frontiers of the Transvaal within forty-eight hours and cease landing fresh troops. The order was not even dignified with a response. Two days later, before the uncomprehending eyes of several million blacks who lived among them on that piece of African paradise, two great white nations who worshiped the same God and believed in the same values, despite their conflicting conceptions of the world, would fight each other to the death to control a few kilometers of underground galleries stuffed with yellow metal.

★

DURING THOSE LAST YEARS of the century the descendants of the Great Trek numbered some 300,000 to 400,000, including women and children—rural people, who through courage, endurance, and fidelity to their ancestral way of life, transformed huge expanses of the African bush into a real Garden of Eden. From hill to hill, as far as the eye could see, the veld was dotted with farms and small, charming trading towns that supplied the southern part of the continent with produce. Curiously enough, the spectacular discovery of diamonds and gold in the bowels of their two republics made little difference in the daily lives of these people for whom the Bible was more important than international financial markets. This vision was perfectly reflected in the army they mustered for their defense: farmers between sixteen and seventy dressed in civilian clothes, mounted on small but extraordinarily swift horses, divided into units of a hundred to two hundred horsemen known as commandos. With their felt bush hats with turned up brims, their magazines stuffed with bullets slung across their chests and their laced up leather boots, they were worthy heirs to the Voortrekkers. For weapons they had the Mauser repeating rifles Kruger had bought from Germany, capable of firing eight rounds with a range and diabolical precision that the British would appreciate to their regret. Above all, however, this citizen army was strong in leaders: all very young and chosen by their fellow villagers for their extensive knowledge of the region they would have to defend. Most famous among them was an athletic man with glasses and a goatee, Jan Smuts. Along with Louis Botha, Barry Hertzog, and other Afrikaner leaders, he was to become a legendary hero with whom the British would partner when the time came to make peace.

Along with their cavalry there were also infantry and artillery units, and several brigades of foreigners who had come to serve the Boer cause: mostly Dutch, German, Irish, but also 250 Russians, one of whom would become a general. Among these volunteers was a colonel in the French Foreign Legion, the Count de Villebois-Mareuil, who saw in this war an opportunity to avenge the humiliation the British had inflicted on France two years previously in the Sudanese town of Fachoda. Promptly dubbed the "South African Lafayette" by the Boers, on April 5, 1900, at the head of his commando, de Villebois-Mareuil was hit by three bullets directly in the chest. Impressed by his bravery, the British shrouded him in a French flag and afforded him full honors.

Against those 60,000 farmer-warriors stood Queen Victoria's celebrated army: disciplined professionals commanded by experienced leaders who had no intention of being humiliated by a few village militiamen. It would invest colossal resources in this war: over 450,000 men from all over the empire, including dominions as far away as Canada and Australia. Even with ten to fifteen times as many combatants, however, this elite force would take nearly three years to finally crush the farmer commandos of the "chosen people."

For a religious people, the call to arms was a call to spiritual fervor. There was not one farm, not one chapel, not one public place where passages from the books of Samuel or Daniel or the

prophesies of Joel were not read out several times a day, reassuring them that God would never abandon the Boers at their hour
of destiny. Dutch Reformed ministers rushed from towns to villages, recalling the Lord's promise given through his prophet Isaiah, to create for his people "new heavens and the new earth" so
that their "seed and their name might remain." But it was the
prophecy of Joel, written as an invasion of locusts laid waste to
the land of Canaan, that most fired the Afrikaners' determination
during those first days of the war: Joel's promise that the Lord
would have pity on his people and scatter the army that threatened them.

★

NEITHER CAMP SEEMED TO HARBOR any illusions. This war would
be neither quick nor glorious. At the outset the Boer commandos
and small artillery, although at a disadvantage in numbers and
weaponry, inflicted a series of stinging defeats on the British adversaries hardened by campaigns in Afghanistan and the Sudan
against warriors as fierce as the Pathans in the Khyber Pass and
the Mahdists of the Upper Nile. The British, awaiting reinforcements, confined themselves to a defensive strategy, which for the
time being allowed the Afrikaners freedom of movement. In Natal to the east and in the Kimberley and Colesberg regions to the
west and south, President Kruger's farmers on horseback were
the victors on the first three fronts of a conflict for which the elderly leader was proud to claim paternity. Sieges and frontal attacks were everywhere turned to his advantage, though victory
was purchased with hundreds of dead, wounded, and captured.

In any event, the war offered the president of the Transvaal
the satisfaction of seeing the Uitlanders leave. Certain the Boers
were about to massacre them, the gold diggers fled Johannesburg
en masse. Newspaper photos showed them piling into cattle
trucks with a defeated air and little else but a pipe in their
mouths, a bowler hat or cap on their heads, and a gold watch
chain in their waistcoat buttonholes. At least, the single-minded

Kruger rejoiced, the Transvaal was rid of the white-skinned ex-
ploiters who had come to plunder its riches for British and American speculators.

★

REPRESENTING ONLY A FIFTH of the population in that part of
Africa, whites on both sides were apprehensive about the blacks'
reaction. Would they remain passive spectators to a conflict
which many of them realized would seriously affect their future?
Boers and British had made a tacit agreement to keep the blacks
out of their confrontation and not recruit persons of color in their
armed forces. This understanding was to be shamelessly violated. At the height of the conflict the British army would in-
clude some hundred thousand combatants of color wearing the
uniform of Victoria's soldiers, many bearing medals on their chests
recognizing acts of bravery. On their side, the Boers set up native
militia to patrol the frontiers of the Transvaal and the Orange
Free State. They showed themselves to be extremely reticent,
however, to involve blacks in a clash between whites. Torn between their haughty nationalism and their policy of strict segregation, the Afrikaners wanted to prepare for the future. Once the
conflict was over, victor and vanquished would have to agree on
the place that people of color would have in its new configura-
tion. For the 450,000 British who would return home, this was a
matter of little consequence. But for the 300,000 to 400,000
Boers convinced that the land they were defending was theirs by
divine right and that blacks were only foreigners passing through,
destined for servitude, it was a matter of life and death.

★

THE GREAT BRITISH WAR MACHINE was on the move. Commanded by Lord Roberts, a mustached veteran of the army in
the Indies, the British launched a general offensive in the direction of the Transvaal and the Orange Free State. On February
15, 1900, they retook Kimberley. The news, telegraphed all over

the world, sent stock exchanges skyrocketing: diamond mining had been resumed in the world's deepest man-made hole. The Boers fought back furiously. Losses on both sides were terrible. Soon ten-year-old boys and white-bearded old men were riding the commandos' horses, flinging themselves at the British troops like grasshoppers. Young Boer generals looking like Napoleonic marshals slowed the British advance north with seven days of hand-to-hand combat. The audacity of these horsemen surging out of the bush and plunging straight back into it was limitless. Derailing trains, blowing up bridges, and wiping out isolated units, they eluded thousands of pursuers and their raids went as far as the Atlantic and Indian Ocean coasts. But all this heroism could not stop the men in scarlet. On March 13, 1900, the British troops reached Bloemfontein, capital of the Orange Free State. Eight days later, Britain proclaimed the territory's annexation to the Crown, renaming it the "Orange River Colony." The event was celebrated with great pomp because it coincided with Queen Victoria's birthday. Four weeks later, Lord Roberts made his entry into Pretoria, capital of the Transvaal. The Uitlanders Kruger so despised could now return to snatch fresh nuggets from the Witwatersrand mines. British imperialism had achieved its ultimate goal.

But the war was not over. The presidents of the two Boer republics did everything they could to keep up the fiction of national independence. As the British advanced they moved their government from city to city. The indomitable Kruger believed he was holding one last card. Wearing his top hat, he sailed for Europe hoping to find support for the Afrikaners' cause. The people of Marseille, where his tour began, gave him a triumphal welcome, and the Boers took heart. Perhaps "Oom Paul" with his international prestige would win a diplomatic victory that would counterbalance the increasingly desperate military situation. It was not to be. The elderly chief of state was greeted coolly by European leaders. No government wanted to risk falling out with Great Britain by openly supporting the Afrikaner cause. Even his friend Wilhelm II closed his door to him. Crushed, Kruger took refuge in Switzerland and died without ever seeing the verdant hills of his beloved Transvaal again. But his name would be inscribed on his promised land forever. In the northeast of the country a territory almost as large as Belgium would become a preserve for African flora and fauna. This wildlife republic, unique in the world, would bear the name of the man who had killed his first lion at the age of fourteen. It would be called the Kruger National Park.

★

TOTAL WAR. Britain deployed great resources, including its most celebrated army general, to bring the Boers' fanatical resistance to an end. A giant of a man with a square head and a salt-and-pepper mustache, he had just covered himself in glory by planting the Union Jack on the great mosque in the Sudanese capital of Khartoum. Fifty-one-year-old Horatio Kitchener would wipe out the militant Afrikaners as mercilessly as he had obliterated the legions of the Prophet from the sands of the Upper Nile. To neutralize the commandos still terrorizing his ranks, he modified his campaign strategy. He would trap the enemy in a spider's web of eight thousand small circular strongholds dispersed across the Transvaal and the Orange Free State. Occupied by a garrison of some fifteen men, each miniature fortress was surrounded by a ditch and protected by a weapon newly emerged from the mills of the English city of Sheffield. Fifty thousand kilometers of wire bristling with pointed barbs would be rolled out, then thousands more for another purpose: to imprison tens of thousands of civilians in the first concentration camps of modern times. Total war as conducted by the new chief of forces did not consist of military operations alone. Kitchener launched a scorched earth policy to prevent the last mounted commandos from finding refuge among the local people. One by one, the farms of the Transvaal and the Orange Free State were systematically set on fire, the cattle killed, the harvests destroyed, the crops laid waste, and the families arrested, separated, and deported to camps, which by the end of 1901 numbered almost forty. More than 118,000 women and children had been interned, along with 43,000 blacks who remained loyal to their masters. Malnutrition and the lack of medical care and hygiene led to epidemics of typhus, typhoid, and dysentery that turned those overpopulated places into death camps. In Kroonstad camp, the mortality rate for adults reached 35 percent; and for children, 88 percent. "Lord, what have we done to deserve such punishment?" wept an entire people with their prophet Jeremiah. In 1901, 28,000 Boer civilians perished, 22,000 of them children—10 percent of the population of the Transvaal and the Orange Free State. An entire generation of Afrikaners was to disappear from their promised land.

But the war went on. In refusing to surrender, the last surviving mounted commandos wrote one of the most glorious pages in Afrikaner history. When they ran out of ammunition for their Mausers, they fought with Enfields taken from the British dead. Their farm clothing in tatters, they put on the scarlet tunics of their fallen adversaries, or sometimes just wheat sacks with holes for their heads and arms. Those left without horses fought on foot, carrying their saddles on their backs until they found another mount. Numbering fewer than 16,000 by the beginning of 1902, they were a mere handful compared with Kitchener's 415,000 soldiers. Public opinion in Europe and America grew outraged. In parliament, the liberal opposition could not find words strong enough to denounce the intransigence of British policy. Secret communications begun the previous year between Kitchener and Louis Botha, the young Boer commanding general, led to a meeting to explore an end to hostilities. But the two sides remained irreconcilable. The British demanded that the Boers renounce any idea of independence while the latter made it an absolute prerequisite.

One year later the horsemen in the last Boer commando unit were almost out of ammunition. In parts of the territory, the native tribes had begun to rise up. The Boers living in the Cape

Colony let it be known that they would not take up arms against the British. At last cracks were appearing in the Afrikaner resistance front. On April 11, 1902, the vice president who had succeeded Kruger as head of the Transvaal Republic and his counterpart in the Orange Free State agreed to open official negotiations with the enemy. Both knew that any agreement would come down to the Afrikaners renouncing their independence.

At the stroke of midnight on May 31, 1902, in a tent erected in the small town of Vereeniging near Pretoria, the treaty was signed that ended the carnage that had bloodied southern Africa for three years. Historians and Hollywood producers call it the Boer War. The cost had been exorbitant: 7,000 dead and 55,000 wounded on the British side and 33,000 dead on the Afrikaner side. Defeat forced the "chosen people" to bury their political identity. Sixty years after their forefathers' spectacular exodus on the wagons of the Great Trek, they now had to stand behind the enemy's shield. In the tent at Vereeniging, the God of Scripture condemned them to the most terrible of punishments: they became subjects of Her Britannic Majesty.

★

DESOLATION. Thousands of villages, hamlets, and farms wiped off the face of Africa. Agriculture destroyed. A century of labor, ingenuity, love, and courage reduced to dust; four thousand men exiled to the distant mists of the island of St. Helena. Thousands of women and children dying of hunger behind 50,000 kilometers of barbed wire.

The British could relish their victory. They had destroyed two states and two armies some nine thousand kilometers from their shores. As they had done before in India, Afghanistan, and Egypt, they would impose the Pax Britannica upon a conquered people. And yet they had not really won this war against the Boers. For the conflict had reinforced like no other event the Boers' mystical conviction that they belonged to a chosen people. From their pitiless confrontation with the regiments of the world's greatest military power, they emerged surer of themselves than ever. The hostilities had provided them with a whole new generation of heroes to admire, new martyrs to honor, new objectives to aim for. An epic of suffering and death had been added to the Great Trek in the Afrikaner people's sacred history. The British did not know it, but this war had awakened Afrikaner national consciousness and unified the nation of farmers they had just defeated.

If the Boer republics had once seemed rather nebulous entities, this was no longer the case. Men, women, and children had fought, suffered, and died for the independence of these states and now believed that this independence was their historical birthright. To keep their patrimony alive, they would have to restore the independence of the land they had made theirs, since without it the Afrikaner people felt they could not develop their culture, language, and identity. Whether the dead had died for the Transvaal or for the Orange Free State, this war had made the Boers conscious of belonging to a single nation: *Ons vir jou Suid-Afrika* (We for you, South Africa).

Heady from their military victory, the British scarcely noticed the swell of nationalist feeling among their adversaries. They had long been developing a plan to strengthen their domination of the former Boer republics. By encouraging mass immigration by British citizens into the two territories, they would establish a majority capable of imposing London's will on the Boer population. As this took place, all Afrikaner activities would be systematically Anglicized, starting with their educational system. The aim of this huge operation was to prevent Afrikaans being taught as a national language and ensure the exclusive use of English. Young teachers fresh out of Oxford were sent into the schools to cast Afrikaans into the dustbin of history. They met with unexpected resistance. Boers everywhere fanatically refused to be robbed of their sacred language that they had invented during the Great Trek to cement their identity. Books in English were burned. Teachers were driven away, sometimes even assaulted, with cries of "Go away! Our children will never be English!" The

plan for a mass immigration of British citizens was also unsuc-
cessful. The promise of high salaries in gold mines or new industries failed to persuade sufficient numbers of Her Britannic
Majesty's citizens to leave their damp island to tip the balance
of the white population under the fierce African sun in favor of
the British. London would have to find other strategies to shape
the future of southern Africa. Perhaps a global entente with the
Boers, to create for the white race the great, unified territory
Cecil Rhodes had dreamed of so passionately?

For the time being the vanquished Boers went home to lick
their wounds. For once the promises of their beloved Bible did
not match with harsh reality. No "new heavens," no promised
perpetration of "their seeds and names" could be seen in the
apocalyptic scenes that awaited them. Besides finding their
farms destroyed, their crops laid to waste, and their animals
gone, many pulled from the ruins the bodies of the wives, children,
and parents they had left behind when they joined their comrades in arms. The British soldiers, harried by Kruger's mounted
farmers, had slaughtered them all. Sometimes the homecomers
found bands of black squatters making their homes in what remained of the farms. There were fierce confrontations with these
intruders, who resisted, fought, and protested their expulsion.
Soon wretched columns were marching northward across the
veld, stopping only to dig a hole by the wayside when they had to
bury some small body dead from hunger or dysentery.

Sad tropics indeed! To compound this misery, the end of the
war coincided with a drought that wiped out the Boers' hopes of
resurrecting their cherished farms. Vast stretches of the country
began to look like the Kalahari Desert. The wretched people of
the veld had no choice but to seek refuge in a city, Johannesburg,
for example. There even at the height of the war the yellow metal
still had fired people's imaginations. A city of 100,000 inhabitants had grown up within a few years. The Uitlanders had returned in droves once the war ended, and tens of thousands of
blacks had descended upon the city, lured by work in the mines

and in the new factories springing up around the world's largest
gold seam. This El Dorado needed so many workers that its pro-
moters had entire boatloads of coolies brought in from China
and India. Glittering, cosmopolitan, and bursting with life,
Johannesburg was already the continent's largest city and the
epicenter of an industrial revolution to whet the appetites of capitalists in London and all over Europe. Because many European
Jews fleeing pogroms had settled there, some nicknamed it the
New Jerusalem, a name which inevitably appealed to the traumatized farmers of the Transvaal and the Orange Free State
making for its lights at the beginning of the 1900s. For them, this
was a new exodus, a new Great Trek, only this time without wagons or *laagers*. It was a sort of interior migration of families on
foot, walking to a destination already known, over plains and hills
inhabited by wild beasts, snakes, and swarms of mosquitoes.
Spurred on by their unshakeable faith in the promises of the
Bible, these trekkers, too, were certain that Isaiah would at last
lead them to the "new heavens" God had reserved for the children he had chosen from among all others. "Do not be afraid.
The Lord is leading us to his sacred domain," the patriarchs repeated tirelessly to their families in the tones of Moses sighting
the Promised Land from the top of Mt. Nebo.

There was nothing sacred about the "promised land" to which
these children of God came. Like all agglomerations born of an
industrial boom, Johannesburg was above all else an inhuman
city. The London capitalists drew no distinctions here when recruiting labor for their factories. Poor whites, blacks, Chinese,
and Indians shared the same predicament in a hive of activity
ruled by poverty. Proud farmers from the veld, used to a limitless
horizon, found themselves confined to a punishingly congested
environment. People who had always believed it their divine
right as white men to build their own universe and feel equal if
not superior to others now had to drink from the bitter chalice of
humiliation. Now they were forced to beg a job, swallow the in-
dignity of having their work timed, and endure bullying and
blows like common blacks. Idealized memories of their farms,

fields, and animals sustained them. They would persevere, haunted by the dream of turning back and going home. Back there, in fields they had cleared with their own hands, the values passed down by their ancestors would endure forever—they were sure of it. In token of this attachment, many families defied the inhumanity of their new surroundings by symbolically keeping a sheep or goat in the backyards of their urban exile.

Two centuries earlier their ancestors had proclaimed their racial superiority by virtue of their skin color. They had solemnly sworn to defend that color by living, everywhere and always, apart from the surrounding black populations. Now their descendants found themselves obliged to renounce that dogma. In Johannesburg and all the other industrial cities of the new southern Africa, the Boers had become poor whites whom the British industrial bosses treated on a par with the blacks. Two parallel competing proletariats formed, engaged in the same fight for survival. The Afrikaners' sole advantage was their white skin, eternal proof of superior racial status. For even in these inhuman hives, the fact of being white still brought the right to dominate. Even an Afrikaner in rags knew that his race promised him a better future than the blacks had, and every Afrikaner believed firmly that the South Africa of tomorrow would belong to white people. Thirty, forty, perhaps fifty years hence. But the Boers were sure that they must start preparing now. Thus their urban concentrations became laboratories for inventing conditions of the future. Sharing employment with black workers was one thing, but living with them was another. For the Afrikaners there was no greater threat to the integrity of the people, no greater danger to their white identity. This enforced intimacy jeopardized the "chosen people's" sense of racial superiority and the blacks' ancestral respect for whites. Worse, it encouraged outright miscegenation, a terrible prospect that only the introduction of total and immediate segregation could prevent.

So separation became the Afrikaners' priority. "Kaffirs out!" became their slogan. Relations grew increasingly tense, and incidents between the communities led to violence. Finally blacks gave up and left the areas en masse where their erstwhile masters were bent on imposing the idea of total segregation devised by their ancestors on their path to African conquest: the concept that would one day be known as apartheid.

★

THEY HAD LOST A CRUEL WAR. They had seen other whites kill their wives and children and torch their farms. They had endured the humiliation of forced labor in factories. Worse, they had been forced to live among blacks. But for all that, it had to be said, the descendants of the heroes of the Great Trek had never given up the hope preached by Holy Scripture. And they were rewarded. Four years after the painful signature in the tent at Vereeniging, there was a political revolution in Britain. On January 12, 1906, the Conservatives who had held power in Great Britain for twenty-one years were defeated by the Liberal Party that had consistently and vigorously denounced Britain's policy in Africa. The Boers had reason to celebrate: the new prime minister, Lord Cambell-Bannerman, had always been sympathetic to them and had held one of their commando heroes, the feisty general Jan Smuts, in particular esteem.

An astonishing offer came of this favorable disposition. Dismissing the past, London proposed to restore the independent Transvaal and Orange Free State republics, each with an autonomous government and parliament. The two states would then unite with the two British colonies of the Cape and Natal to form a Union of South Africa encompassing all territory in southern Africa. Cecil Rhodes's long-standing dream would at last see the light, the dream of a South Africa in which religious, cultural, and historical antagonisms among whites would be reconciled, a South Africa that would beat with one heart, Boers and British reconciled around the same national vision. Not that this would be easy. Negotiations would have to overcome significant differences, first over the choice of the capital. The British in the Cape claimed that only their city merited this honor, while the Afrikaners in the Transvaal, supported by the British in neighboring Natal, argued that Pretoria was the ideal site because of its central location and the proximity to the gold mines. As for the representatives the Orange Free State, they suggested the "city of roses," Bloemfontein on the high plateau of the veld, as an ideal compromise. In the end all these proposals were taken into account. Pretoria became the administrative capital, Cape Town the parliamentary capital, Bloemfontein the judicial capital. It would be a three-headed state.

About the future of the black population, the four founding countries could not reach agreement. Blacks had hoped after the Boers' defeat that British liberal policies in the Cape Colony, where they had enjoyed a limited right to vote since 1854, would be extended throughout South Africa. This hope was swiftly dispelled. Traumatized by the nightmare of cohabitating with the workers in the industrial suburbs, the Boers refused to grant the blacks any right to vote in the new Union of South Africa. Thus the dream of an integrated future that had been nurtured by certain tribal chiefs and members of the Protestant elite vanished forever. Worse still, the Afrikaners, given the leadership of the country in the 1912 elections, immediately excluded blacks from the national community by passing the Native Land Act. It led to one of the greatest acts of dispossession in history by dividing the country into areas reserved for whites and areas allocated to blacks. Teams of surveyors divided up a map of the union into a mosaic of distinct plots of land, each marked out, measured, surveyed, and registered. Although there were twelve times more black people than white, they inherited only 7.3 percent of the total area of the country. The division deprived them of the best land as well as all mining and industrial resources. Furthermore, the law prohibited them from acquiring land beyond the plots allotted to them and from living in areas reserved for whites. Overnight hundreds of thousands of poor blacks found themselves obliged to leave their villages, their farms, their schools, their churches, and their cemeteries to go to the reserves assigned to them. Ten years later a new law, the Urban Areas Act, would create ghettos known as townships into which blacks working in industrial concerns and the mines had to regroup. The general tenor of the new Afrikaner policy toward blacks was established: they belonged to an inferior race and must be geographically separated from the white communities. They would thus be regarded as foreigners in their own country, which from now on belonged to the people God had chosen to bring Christian revelation to the land of Africa. This division was the last avatar of Jan van Riebeeck's line of bitter almonds, the trees he had planted two centuries earlier to divide the first colonists' territory from the rest of the continent.

★

THE AFRIKANERS HAD WON THE RIGHT to govern the new Union of South Africa. They had carried the elections, being in the majority among the white population. But the British capitalists who presided over all national economic activity were the ones who actually ran the country. They controlled the production of gold, diamonds, and coal and directed the principal companies. This gave them deciding power over domestic and foreign policy. The Afrikaners were resigned to the country they governed being a dominion of the British Empire and entering the Commonwealth. The Union Jack fluttered in the African sky over the seat of government, as over all official buildings, though the descendants of the Voortrekkers lessened the humiliation by integrating the flags of the Transvaal and the Orange Free State, and above all by having Afrikaans proclaimed a national language of the new union with the same standing as English.

Such political considerations were trivial next to the extreme poverty experienced by a large number of poor whites who had taken refuge in "English cities" since the end of the war. Not only did they have to compete with a cheaper black workforce, but the interracial mingling they had to accept ultimately threatened their identity as whites. Persons of mixed race soon numbered a million. Nearly all of them bore Afrikaner names and spoke only Afrikaans. Terrified by the extent of this hybridization, thousands of families returned to the countryside, where they soon formed an impoverished agricultural proletariat. One day these poor whites would vote for the champions of an extreme form of nationalism who promised to guarantee the supremacy of whites over the whole country forever. For the refugees from the "English cities," as for all the other descendants of the Great Trek, the political victory of those extremists would be God's final gift to those who had struggled and suffered over three centuries to create a place of their own under the scorching sun of southern Africa.

★

AT THE BEGINNING OF the twentieth century, however, these poor Afrikaners were far from realizing their dream. Numerous threats loomed on the horizon, beginning with members of the black elite who were trying to make a stand against their white oppressors. Fresh from Columbia and Oxford, a thirty-four-year-old lawyer with the airs of a London dandy had launched an opposition movement. His name was Pixley Seme. He gathered around him the leaders of the country's main ethnic groups, tribes, and kingdoms. His inspiration was a fellow lawyer, the Indian Mohandas Gandhi who, with the weapon of passive resistance, had succeeded in freeing the million Indians in South Africa from the chains of segregation. On January 8, 1912, Pixley Seme assembled the principal members of the black community in the large theater in Bloemfontein, the small city in the Orange Free State that was the country's judicial seat. Several hundred activists, observers, and journalists were present. Suppressing for the moment their ancestral rivalries, the Xhosa, Fingo, Zulu, Tsonga, Sotho, and Griqua chiefs opened the meeting by singing in unison the ancient African hymn: "Lizalise Dinga Dingalako Tixo We Nyaniso!" Fulfill Thy Promise, God of Truth!

Pixley Seme proposed the immediate creation of a militant organization to struggle for the unity of all Africans and defend their rights. Thus was born, on the evening of a stifling summer day, the African National Congress, the incarnation of black South Africans' nonracial and nonviolent crusade for equality and liberty. Its initials, ANC, would signal for three generations the black population's hopes for an Africa of justice and reconciliation. After spending twenty-eight years in white prisons, one of its heroes would become the first president of a multiracial and democratic South Africa.

★

THE AFRIKANERS' ANSWER to the mass assembly in Bloemfontein came six years later from three whites nursing tankards of beer in the smoky backroom of a Johannesburg café. On June 5, 1918, they were barely in their thirties. The first was a railway worker, the second a Dutch Reformed Church minister in a working-class suburb, and the third a builder on a mill construction site. His name was Henning Klopper. He had the typical square-jawed face of farmers in the high plateaus of the veld. At sixteen, with nothing but a Bible given to him by his mother, he had left the small family farm to look for work in the big city that was still growing fast with the gold rush. Henning Klopper shared with his two accomplices the precarious day-to-day existence of a white proletariat under the pitiless laws of a capitalism always seeking cheaper labor. Neither strikes nor popular protests captured the attention of Pretoria's rulers, so hope would have to come from the bottom. Convinced Afrikaners were being treated unjustly in their country of birth, Klopper and his companions decided to create an organization to take control of their destiny. The prime mission of the Broederbond (League of Brothers), the secret fraternity they founded, would be to help the poor in the cities, assist underprivileged farmers, and create Afrikaner businesses, including banks and moneylending bodies. But the league would be more than an aid organization. It would represent the mystique of Afrikaner destiny. Hadn't God wanted the Afrikaner people to prevail on this piece of Africa? Called by God to take dominion over other races, this people thus had the right to replace the current coalition government of moderate

Afrikaners and liberals with an ultranationalist executive that would champion the cause of the white race. As this message spread through white society, teachers, lawyers, doctors, and bankers joined the covert Broederbond that, for reasons of secrecy, had no address or telephone number. Members were accepted only after extensive investigation. Were they faithful members of the Reformed Church? Did their children attend an Afrikaans school? Was Afrikaans their everyday language? Was there any divorce in their family? In an initiation ceremony with religious overtones, they had to swear never to betray the organization or any of its members, and never to discuss its activities, even with their spouses. Thus the Broederbond became the backbone of rigid Afrikaner nationalism and a racist ideology that would bring South Africa near disaster.

★

ONE OF ITS PRINCIPAL ARCHITECTS was born in a suburb of Cape Town named after the mythical Van Riebeeck, the first Dutchman to set foot on African soil almost three centuries earlier. He stood six feet two and had a double chin and a severe-looking long face, with his metal-rimmed granny glasses and immaculate white bow tie. Daniel François Malan had been a minister in the Dutch Reformed Church and then a journalist, founding the first South African daily newspaper in the Afrikaans language. But it was his activism in the ranks of the ruling National Party that had made him a symbol of white mobilization against the black peril. He was vehemently critical of the racial segregation laws instituted by the first Afrikaner government. Yes, blacks had been driven into a tiny part of the country or confined to ghettos in the places where they worked, but such laws existed only on paper, he claimed, because much to his great indignation, they had not been voted on in parliament. He wanted the racial separation of blacks and whites to be inscribed into the constitution itself.

This fanatical nationalist with the little round spectacles was no orator, but his raspy voice always drew crowds when he spoke of the Afrikaners' holy mission to make the southern tip of Africa a fortress of Calvinism. "Our rebirth and survival depend upon our belief in our God-given mission," he would tell them at every opportunity. His assertions alarmed more moderate Afrikaners, and especially the British liberals who shared power with them. But they bolstered those in whom Malan sought to nourish the myth of their divine superiority. Spurred on by his Broederbond friends, he broke with the National Party and those in power to create his own political group. Defiantly, he called it the Purified National Party. In the legislative elections of 1934, it won only 19 out of the 150 seats in the white South African parliament. But with these nineteen members fanatically convinced they were the guardians of the Holy Grail, the celestial vessel representing the long march of mankind in quest of redemption. Daniel François Malan was sure of having the perfect instrument for one day imposing on the country his diabolical vision of a South Africa finally free of the black menace.

★

THE EXTREMIST ENDS of the Purified National Party's president were served unexpectedly by a mysterious German aristocrat who turned up one morning in 1934 in the office of the director of Stellenbosch University. Gustav, Count von Durkheim, introduced himself under the auspices of the cultural department at the Third Reich's embassy, stating that he had been charged by his country's minister for culture to invite some thirty South African students to complete their higher education at German universities. This proposal was so tempting that the heads of some universities in Cape Town and Pretoria had no difficulty recruiting candidates.

One was Hendrik Verwoerd, a brilliant twenty-seven-year-old psychologist whose father, a Dutch clergyman, had emigrated to South Africa when Verwoerd was two. His childhood and adolescence had been bathed in the mystique of the Afrikaner cause. The Verwoerd home in the Cape Town suburbs was a welcome haven for outsiders in the economic competition between the Boers and the British. As soon as he left secondary school he joined the Broederbond and became one of its driving forces in the Cape region. During a parliamentary session, he met the man who was to become his messiah. The founder of the Purified National Party and the psychology student felt an instant bond. They shared the certainty that the Afrikaner people were divinely ordained and that their elite had a duty to promote ethnic mobilization against the dangers menacing them.

Malan didn't know that Verwoerd's visit to Germany would shape the man who was to become the strong arm of his racist policies before he became their all-powerful master.

★

As COUNT VON DURKHEIM had promised, the young South Africans received a red-carpet welcome. Sent to the history faculties of the best universities, they were given an education that was the privilege of the Third Reich's young elite. Their initiation began with a journey back in time, an encounter with the German romantic writers who, one and a half centuries before Hitler, had rekindled the flame of Germanic nationalism. Their names were Fichte, Herder, and von Schlegel. Above all they advocated the rehabilitation of the *Muttersprache*, the mother tongue, which in their eyes embodied the German soul. Their message resonated keenly with the young visitors. Their fathers, after all, had to forge their own language—Afrikaans—to assert their identity and resist subjugation by the English-speaking world. The German writers had claimed that only the shared characteristic of being German could guarantee the nation's redemption. And finally, they all exalted the values of blood, the individual, land, and race.

Hendrik Verwoerd and his companions were enthralled by this message. It was not, then, merely a product of Adolf Hitler's imagination. It sprang from the very depths of German history. How could this discovery fail to impress them? As Hitler appealed to the crowds to unite in the shared ideal of *Blut und*

Boden, blood and soil, and exalted the notion of "people" and "race," the master of the Third Reich spoke of historic revival with a revolutionary vision that was both nationalist and anticapitalist and condemned both communism and liberalism. These themes were crucially relevant to representatives of a minority people pressured simultaneously by the industrial and commercial imperialism of the British and the hunger for justice of millions of blacks.

The visitors quickly realized that the sacred words "blood," "soil," and "race" had a precise significance in the mouths of their hosts. One day Verwoerd read in a Berlin newspaper that the Nazi Party congress had just passed a law relating to German citizenship that stripped all Jewish citizens of their civil rights. A few days later, another short piece announced a new "law for the protection of German blood and honor" that prohibited marriage between Jews and Germans. Unions already contracted would be dissolved and sexual relations between the two races henceforth banned. The new law also prohibited Jews from employing Germans under the age of forty-five as domestics.

★

OF ALL THEIR EXPERIENCES in Germany, none would have a greater impact on the young South Africans than the regime's great rallies. "They are always spectacular demonstrations carried out in a sea of flags, and red and black banners decorated with swastikas," Verwoerd would recount in a letter. "All along the routes overexcited crowds cheer the troops and the dignitaries in their enormous open limousines flanked by bodyguards. Sometimes Hitler is there, standing up in one of the vehicles, saluting interminably with his arm raised. The sight of their beloved leader gives rise to more cheering, bordering on hysteria. Our German friends acting as our guides join in this collective delirium like insects in a crazed ant heap. Then come the speeches, which the crowd listens to in religious silence. When the Führer's voice starts hammering his words into the air, it is as if God were speaking to Germany. Our companions assume a quasi-mystical air when they translate his words. His speeches are always about the superior people, the chosen race, pride regained, the purification of the nation and of course, the coming of a Reich to reign for a thousand years over Germany and the world." In Nuremberg once, a young woman named Helga who often accompanied the South African to these rallies seized his hand. She kept her grip all through Hitler's speech, at times sinking her nails deeply into his palm. It was as if she wanted to force into his flesh the words issuing from her idol, relayed by the loudspeakers positioned all across the vast square full of banners. Helga was blond. Hendrik liked her determined face and slightly sad blue eyes. She was the incarnation of the young German girl he had imagined from his reading. One day, at the end of a *stryddag* (political rally), one of the torchlit retreats of which Nuremberg was so fond, Helga took her companion's hand once more and told him fervently, "Hendrik, you can be sure of one thing: the Führer is not addressing the German people alone. His vision is universal. His concept of a master race applies to all nations who are struggling to impose the purity of their inherited values on their enemies. South African whites are among those privileged nations. One day they will choose a leader capable of making the values of their language, race, and skin color prevail."

The young German girl completed her friend's initiation by taking him to the opening ceremony of the Olympic Games in Berlin, to be held in the presence of Adolf Hitler. As luck would have it, the couple sat in a grandstand next to the one occupied by the Führer. At the end of the opening 100 meter race Hendrik Verwoerd saw the dictator's face suddenly turn pale, his thin lips contorting into a grimace of anger under his small mustache. Hitler jumped up like a jack-in-the-box and disappeared, his assembly of accompanying dignitaries trailing after him. Down below on the track, athletes formed a circle three deep around the winner, to thundering cheers and applause from the tiers of the immense, packed stadium. The runner had won this championship race in a record 10.2 seconds. He was a twenty-two-year-old American named Jesse Owens. Flouting the rules of hospitality and the Olympic tradition, the prophet of the Aryan race refused to shake hands with an athlete who had just entered the pantheon of modern sport by beating the best German sprinters. His victory humiliated Germany because the American belonged to a race of subhumans. Jesse Owens was black.

★

PREDICTABLY, WHEN THE young visitors to Hitler's Germany returned home, their fellow Afrikaners flocked around them to hear about their experiences and discuss what might be learned from them. Could the Nazi dictator's methods of imposing the concept of a master race be applied in South Africa? Did his messianic cries, to one of the planet's most sophisticated peoples, that the time had come for the "race's decisive battle against the masses" contain a lesson for them? Should they remain insensible to the myths of Volk, blood, and soil the German dictator used to rally his people?

As Daniel François Malan and his friends in the Broederbond would discover, Hendrik Verwoerd returned from Germany having reached conclusions to all these questions. One of his fellow students also back from the Third Reich, a young political history graduate named Nico Diederichs, published an account of his experiences in a pamphlet entitled *Nationalism as a Philosophy of Life*. A blistering text inspired by the most extreme elements in Nazi ideology, it urged Afrikaners to get rid of the existing order in favor of a system based on the racial supremacy that set them apart from other peoples. Malan and the Afrikaner Nationalists were not yet prepared to embark on such a radical course, but the seeds of the storm had been sown. Within a few years the lives of millions of human beings would be devastated, entire communities destroyed, and a whole country turned into an ugly patchwork of colors, races, and tribes based on what a young student returning from Germany, won over by Nazi propaganda, would call "God's natural law."

In the meantime, acting in strict secrecy, the Broederbond fraternity set about helping Afrikaners gain control of their own destiny. Making itself the absolute champion of white supremacy, it devoted itself to clearing the way for the assumption of power by systematically eliminating all moderate Afrikaners and liberal English speakers from the various wheels of state.

★

THE MEETING HELD on May 15, 1938, behind the drawn curtains of an elegant house in the center of Cape Town was not reported in any newspaper. Even specialists would find no record of it. Yet it was the day when South Africa's destiny tilted toward ineluctable tragedy. Four men gathered around the drawing room table to work out the last details of an electoral campaign to bring Daniel François Malan's Purified National Party to power and to decide what actions to take once they controlled the government. The house belonged to an eminent member of the Broederbond fraternity. The visitors could sense the gathering's importance the moment they entered the drawing room. On its walls hung portraits of the principal heroes of Afrikaner history: Jan van Riebeeck in his white collarette; the indomitable Paul Kruger with his bulging eyes and top hat; Andries Pretorius, the heroic commander who had crushed the Zulu army; General Jan Smuts, who had routed the squadrons in scarlet tunics, then made peace with the British and governed the first State of South Africa. The heroes of a short but glorious history were all assembled on the walls of the room where now gathered those who might themselves be the new generation of leaders awaited by South Africa's whites. One last portrait rested on a console lit by a discreet spotlight edged in a sober green, the color of the Transvaal and the Orange Free State. There was no mistaking John Calvin's severe face, with his long triangular beard and a black velvet calotte on his head. The four visitors no doubt looked to him and the other figures on the drawing room walls for inspiration.

Around Daniel François Malan sat his three closest collaborators. The first was Hendrik Verwoerd, who since his return from Germany had worked full-time alongside Malan. His main task was to keep in constant touch with the grassroots Afrikaner vote, so that at any given time he could mobilize working-class whites in support of a Nationalist objective. Opposite Verwoerd sat a big fellow with a bushy mustache and rimless spectacles. Piet Meyer was the son of one of Malan's fellow students at theological college. Though only thirty, he was already one of the principal leaders of the local Dutch Reformed Church. After completing his theological studies in Amsterdam, he, too, had made the journey to Berlin to study history at Nazi universities, where he turned into an unconditional admirer of Hitler. He had married on his return to the Cape and named his first son Izan. Rumormongers had it that Izan was an anagram of the word "Nazi," something Piet Meyer always strenuously denied. But Malan valued the young ecclesiastic less for his German sympathies than for his position in the bosom of the Dutch Reformed Church. He knew how vital the support of the Nederduiste Gereformeerde Kerk would be in gaining the helm of government. Malan did not underestimate the respect he himself commanded in church circles. He had been after all a dignitary of that venerable institution. Had he not on many occasions given the church's blessing to those seeking to bring "the dazzling, pure light of Christianity to the black continent"?

No one understood the mentality of the masses who could elevate Malan to power better than the meeting's fourth participant, Henning Klopper, who had founded the Broederbond. By now the secret society had several thousand members and its network extended into every economic and political sphere. It was a formidable instrument of conquest and everyone knew that Klopper was its covert leader.

After a few brief words of welcome, Malan opened the discussion in his raspy voice. "We need an idea for our people to rally around in our bid for power," was the gist of what he said. "But what idea? That's what we're here to talk about. I'll put it to you straight: the apocalypse is at our door. The black tide is about to drown us. What few segregation measures the current government has introduced have had practically no effect. The blacks have never respected the provisions of the Land Act excluding them from 92 percent of the national territory. For thirty years, I have been going hoarse calling for a political system in which a kaffir would remain a kaffir. And for what? Neighborhoods like District Six and Sophiatown where blacks and whites fornicate and even marry just as they like!"

Grimacing with disgust, he then hammered home his message: "Until the laws regulating the coexistence of whites and blacks in this country are part of a legislative arsenal formally inscribed in the constitution of a South African state, this racial pollution will only get worse. With consequences I will leave to your imaginations. . . ."

Malan sighed, a look of defeat passing briefly over his face, then asked Verwoerd what he thought. In the two years since Hendrik Verwoerd returned from Germany, the specter of a black tidal wave engulfing his country's white minority had haunted him: 4 million whites facing 24 million blacks. The Jews were only a tiny fraction of the Nazi dictator's Reich so he might be able to expel them beyond the German frontiers or shut them up in camps. By the enormity of their numbers, the South African blacks could not be the Afrikaners' Jews. Hendrik was convinced that there was only one way to solve the problem.

He tapped the table with the point of his pencil: "We must come up with a system that will permit us to coexist with the nonwhites of this country," he declared. "We have no other choice. Coexistence to me does not mean mixed existence. It means 'living alongside.' Alongside but separate. We should now formally put to the South African people the ancient idea our forefathers advocated, according to which we should live next to but separate from the blacks. We should base this coexistence on a principle, a doctrine, an ideology that for the long term will preserve our survival as a people—apartheid—total, absolute, uncompromising separation between us and the other South African races and cultures."

The word that would make South Africa an outlaw among civilized nations was an Afrikaans expression signifying this idea of separation. It fell like a thunderclap in that portrait-lined drawing room.

Malan nodded his head with relief. "A wall between blacks and whites is our only real hope of escaping the perils of our numerical inferiority," he continued. "It may also be our only hope of avoiding civil war between our country's communities."

Thinking of the Afrikaner people's fearfulness about the future, he added, "To be sure, the promise of physical, political, and administrative separation between the colors, races, cultures, and languages of this country would strengthen our people's resolve to assume responsibility for governing South Africa," he explained. "But first they must be convinced in their souls and consciences that it is God's will."

He turned to Piet Meyer, the young leader of the Dutch Reformed Church: "Piet, no voice can better encourage this conviction than that of our church. This apartheid we're calling for starting today will of necessity bring injustice, discrimination, and perhaps brutality. Our people are deeply religious. They may recoil from the prospect of causing suffering to other children of God. To reassure them, we need our church's 10,000 representatives to offer them a justification that is in some sense 'theological' to absolve them from any feelings of guilt."

Meyer thought for a moment. "That shouldn't be difficult," he said. "Most of our churchmen have long agreed with this idea of physical separation between the races in our country because it's actually supported in the Old and New Testament. Recall verses 6 to 9 in Genesis, Chapter 11, for example, about the Tower of Babel, which show that God's clear intention is to separate the peoples of the earth."

Verwoerd broke in. "Biblical references are important, Piet, I agree, but no matter how sound they are, I don't believe they will calm the fears that will arise with imposition of a system as radical as apartheid."

He studied his comrades one by one. "Forgive me for again coming back to Hitler. But what strikes me most about his project is that he has succeeded in convincing an entire population of decent farmers, tradesmen, laborers, public service employees, and intellectuals that they belong to a 'superior' race. And this superiority gives the German people warrant to demand the physical elimination of all those their leader has classified as subhuman—Jews, gypsies, homosexuals, the mentally disabled, and whoever else. . . . In the land of Goethe, Kant, Nietzsche, Rilke, Wagner, and Beethoven, a single man has persuaded 70 million ordinary people that they constitute a race of overlords! Isn't that extraordinary?"

His admiration resonated through the room.

"We should emulate Hitler," he concluded. "To allay their fears, we must convince our white countrymen that they belong to a superior race."

"I agree completely!" exclaimed the Dutch Reformed representative. "Didn't God himself proclaim the racial superiority of the Afrikaners when he gave them this parcel of Africa as a promised land, as he once granted the Hebrews the land of Israel? With this gift, the Afrikaners were vested with a divine mission: to separate the different races and cultures in this country so that each may bloom and thrive in a place appointed by God. The Bantus in the Transkei, the Zulus in Natal, the Xhosas in the Transvaal, the Coloreds and Indians elsewhere. . . . My friends, I'm sure I speak for our church theologians when I tell you that introducing apartheid in this country will be neither a sin nor a crime. On the contrary, it will be a way of serving the will of God. What's more, apartheid will be in the Afrikaners' imagination a rampart protecting their race, which God has chosen to have dominion over the rest of his creation."

"Piet, have you thought of how we're going to convince them they belong to this superior race?" Malan asked.

"Of course! We work from the ground up. We enlist all our ministers, our *dominees*, to organize seminars, conferences, retreats, and debates in parishes throughout the country. It may take months or years. But in the end we will have an army of crusaders ready to begin a quest for the Holy Grail!"

The allusion to the chalice symbolizing man's quest for redemption brought a smile to everyone's lips. Then another voice joined the discussion. The natural reserve of the former Johannesburg builder Henning Klopper was well-known to his companions and they listened all the more closely when he finally spoke. Although he had not actually seen the great Hitler rallies with his own eyes, Klopper probably knew more than any other South African about the techniques Hitler used to deliver Germany to the many-headed Nazi hydra.

"It's as much by the theatrical use of symbols as by any ideological preaching that Hitler has managed to spellbind the German people," he pointed out. "Our political leaders would do well to imitate the style of the head of the Third Reich. As our dear Daniel François Malan here knows better than anyone, these days poor whites seem to be paralyzed by a certain apathy. To shake them we should resurrect some of the great myths of their history, organize celebrations and parades with brass bands, flags, and banners commemorating their glorious past. Just like at Nuremberg!"

The notion of Nuremberg-style gatherings in the Cape, Durban, Pretoria, and Johannesburg startled his friends. Malan removed his glasses and began wiping them with his handkerchief. Verwoerd and Meyer tapped their pencils nervously. Klopper hastened to reassure them:

"Our national history is full of symbols and magnificent epics capable of firing our countrymen's imaginations and rousing them to action. Most beautiful to me is the great migration of a century ago, when our ancestors left the Cape with their wives, children, and Bibles, in ox-drawn wagons to go out and conquer new territory. The Great Trek is our history's emblematic episode, the one all Afrikaners hold sacred. I'm suggesting that we reenact that adventure on the roads and trails from the Cape to Pretoria.

Twelve hundred kilometers of a new great trek will remind our people of their incontrovertible right to the land bestowed upon them by God. Their epic lasted five years. It wedded our fathers to the land of Africa forever."

Klopper's words created a sensation. The meeting came to a close, spirits buoyed by this plan. The idea for resurrecting the past could come from a Third Reich choreographer. Klopper got to work the next day, his imagination brimming. He commissioned the building of nine wagons identical to those used in the Great Trek, each one named for a heroic person, place, or event engraved in people's memories. "Piet Retief," named for the Afrikaner who sought to negotiate with the Zulus but was stoned to death by their king; "Andries Pretorius" for the heroic officer whose portrait watched Malan and his friends from that drawing room wall, who had led 468 trekkers to wipe out 3,000 Zulus on the banks of the Buffalo River; "De Weenen, the Vale of Tears" for the place where 281 men, women, and children and their two hundred servants were slaughtered in their sleep; "Sarel Cilliers" honoring a preacher from the Cape who, in the heat of battle, had climbed on a gun carriage and called on his companions to promise God that they and their descendants would ever after observe that date with an act of thanksgiving. Ever since that day in 1838, December 16 had been a sacred date on the Afrikaner calendar. The other wagons honored children like Dirkie Uys, who died beside his father's wounded body rather than run away, or little Johanna, who was hidden in the back of the family wagon by her mortally injured mother.

★

IT WAS THE GREATEST CROWD EVER ASSEMBLED on Adderley Street, Cape Town's famous main road. On August 8, 1938, over 100,000 Afrikaners came to witness the departure of the great pilgrimage dreamed up by Henning Klopper. Before hoisting himself up to the tiller of "Piet Retief," he doffed his top hat to the imposing statue of Jan van Riebeeck, the first Dutchman to arrive in Africa. "My friends, let us pray that our journey will unite all Afrikaners of this country," he cried. Then to the crowd's cheers the nine wagons, each drawn by eight pairs of oxen, set off. They would take different routes to reach Pretoria, twelve hundred kilometers away. In all the places they went through a welcoming party awaited them, presided over by the *dominee* of the parish and the local representative of the Broederbond. At each stopping place, farmers replaced the exhausted team with fresh animals. Everywhere such emotion was unleashed by the pilgrims' passing through that streets were renamed after great figures in the migration of the previous century. For instance in Boksburg, Seventh Street became Sarel Cilliers Road in memory of the former Cape Town cleric. In an even more vivid tribute to their ancestors, thousands of men grew out their beards, donned leather trousers and waistcoats, and wore hats with turned-up brims like the Voortrekkers. Women wearing long floral dresses like housewives of old ran out to the wagons to have their babies blessed by the crews.

Brass bands and fluttering flags greeted the pilgrims on the previous century's battlefields, poignant testimony to the Afrikaners' fidelity to the myths of their past. In Fordsburg, factory workers in traditional costume showered a passing team with flowers. Near Johannesburg coal miners emerged black-faced from their pit to cheer on the travelers and their teams. At the entrance to the capital thousands of Boy Scouts raising torches flooded the arrivals in a sea of fire. Two huge flares symbolizing liberty and the white race headed the torchlight procession brought by relays of young runners who had started from the Cape a fortnight earlier. A river of light more than a kilometer long escorted the wagon train up the hill where a monument to the glory of the original Voortrekkers stood. As they arrived, the torchbearers cast their flames into a gigantic bonfire. Women rushed to the brazier to light a corner of their handkerchief or a fold of their dress to preserve the memory of this impressive celebration. Other fires lit the hillsides surrounding Pretoria. Soon the entire capital was encircled by an incandescent ring symbolizing the freedom and glory of the white man. "The hill is burning with Afrikaner fire! The enthusiastic fire of the young South Africa!" exclaimed one sixteen-year-old torchbearer.

Soon a human sea of at least 200,000 people covered the hill. It was the biggest assembly in the history of the Afrikaner people. Visibly moved by the spectacle's magnitude and its magical aura, Daniel François Malan climbed the rostrum erected in his honor. At first breaking with emotion, his voice quickly recovered. Malan spoke stirringly. "As the heroes of Blood River saved the white race by their sacrifice," he cried, to thunderous applause, "so today must Afrikaners fight for South Africa to remain the white man's forever!"

★

EIE VOLK, EIE TAAL, EIE LAND! Our own people, our own language, our own land! It could have been one of the slogans Hitler shouted at the German crowds. It would be Daniel François Malan's the day after this great wagon rally on the hillsides of Pretoria. Galvanized by his young followers' accounts of their visit to the Third Reich and reassured by the unanimous support of the Broederbond members, the leader of the Purified National Party did not hesitate to compare his fight for power with Hitler's. True, the doctrine of apartheid he was introducing to his electorate was not the same thing as National Socialism, but both came out of the same cauldron of national dissatisfaction and economic hardship. The flames of revival ignited by Hitler, the vision of a nationalist and anticapitalist revolution that rejected both communism and liberalism while exalting the notions of people, blood, and race, had definitely seduced Malan and the Afrikaner ideologists. Wasn't the Afrikaner's battle for "blood" and "soil" the same as the Israelites' struggle to reach the Promised Land? Wouldn't taking power prove that God wanted South Africa to be the property of whites forever?

Die Kaffer op sy plek—The Kaffir in his place. In the perverted cosmology that inspired the Purified National Party's election platform, this motto became an article of faith. Racial segregation already permeated most aspects of South African life. Every city had its separate black area made up of wooden barrack huts, known as "the location" as if to underline the nonidentity of the blacks who lived there. In the evening at the curfew bell white residences and businesses abruptly emptied of their servants and employees of color. Buses and trains were segregated. Post offices and banks had specific counters for blacks. In hospitals, even in operating theaters, blacks and whites were treated separately. Blacks went to separate schools and were buried in separate cemeteries. Except in the workplace, however, such separation was not mandated by any law or regulation. This was how it was, more or less by habit. Blacks and whites lived in different worlds. They never met, outside their roles as masters and servants. Although not technically prohibited, mixed marriages were extremely rare. In the Cape Province, males of mixed race benefited from the right to vote in parliamentary elections. Whites, however, still regarded these privileged people as members of an inferior race who would never belong to white civilization. It was less a system than a way of life. Its pragmatic rather than ideological nature made possible a few exceptions, such as District Six or Sophiatown, where blacks, coloreds, and whites practiced a racial coexistence that made progress seem not altogether impossible. Malan fiercely denounced such deviations as threats to the purity of the race. With apartheid in place he would have the means to put a stop to them, a political system he promoted without qualms because its objectives were in conformity with the law of God and blessed by the church. Woe to any Afrikaners who dared oppose it! They would be sanctioned immediately as "traitors to their race." The descendants of an individualist people were to become a nation of conformists. The time had come for all Afrikaners to be cast in the same implacable ideological mold.

★

MALAN HAD GIVEN THE VITAL MISSION of working out the practical application of this ideology to the one among his close associates who had first uttered the word "apartheid." The former student who had seen Hitler flee the stadium at the Berlin Olympics to avoid shaking hands with a black athlete had become the high priest of the purified Nationalist Party's crucial election campaign of May 1948. With limitless imagination and exceptional competence, Hendrik Verwoerd worked out what the party's strategy should be in the event of victory. Implementing the system of apartheid was of course his first priority. The separation of communities throughout the country in every aspect of their existence was a mammoth undertaking without precedent in human history. Legions of surveyors, ethnographers, land registry experts, urban planners, property tax inspectors, police, bulldozer operators, movers, practitioners of other urban and rural skills had to be recruited and trained. Tens of thousands of maps, plans, and title deeds had to be drawn up and printed. There would have to be files for several million individuals. Hundreds of laws would have to be drafted and put before parliament. Buildings and offices for a gigantic general headquarters to conduct any operations decided upon would have to be requisitioned.

Who could have known at the end of the 1940s that Hendrik Verwoerd and his antlike team of associates were already prepared to promulgate no fewer than 1,750 different pieces of legislation designed to give whites sole rule in South Africa forever?

Two

The Prime Minister's Bulldozers

THE JOURNEY OF THE GREAT TREKKERS was over at last. On May 28, 1948, 296 years and 21 days after the first Dutchman set foot in Africa, and ten years after Daniel François Malan's solemn appeal from the Pretoria hillsides, the time of redemption had come. God was about to grant his people the place he had chosen for them on the continent of Africa. With a majority of 624,500 votes and 89 seats out of 154, the Purified National Party and its allies had won the Union of South Africa's general election.

The Cape Town cannon fired its traditional noon volley as the architect of this achievement rose to speak to the parliament. To signal that this victory truly heralded a new era, he addressed his peers not in English, the official language of the country's previous leaders, but in Afrikaans, the guttural language the Afrikaners had forged for themselves during their long pilgrimage across Africa. Lifting his arms, Daniel François Malan exclaimed to the members, "In the history of the Afrikaners can be seen a will and a determination that suggest our people's destiny is not the work of man but the creation of God. South Africa at last belongs to us. Let us pray to God that it will always be thus." With this sober speech the hitherto silent house erupted. People stood up, stamped their feet, applauded, and cheered. There was a sudden upwelling of pride, a vision of revenge. The teak paneling on the walls of that noble institution had never reverberated with such an uproar. People wept and embraced and congratulated each other. The wave of cheering swept the benches, including those of the opposition. Suddenly the sound of singing filled the bays—powerful, expansive, martial, the whites' national anthem glorifying their epic in the land of South Africa. It was a strange victory won by a little over half the white minority, which represented only a fifth of the total population. Inhabited by 5 million whites and 25 million blacks in an area three times the size of California, the country the former clergyman now headed was a mosaic in which the best and the worst existed side by side with an intensity and brutality matched nowhere else in Africa. It was a country where wild animals were collected in sumptuous reserves but millions of people were packed into degrading ghettos; a country that had supplied a 590 carat stone for the English King Edward VII's scepter, but condemned two out of three of its black or colored children to walk to school barefoot—if they had a school to go to. It was a country that compensated for the destitution of the majority of its population with a cultural richness and a religious fervor unseen anywhere else on the continent; a country of intense spirituality in which 90 percent of blacks and coloreds worshiped the same God of justice and love as their white oppressors but 600,000 Hindus revered as many deities as Africa had inhabitants; a country whose hospitals were among the most modern in the world but where thousands of families resorted to quacks; where rural women warded off sterility by wearing talismans they relinquished only at death; where young Zulu males had to kill a lion with an *assegai* to gain tribal acceptance. It was a country that produced more steel, coal, copper, uranium, and precious woods than India and Brazil consumed, but it failed to provide millions of its children with a daily dish of corn or sweet potato. It was a country whose road, rail, and air infrastructure would be the envy of many European nations but that allowed an incalculable number of its workers to stagnate in sordid dormitories comparable to the shacks of Nazi camps or Soviet gulags. It was a country constantly being urged to revolt by a myriad of political parties and organizations; a country where between 300,000 and 400,000 whites working on farms or in the mines lived at the edge of poverty because they were competing with a black workforce paid even less. In short, it was a country of extremes, overflowing with resources and wealth but corrupted by brutalities and injustices that only an iron hand following a political plan could hope to master.

★

BY A MISCHIEVOUS TWIST OF FATE, there was another historic meeting in South Africa on the morning of May 28, 1948. As the representatives of the Africaners celebrated their electoral victory within the splendid Victorian facades of the Cape Town parliament building, a ceremony began in a suburb a stone's throw away from the opulent white city. "You are about to enter wonderland!" proclaimed the graffiti on the wall of a small Victorian house with wrought iron railings that stood at the entrance to District Six, as the neighborhood was called on city maps. Here, in a maze of alleyways, squares, and old buildings harboring a jumble of stalls, taverns, cafés, spice vendors, dives, artist studios, and lodgings, 60,000 blacks, coloreds, Indians, Malay, and whites cohabited. Every evening whites from middle-class neighborhoods came to savor the spicy stews at Alex's bistro or get drunk on bottles of cheap wine from the Paarl region. Then they would smoke a cannabis joint or an opium pipe next door to the Grand Canyon hairdressers. As for the innumerable brothels, everyone agreed they did more to advance racial harmony in South Africa than the sermons at all the churches put together. District Six was an oasis of tolerance and fellowship where poverty had managed to erase most differences. The place breathed an energy, an optimism that stirred the pride and admiration of everyone, white, black, or colored, and even spilled over into the rest of the metropolis. After all it was in the taverns and small squares of District Six that, among other things, African jazz was born, music whose connoisseurs swore equaled that of the New Orleans cabarets, whose idol was Hugh Masekela, a trumpeter as adulated as much as the legendary Satchmo.

The neighborhood's most original feature was its love of partying. Almost daily, its alleyways and squares were filled with the sound of band music from a parade marking some event or festival of this microcosm of religions, cultures, and traditions. The poor of District Six were in no way rootless or victimized by bad karma. On the contrary, they were vibrant proof of humanity's eternal capacity to rise above adversity.

The festival that day in May was a replica of the famous Coon Carnival that set the area alight every New Year's Day with its dancing, singing, and glittering costumes. At its head strode one of the best-known local characters, a tall, muscular black man with scars across his torso, who had sponsored many of the initiatives that made District Six bubble with life and imagination. Thirty-seven-year-old Barnabas Zanzibari owned a tavern in Eaton Square, a piece of ground lined with dilapidated Victorian houses that had seen better times. Following Zanzibari were his usual two acolytes: Apollon Davidson, a colored man in skintight jeans who worked as a tattooist in Upper Ashley Street, and another African dressed in a *gandoura* trimmed with sequined ribbon. Everyone knew Salomon Tutu. He was the neighborhood's "jet" hairstylist, a true sculptor of Afro hair, whose reputation reached far beyond the walls of District Six. These three were followed by a band of trumpets and drums bringing in its wake a crowd of men, women, and children in multicolored costumes and hats.

That May morning District Six was popping. The event that was stirring up the neighborhood was symbolic of the determination of men and women of color to resist the racist tyranny their white fellow citizens were preparing for them. The tavern owner Barnabas Zanzibari, the tattooist Apollon Davidson, and the hairstylist Salomon Tutu were about to christen on behalf of District Six's population the first public urinal in "wonderland."

It stood at the bottom of Upper Darling Street, in the middle of a small square planted with a few puny acacia bushes. It was attractive with its terraced roof and two entrances decorated with painted ceramics. The inside was spotless with gleaming white porcelain bowls fixed to the walls and shiny copper taps and pipes. A sign warned of the dangers of venereal disease. Another advised users to stand as close to the receptacles as possible to avoid getting the smallest drop of urine on the floor. Another proclaimed spitting an offense punishable with a fine.

When everyone had gathered around this small edifice, Zanzibari climbed onto a stone and addressed his fellow citizens: "What we inaugurate today is very much more than a public urinal," he declared. "It is a place where men of all races and colors can answer the call of nature together." Then, sticking out his chest, he added, "Beneath this roof there will be no more blacks, coloreds, Indians, or whites, just children of God sharing an interlude of racial peace!" Someone in the audience raised his hand and shouted, "Brother, won't the government be in a hurry to close our urinal because it violates the racial segregation rules?" Zanzibari gave them a faint smile of reassurance: "For the moment this country's racial laws apply only to public places," he replied briskly. "A urinal is not exactly a public place because the activity pursued in it is by its very nature private. To prohibit it, they would have to pass a special law banning the interracial exercise of a natural act intended by God." The explanation was a little complicated, but it delighted his audience members, who began applauding enthusiastically. Zanzibari then raised his arms to appeal for silence. His face lit up with happiness. The crucial moment had arrived. "Gentlemen," he exclaimed, "I invite you to take possession of your urinal."

A dozen men came forward. Among them were blacks, coloreds, Indians, Malays, as well as two members of the neighborhood's white minority. Each bowed respectfully as he went in. Soon there was the sound of flushing, drowned out by a burst from the band. The residents of District Six had succeeded in defying the victory song shaking the walls of parliament. One day, for sure, the whole of South Africa would piss together in racial harmony.

★

AMONG SOUTH AFRICA'S 25 million disenfranchised blacks and colored, there was consternation. Just when ideas of equality and dignity were spreading throughout the colonized world, when the great Western imperialist nations were renouncing their hegemony over the peoples they had dominated for generations, when a hundred new independent nations had just joined the United Nations, white South Africa was moving in the opposite direction.

Throughout the country, people were gathering to talk about how this terrible reality would affect their future. One of these meetings would have the greatest consequence. On the afternoon of May 28 three men arrived at 8115 Orlando West, a township on the outskirts of Johannesburg. The address belonged to one of the two thousand dwellings with corrugated iron roofs stretching as far as the eye could see across the dry plateau that would one day take the name of Soweto. Only families with proof of a job in a white area had the right to rent one of these homes, which often lacked running water, electricity, or sanitation.

The building contained a kitchen recess and two tiny rooms that served as a sleeping, dining, and living area combined. It was home to a twenty-nine-year-old legal intern, the descendant of a royal family in Xhosa country, his twenty-seven-year-old wife, Evelyn, and their two children, aged two and one. Tall, robust, his face partially covered by a downy beard, his frizzy hair carefully parted, elegant in his only suit, the man had presence. His soft voice that seemed to come from deep inside his chest and his smile radiating like a halo around his face gave him a natural distinction that commanded respect. His first name had been given to him by the British clergyman at the small school in the Transkei where he had learned to read and write. One day millions of ecstatic Africans would shout it as the name of a messiah. His name was Nelson Mandela.

Mandela looked up at the companions who had joined him to assess the situation. "We must prepare for the worst," was the substance of what he said. "Their entire campaign is based on the *swart gevaar*—black peril—and their slogan 'The kaffir in his place.' Wake up to reality, my friends. Their apartheid may be a new concept but it's an old idea. It's nothing less than a system of oppression by which they will be able to codify once and for all the laws and practices which have subjugated this country's blacks for three centuries. We must immediately prepare to defend ourselves."

"Yes!" agreed twenty-six-year-old Oliver Tambo, who taught mathematics in a Christian school in Johannesburg. Like Mandela, Tambo was a committed activist in the black struggle against white oppression.

"We cannot let the Afrikaners' election victory frighten us," interjected the placid voice of Walter Sisulu, the third man at the meeting. "At least now we know who our enemies are."

It would be hard to imagine anyone more different from Mandela than this thickset thirty-two-year-old who worked as a clerk in a real estate agency in Johannesburg. Dressed in a leather jacket and longshoreman's boots, he was a man of quiet strength who tried to see the positive side of any situation.

"Whoever our enemies are," Tambo observed sharply, "it's war they want with us, with their apartheid."

"War or not, the ANC's response must be firm," Mandela declared. "Malan and his Afrikaners must be made to realize that we are ready to fight for our basic rights. For an immediate end to land redistribution, for example, and to the prohibition against Africans doing certain jobs." He cleared his throat. "As for freedom of domicile, universal education, marriage between blacks and whites, we'll see about them later."

"You are right, Nelson," agreed Sisulu, "but you know not much can be expected from the current ANC leaders. These days the ANC is more concerned with holding onto past gains than promoting our people's rights for the future."

The legendary organization defending the black cause born one evening in 1912 in a theater in Bloemfontein opposed discrimination through nonviolent means, denounced racism, and struggled to make Africans full citizens. Buoyed by the wind of freedom that World War II had brought the colonial world, it had drawn up a charter of African demands, led by the blacks' right to South African citizenship. As Nelson Mandela would later write, "We hoped that the government and ordinary South Africans would see that the principles they were fighting for in Europe were the same ones we were advocating at home."[1]

Persuaded that the ANC needed new blood to confront the white extremists, Mandela, Sisulu, Tambo, and a handful of young activists had created in 1943 a Youth League within the old organization. Calling for a hard-line African nationalism and a single nation comprising all tribes, the Youth League had openly advocated for five years the overthrow of white supremacy and the installation of a truly democratic form of government. In their manifesto, the three activists meeting in Orlando West would solemnly reaffirm their conviction that the national liberation of Africans would be achieved by Africans themselves and that "the Congress Youth League must be the brain-trust and power-station of the spirit of African nationalism."[2] Their credo still held to the ideal of nonviolence the ANC had originally taken from Mohandas Gandhi. But how much longer would it continue to do so?

In their moment of triumph, the champions of apartheid would have ridiculed the defiance voiced by those three young blacks. In the buildings that housed their new government, perched on Pretoria's flowering hills, the racist crusade to horror had already begun.

★

CARNAL LOVE: the greatest peril to the integrity of the race. Once the obsession of Adolf Hitler and his ethnic cleansers, it was

---

1. Nelson Mandela, *Long Walk to Freedom* (London: Little, Brown, 1994), p. 10.

2. Mandela, *Long Walk to Freedom*, p. 93.

taken up by Malan and his accomplices as they launched apartheid. Hendrik Verwoerd attacked the problem from the moment his party took occupancy of the first floor of the Union Buildings, the administrative seat of government. In a matter of hours he conceived two laws. Called the Immorality Act and the Prohibition of Mixed Marriage, they made sexual relations between members of different races illegal. Any infraction was punishable with seven years imprisonment. Though they affected only a very small minority of the population, still the right to love freely had until then been one of the few privileges shared by all South Africans regardless of their skin color.

In the rare places where racial mixing was open, people were stunned. Apollon Davidson, the neighbor of District Six's jet hairstylist, was overcome when the hairdresser arrived at his tattoo parlor brandishing the front page of that day's *Cape Times*. Its enormous headline proclaimed "New Power to Impose Apartheid," and a subheading announced the banning of all sexual relations between blacks and whites, on pain of imprisonment.

"Apartheid?" the tattooist asked anxiously. "What exactly does that mean?" Someone suggested getting the tavern owner Zanzibari, the man responsible for the newly inaugurated interracial public urinal. He came running trailed by other locals. Soon the tattoo studio was packed, nothing unusual since it had always been the main political meeting place in the neighborhood. In his capacity as official tattooist, Apollon enjoyed special respect. He had become a sort of confessor to whom people came to exorcise their fears and satisfy their secret fantasies. Plying needles, scissors, and vials of dye, his long, sensitive fingers regularly traced appeals for happiness, luck, or fortune onto his clients' skin. A whole catalog of desires, too, sometimes even lunacies. White women would come from wealthy neighborhoods to have erect black phalluses tattooed on their stomachs. Others asked for serpents, dragons, phallic symbols. Men preferred cockerels, eagles, lions, sabers. Beggars had "Please" tattooed on the palm of one hand and "Thank-you" on the other. Gangsters

wanted four black dots in a square on their arm symbolizing the
four walls of a prison, with a fifth in the middle representing
the detainee about to escape. Herbalists, drug addicts, homosexuals, lesbians, and prostitutes crowded the parlor to have fetish
symbols engraved into their flesh. One eccentric had a zipper
drawn over his appendix with the caption "opened by mistake."
Apollon himself had a shirt collar and bow tie tattooed round his
neck. As for the naked pinup girl he'd tattooed on the chest of
the Muslim butcher, it had taken all Apollon's skill to cover her
with a veil when the tradesman found himself a wife.

Everyone was waiting for the tavern owner's reaction to the
headline. "It's bad news," he declared. "The whites are going to
put up a wall between them and us."

"You mean they're going to take the best of the country and
leave us what they don't want?" asked the hairstylist.

"You've got it, my friend," confirmed the café owner, per-
turbed. "Apartheid is Afrikaans for 'separation.' Whites on one
side, and everyone else on the other."

Zanzibari drew an imaginary line with his hand.

"And on which side are they going to put us District Six
whites?" asked the little man with the mustache who owned the
hardware store on Windsor Street. Julius Samuel was Jewish and
his wife was colored. His grandparents had emigrated from
Lithuania after the pogroms at the end of the nineteenth century.
His family was one of the oldest in the neighborhood. Together
with a few other mixed-race families, the Samuel family exemplified the racial harmony that prevailed in District Six.

The tavern owner groped for words.

"Perhaps the whites will force you to separate from your wife
and live with them," he said eventually, raising his arms sadly.

This possibility seemed outrageous. District Six was one
community. No one should be threatened with being torn away
from the group.

"I've got an idea," the hairstylist suddenly announced. "We'll
have Apollon tattoo 'Everyone against apartheid' across our

chests. And then we'll march bare-chested outside parliament in Cape Town."

All heads bowed, as if in solemn contemplation of the hairdresser's extraordinary suggestion. Then someone shouted: "Yes, everyone against apartheid!" Malan and Verwoerd never heard it, but the cry, taken up by everyone, filled the tattoo parlor.

★

TO PREVENT THE INTERMINGLING OF BLOOD, the new government had decided to make a show of inflexibility. To detect relationships that could blot the purity of the race, it would spy on its citizens in their beds. This would require a new sort of detective work. Along with District Six, one of the government's prime targets was a mixed suburb about four miles from the center of the country's largest city, Johannesburg. With its baroque church tower and red tiled roofs nestling among eucalyptus trees, from a distance it looked like a town in Tuscany. Close up, it was a jumble of shacks squeezed along narrow dirt alleyways. The neighborhood was called Sophiatown after the daughter of the Jewish developer who, at the turn of the century, had dreamed of building a residential suburb here for the white managerial staff in the mining industry. But Sophia's father had hardly sold his first lots when the Johannesburg council decided to sink an enormous open sewer on its periphery. The white clientele promptly left and was replaced by black buyers, only too glad to get title to property at low cost enabling them to live near a white city. In fact possession of this document gave the African residents of Sophiatown a sense of security and independence that was expressed in an unusually carefree lifestyle. Almost unique in South Africa, blacks here could lead an existence free of humiliating restrictions, political barriers, and racial prohibitions. As apartheid's ravages were beginning, South Africans of all races and colors could still settle freely in Sophiatown. Attracted to this atmosphere, many whites had even come to build houses. From this amalgam had resulted a multiracial society made up of journalists, writers, musicians, and even politicians. Though of course by official standards a shantytown whose population density and types of habitation violated the norms of urban planning, Sophiatown was a vibrant community, a place with soul, where laughter, music, and dance could make people forget the precariousness of their day-to-day lives.

One of the most popular personalities in this unusual place was a tall white man who wore the clerical collar of an Anglican priest. Forty-eight-year-old Trevor Huddleston was vicar of a local church, Christ the King. His impassioned sermons calling for the integration of blacks into a reconciled South African society had assaulted the racist ears of the Nationalists in Pretoria for the past twenty years. Other prominent white figures living in Sophiatown included playwright Athol Fugard and novelist Peter Simpson, as well as several well-known journalists. These whites appreciated living in the heart of a detribalized, modern black society that included intellectuals, artists, and musicians. Sophiatown was also renowned for the beauty of the women who kept its *shebeens*, the somewhat clandestine bars that formed an integral part of the culture of any African neighborhood; for its procurers, its ladies of the night, and its *tsotsis*—two rival gangs: the Americans, so called because their members were known as Gary Cooper, Humphrey Bogart, and Clark Gable, and the Berliners, recognizable by the small swastika painted on their foreheads. But above all it was a passion for jazz that earned the neighborhood its exceptional reputation. As in the cafés and alleyways of District Six, jazz in Sophiatown was a culture in itself, a way of drowning conflict in the blasts of trumpets and saxophones.

Each night the Odin cinema, a huge hall that stood at the entrance to the neighborhood, hosted musicians as celebrated as Hugh Masekela, the renegade from District Six whose muted trumpet was legendary as far away as New Orleans, and the mythical saxophone king in dark glasses, Kippie Moeketsie, and his partner Miriam Makeba, whose beguiling voice drew fans from Johannesburg and even Pretoria. Every Saturday until dawn, the Odin would show enraptured audiences the latest Hollywood movie hits with Lena Horne singing "Stormy Weather" or "Black Velvet." In the early hours of the morning the musicians paraded through the streets and squares bringing with great flourishes of trumpets and cymbals the musical message of their black brothers on the far side of the Atlantic. The most adored of these small bands were the Manhattan Brothers and the Jazz Maniacs. Their orgies of sound would linger in the smoke and alcohol of the *shebeens,* ending up in the morning at the head of some marriage or funeral procession. Like District Six in Cape Town, Sophiatown in the suburbs of Johannesburg presented a symbolic image of what South Africa could be if only it were rid of its fears and hatreds.

For the current oppressors this was a horrifying black spot marring the environmental purity of South Africa's largest white city, the embodiment of the tragedy of racial mixing that hung like a specter over their country.

★

THEY WERE ONLY A FEW HUNDRED out of 25 million South Africans, these men and women who dared to defy the Immorality Act by loving each other openly despite their difference in color. Twenty-six-year-old Monika de Villiers was a tall blonde with a pretty, freckled face. She was born near Cape Town where her parents, descendants of Huguenots, had a prosperous wine-growing estate. After she graduated with a degree in sociology from the Afrikaans University of Stellenbosch, her father had sent her for a sabbatical year at the University of Birmingham in England, secretly hoping that she would find a husband there. Many white parents tried to extricate their children from the uncertainties of a future in the land of apartheid by sending them abroad during the 1950s. But Monika would not hear of leaving her native country. One day she saw a small newspaper advertisement seeking volunteers to go into the townships to teach

African women their rights. Attracted by this bold idea, Monika packed her bag, caught the train, and presented herself at the address indicated. The organization occupied a small room in an apartment building in Johannesburg. A black man of about thirty received her. His name was Willi.

"I was immediately struck by the gentleness in his expression and his voice," the young woman would later say. "He told me he lived with his parents in Sophiatown and that he was looking for civil rights specialists to give instruction there. I was just the sort of person he needed. At university I had studied history and human relations. I knew most of the civil administrative code by heart. Next day Willi invited me to go with him to Sophiatown. He introduced me to his family and friends. I fell under his spell. I had never known any blacks. There was something so reassuring about him. I started working at once.

"Every evening I drove back to Johannesburg where a friend of my parents had loaned me a small house called the White House. But one evening I stayed in Sophiatown. That night, Willi and I made love on the carpet in his living room, like two curious children. We could hear his parents snoring in the next room and the iron beds creaking in his brothers' and sisters' room. The fluorescent numbers on the alarm clock cast a green light like a lunar veil over our bodies. Now and then through the curtains on the windows, headlights of passing cars would shower us with a burst of light. The Immorality Act had just been promulgated. I was paralyzed with fear. I imagined Peeping Toms outside the door. Rapists! Moralizers from the vice squad! I imagined them bursting in, their flashlights aimed at us, and their coarse laughter and obscenities. 'Aha! In flagrante delicto, a white fucking a black!' Willi seemed less worried than me even though the risk for him was much greater: up to seven years imprisonment. . . . But no. The headlights receded and our love was once more just moonlit.

"For days and nights our idyll went on undisturbed in Sophiatown, never encountering hostility. Willi's parents adopted me as their daughter. His sister did my hair African-style. I went with

Willi to the *shebeens* where we drank brandy and Coke and listened to funky American music. I forgot I was white. I had no color, was transparent, a sort of mutant accepted in complete simplicity by the other inhabitants of this amazing neighborhood.

"Our carefree honeymoon lasted until that unforgettable night when I thought Willi's house was going to be broken down. Police were banging on the door and walls with their rifle butts and boots like madmen. They were shouting: 'Police. Open the door!' There were at least four of them. They wanted to be able to write in their report that they had caught a white woman and a black man in the act of violating the Immorality Act. We got dressed as fast as we could and Willi motioned to me to go out the back of the house. His brother's children were screaming. His father and mother had gotten up. Outside a neighbor intercepted me and threw a cover over my head. Then he pushed me toward the small outhouse at the far end of the garden and shut me inside. I could hear the policemen yelling: 'Where is she? Where's your whore bitch?' After a moment one of them screamed at Willi: 'Liar! Smell this sheet with your filthy kaffir nose. It stinks of fucking!' They started shouting again: 'Where's your slut?' I realized that every question was punctuated with a punch to Willi's face. It was frightful. I fought with the idea of going to help him and giving myself up to those bastards, but Willi's friend who had thrown the blanket over my head held me back. Not finding me, they abandoned the idea of taking Willi away. When the coast was clear and I went back in the house, I suggested we go to my home in Johannesburg until this blew over. In the car Willi suddenly clammed up. Looking back, I realize it wasn't tiredness that made his shoulders slump and his eyes go dead. It was suffering buried deep in his brain that resurfaced as we approached the White House. Centuries of humiliation and slavery are not erased by a few nights of love.

"We arrived at the villa with our lights out. Willi crept in like a thief. And in bed when he wanted to take me in his arms, he couldn't get an erection."

★

AT THE START OF THE 1950S, the terrified screams of a little white girl in the eastern Transvaal emblemized more than any blood crime could the madness set in motion by the apartheid regime of Daniel François Malan and his accomplices. Her name was Sandra Laing, and she was eight years old. She lived in Piet Retief, a small town named after the Afrikaner leader stoned to death by the Zulus in the previous century. Her parents were shopkeepers respected by the local white community. Sandra was a model pupil at the public school. With her long plaits and slightly tanned skin, she looked like all the other little girls in an institution attended exclusively by white schoolchildren. Then one day the parents of one of her friends complained to the headmistress that Sandra Laing was not really white but colored. Although the accusation seemed unfounded, the headmistress was obliged to notify the South African Bureau of Racial Affairs in Pretoria. This newly created body was the ultimate authority on matters of racial classification and had branches scattered all over the country, each with its own magistrate. These agencies were charged with ruling on the color and the race of any South African citizen. One of these magistrates turned up at the Piet Retief school escorted by two assistants to examine little Sandra. Was she white or colored? They were perplexed. In a country where the sun could turn white skin so many different shades, it was very difficult to be certain who belonged to one race or another. There was just one test that was reliable. Devised by one of Verwoerd's henchmen, this procedure would soon constitute one of the new regime's most moronic follies.

The representative from the commission for race classification carefully undid the little girl's plaits. Then he placed a pencil in the parting of her hair. If Sandra really belonged to the white race, the pencil would slip between her locks and fall to the ground. In this particular case the slender shaft of wood came to rest against a curl. This was proof that Sandra was colored. She

had been betrayed by her slightly curly hair. That same day, despite her tears of despair, she was cast outside the school gate as
if she had the plague.

Thousands of other pencils would inflict similar trauma in
the nationwide enforcement of a new law even more vicious than
the one prohibiting sexual relations between blacks and whites.
Just as Hitler had divided Germans into privileged or despised
classes according to whether they were "Aryan" or Jewish or
gypsy or some other, so Verwoerd divided the South African population into four distinct categories: whites, blacks, coloreds, and
Asians. The law sanctioning the long-standing white dream of
living in a country where all races were clearly identified bore a
banal administrative name—Population Registration Act—three
words that represented a national nightmare. Verwoerd's troops
suddenly found themselves confronted with the superhuman
task of classifying and registering millions of South Africans;
blacks, coloreds, and Asians were to discover that from then on
their existence was defined by a single criterion that ignored character and merit and judged them only by the color of their skin.

★

A BUZZING HIVE. Day or night, the splendid colonnaded edifice in
Pretoria, the seat of South African government since 1913, was
never still. Hendrik Verwoerd and his teams of surveyors, ethnographers, and urban planners occupied an entire floor of the
enormous building that had been the model for the viceroy's
palace in New Delhi. Large-scale maps, town plans, synoptic
pictures, and charts lining the walls of offices, reception rooms,
and corridors mapped the locations of the various populations,
ethnic groups, and tribes. On some walls there were even aerial
photographs. Although satellite detection did not yet exist, Pretoria's inquisitors had gone to impossible lengths to ensure that no
village, farm, or hut in a country three times the size of California escaped their investigation. Inspired by the Nazi census of
Jews in Germany and other countries occupied by the Reich, the

Population Registration Act required every citizen to declare his racial group to the local authority where he lived. To be recognized as white an individual had to prove that both his parents were white and that he was accepted as such in the neighborhood where he lived. If there was the slightest doubt (for example, if a colored person wanted to pass himself off as white), experts would intervene. They would question relatives and friends, resort to the pencil test, and look for signs of pigmentation around nails and eyes. In a country with such a diverse population, trying to determine an individual's race for certain was a total folly. How many whites had the unhappy surprise of finding themselves suddenly described as colored; how many Cape coloreds were demoted to the ranks of Malay coloreds—there were no fewer than seven categories of coloreds based on darkness or lightness of skin; how many Indians of South Indian origin saw themselves downgraded to the unenviable status of black because of their very dark color? The race classification board's report for the first year of apartheid showed that eight hundred South Africans had been forced to change race. Among them fourteen white and fifty Indians had become coloreds; seventeen Indians, Malays; four coloreds and one Malay, Chinese. Eighty-nine blacks had the good luck to be reclassified as colored and five coloreds had the misfortune to become blacks. But 518 coloreds hit the jackpot by officially joining the white Afrikaner race.

What tragedies were brought on by these brutal transfers from one race to another! Those whose racial category was reassigned had to move, find another school for the children, look for another job. Not to mention the marriages or liaisons that became illegal overnight. Or the people who suddenly belonged to a different race than their own family. There was the case of three abandoned children whom the authorities kept locked up in a secret place for six months before identifying them as white. A well-known television announcer seriously injured in a car accident died without medical aid because the emergency room could not decide which department to admit him to—white or colored.

The official racial classification of every South African citizen was only the prelude to a great plan Verwoerd and his teams in Pretoria were drawing up. With the passage of the Group Areas Act, Hitler's admirer sought to carve up South Africa to geographically separate the various communities from one another. This law, the real cornerstone of apartheid, defined the places where nonwhites were to regroup. Shrewd districting would confine blacks to a few urban developments designated as townships, and especially to the distant "homelands," reserves, or Bantustans, destined one day to become autonomous states. This new law would get rid of what its inventors considered anomalies—the rare neighborhoods like District Six or Sophiatown occupied by people of color at the center or on the immediate fringes of white cities. Finally, the law was intended to systemize ethnic separation inside the townships; each group would be apportioned its fraction of the locality according to whether it was Zulu, Xhosa, Sotho, Tswana, or other. Ultimately this law and all the appendixes that extended its reach over the years would lead to the forced expulsion of several million blacks from areas it classed as white to peripheral, often impoverished regions. To the organization in charge of these deportations, the imaginative Verwoerd gave a name that cleverly disguised their finality: Department for Cooperation and Development. It was a way of reassuring ministers in the Presbyterian Church who were disturbed by people being uprooted en masse. Verwoerd was quick to allay their fears by declaring, "The displacement of blacks is intended to promote their national unity, protect their ethnic and political interests, and improve their living conditions." He added that precautions were always taken to ensure that displaced communities found job opportunities "comparable to those they had enjoyed where they came from." He even went so far as to announce that "everything is done to make these transplantations as attractive as possible to obtain the cooperation of the people concerned." For individuals or groups who resisted these expulsions or contested their legality by appealing to the courts, he came up with the Black Prohibition of Interdicts Act, which prevented the judiciary from opposing government action and authorized the use of force against any rebellion. Another law prohibited the disclosure of any military action.

Finally, Verwoerd and his accomplices produced a flurry of laws limiting interracial contact in virtually every aspect of life: housing, education, employment, entertainment, sports, transport, and personal relationships. They extended the enforcement of apartheid to park benches, buses and trains, public urinals and elevators, station waiting rooms, theaters, music auditoriums, and even beaches. They excluded blacks from state universities and sought to ban them from taking part in white church services. In the Catholic cathedral in Cape Town, the congregation's members of color could not receive the Eucharist until the last white had left the communion table. Nothing would convey the tragedy of apartheid more effectively to the world than the legislative harassment that even many South Africans referred to as "petty apartheid."

Petty or not, apartheid expressed the Afrikaner Nationalists' fanatical will to impose everywhere and always physical distance between whites and others. The policy of transplanting the various black communities into a multiplicity of ghettos was intended to demonstrate that South Africa was not one country but a patchwork of different countries. There was no room for any kind of melting pot. The white need for black manpower must not involve cohabitation. Never short on creativity, Verwoerd even created a law imposing a buffer zone of at least five hundred yards between any black township and the white city that profited from the sweat of the black laborers. Five hundred yards of empty ground, a no-man's-land meant to convey the divide between peoples, between Christian civilization and African barbarity, between Jan van Riebeeck's white descendants and the Bushmen of the African jungle.

★

THE NAZIS FORCED JEWS TO DISPLAY their pariah status through a yellow Star of David sewn onto their clothing. To oblige blacks to acknowledge their subhuman status, the implementers of the apartheid system thought up another symbol: a small ninety-two-page notebook with a red or green cardboard cover that every citizen of color must be ready to show to any authority on pain of immediate imprisonment. Called the "reference book" or simply "pass," this identity document was a kind of internal passport without which a citizen of color could not move about or work anywhere in the country. It contained detailed information about its owner: a photograph, fingerprints, ethnic group, tax status, place of residence and work, lists of previous jobs together with addresses and duration, and so on. The pass even contained a certificate specifying where its holder could be buried. In short, this was a document in which all South African blacks, from university professors to farm laborers, saw their lives pitilessly and minutely charted by the authorities. But for the whites in power it was to be a vital means of controlling the comings and goings of 25 million South Africans of color and of ensuring that members of the various tribes actually reported to their new living areas.

★

THE MASTER OF PRETORIA remembered the lessons of his youthful stay in Nazi Germany. "Africans who disagree with our policy must be constrained, if necessary by force," paraphrasing Hitler's speeches about the Jews. Luck was on his side. A heart attack suddenly removed Daniel François Malan, who had led South Africa's small white minority to power. Verwoerd, his natural successor, was elected to replace him. He was just fifty-seven years old. The Afrikaners rejoiced: their future was in safe hands. The new head of government began by instituting what amounted to a politics of terror. He dissolved the South African Communist Party, one of the last bastions of freedom of opinion where blacks and whites still collaborated. Then he outlawed all protest against the laws of apartheid. Finally he threatened to imprison anyone attempting to oppose the freedom to work in case of a strike.

Despite his authoritarian leanings, Verwoerd had never cared for Hitler's exploitation of his own personality to sway the crowds of the Third Reich. He had none of the charismatic appeal on which the success of dictators usually depends. Though he had presence, it was cloaked in a professor's paternal airs. He was not a gifted public speaker. No flashes of humor or surges of passion ever relieved the monotony of the long speeches he delivered to the Cape Town parliament. But that did not prevent his audiences from listening to him with an almost religious attention, for Verwoerd conveyed to the Afrikaners the assurance that their destiny was under his control. Above all, he was able to give them a clear conscience in a world where criticism was beginning to mount at home and abroad. His vision for the future did not involve only the advent of *wit baasskap,* white supremacy. It also involved giving blacks their rightful place—territories where they could develop their own nations exactly as the whites had done in the areas they had allocated to themselves. Thus blacks would no longer be considered inferior but different. Moreover, he claimed, it was not because they were "inferior" that Africans must be excluded from the South African political system but because they were not really South Africans. Over time, Verwoerd even stopped using the term "apartheid" and replaced it with "separate development" and sometimes even "separate freedom."

The fact that the territories to which the regime expelled people of color were poor enclaves amounting to only 13 percent of the area of South Africa, while the masses they were supposed to accommodate formed more than 75 percent of the country's total population, was of little importance. It was the myth that counted, not the reality. To give substance to that myth Verwoerd built capitals in the various reserves, set up legislative assemblies, had flags designed, national anthems composed, and heads of state appointed. He went out in the field to ensure that this monumental operation, this unprecedented deportation would go smoothly. "Purifying" southern Africa, the sovereign property of whites, was his priority. Blacks must leave all the areas that whites had reserved for themselves and move to their rural "homelands" where they could exercise their rights as citizens and develop their national independence. Verwoerd was convinced that the lure of "separate independence" would even empty the enormous black concentrations living in townships like Soweto in favor of these nation-states. Then only a few thousand migrants would be left in white South Africa, working under contract and only short-term in white cities. These temporary workers would not be treated as South Africans but as foreigners.

Pretoria's social engineers applied themselves with a vengeance to keep the system functioning effectively. They saw to it that the coloreds staying in white areas on work permits could not put down roots. A pitiless Land Act prohibited them from buying their temporary lodgings. Apart from selling wood, coal, milk, and vegetables, migrants could not conduct any commercial activity. In their townships, no public services, banks, clothing stores, supermarkets, or any other businesses likely to make them seem permanent were allowed. All commercial licenses had to be renewed at the beginning of each year. The white administrators handling this formality were required to check that no black business had been unduly successful. If a small businessman in a township actually did make a profit, he automatically had to return his capital to the Bantustan from which he had come.

Verwoerd busied himself promising blacks a return to their past, their traditions, the life of their ancestors, a way of life finally free of the afflictions of city living and vexation from whites. To the descendants of the people of the wagons he liked to project himself as a man chosen by God to give them the Africa they had dreamed of for generations, an Africa where whites and blacks would live in peace but *separately*. Newspaper cartoonists regularly portrayed him sitting on a cloud, talking on the telephone to the Creator. For Afrikaners this satire would gain significance

one day in 1960 when their messiah miraculously escaped two
bullets fired straight at his head by a deranged white farmer.

★

THE THREE YOUNG BLACKS watched silently as the coffin was lowered into a hole dug in the highveld's red earth, consumed with
outrage against the racial politics of Pretoria's tyrant. Nelson
Mandela, Walter Sisulu, and Oliver Tambo had come that icy
winter's day to bid farewell to Pixley Seme, the lawyer who in
1912 had founded the African National Congress to give voice to
the blacks' opposition to white oppression. But in forty years of
reticence and attachment to the principles of nonviolence, suc-
cessive leaders of the ANC had won no significant victory. Out of
this bitter recognition had been born the Youth League, a more
militant group of which Mandela and his companions were now
the main leaders. As the last shovelfuls of African soil covered
the coffin, the three men made a decision: they would launch a
spectacular operation to restore the prestige of the organization
Pixley Seme had founded. This operation would be called the Defiance Campaign and would have a single objective: the abolition
of the heinous laws recently promulgated by the apartheid state.

D day was set for June 26, 1952. Across Natal, the Transkei,
the Orange Free State, and the eastern Cape groups of nonviolent
protesters, cheered on by crowds delirious with hope and pride,
undertook to break the chains of white tyranny. They publicly
burned their passbooks, burst into white neighborhoods flouting
signs that said "Europeans only," violated curfew, entered hotels
forbidden to people of color, went swimming at the whites-only
beaches, occupied cinemas and railway cars strictly reserved for
Europeans. A wave of almost mystical fervor accompanied these
acts of defiance. The churches immediately announced days of
fasting and prayer in support of the militants. Verwoerd and the
full apartheid apparatus counterattacked violently. Thousands
of demonstrators were arrested and jailed. Mandela was undaunted. "At least the authorities in Pretoria are finally aware of

our existence!" The response was harsher than ever. A torrent of emergency legislation was passed to punish with unprecedented severity those participating in the Defiance Campaign. The police searched hundreds of offices and homes. Soon 20,000 people were behind bars. But for every arrest there were ten new recruits to the ANC. Mandela and his fellow Youth League members were jubilant: 200,000 new activists had joined their organization in a few weeks. It was a spectacular result achieved almost without bloodshed. As the illegal actions and the number of arrests grew, however, the situation worsened. Riots broke out in Port Elizabeth, Johannesburg, Kimberley, and East London, and this time blood was shed—by blacks as well as whites. Mandela and his companions were arrested and banned from all political activity for a period of two years. When the resistance campaign did not let up, the government outlawed all acts of protest. A state of emergency could be declared at any moment.

This time there could be no doubt. The greatest confrontation between blacks and whites since Jan van Riebeeck landed on the shores of the Cape in 1652 had begun. Over forty years it would claim hundreds of thousands of victims and expose South Africa to world condemnation.

In his office, with the scent of jacaranda blossoms wafting from the Pretoria heights, the man primarily responsible for this anathema had no qualms about spreading the cancer of apartheid. Having registered and then deported several million Africans to the townships and reserves, Hendrik Verwoerd now turned his sights to what constitutes the most precious asset of any people and its potential for forging a better future: the education of its children. On September 15, 1953, Verwoerd announced, "An African child should not be allowed to glimpse the green pastures of the European community, on which he will never have the opportunity to graze." The Bantu Education Act established total segregation in the South African educational system. No private black school would have the right to open and function without consent of the authorities. Anyone breaking this ban would be found guilty of "the illegal propagation of knowledge." This at a time when the state devoted 1,385 rand a year to educating every white pupil, 593 on each colored child, and 192 on each black. Subjects such as mathematics, physics, and biology were simply crossed off the black school syllabus. These measures provoked an outcry among ANC activists, black public opinion, and even moderate whites. In response, Verwoerd waved the banner of a clear conscience. "What is the point of teaching mathematics to a black child if he will never be called upon to use it? There is no place for the native in European society above the level of certain menial jobs," a profession of faith which he concluded with this lapidary refrain: "We must get it into the blacks' heads that they will never be equal to whites."

★

RESISTANCE TO PRETORIA'S state terror continued. One day in 1955 the white woman Monika de Villiers announced she was expecting a baby with Willi, the black worker whose life she shared in Sophiatown on the outskirts of Johannesburg.

"This infringement of the Immorality Act exposed us to terrible trouble," she would later recount. "Afraid I might lose my baby while being jolted about in traffic, I had moved in with Willi for good. His father had arranged a private corner for us in the middle room where we had made love for the first time. The police had not come back. We weren't hiding. Sophiatown remained a marvelous island of liberty amidst all the turbulence of apartheid.

"But we knew we had everything to fear from the prime minister of South Africa. He had studied in Germany and absorbed the Nazi methods of eliminating the Jews. We knew he was a very dangerous man. He would not tolerate for very long the existence of a multiracial neighborhood like ours at the edge of the great white city of Johannesburg. It defied all the apartheid policies designed to remove blacks from white residential areas. According to the Reverend Huddleston, who always knew about these things, the government had requisitioned a vast area of uncultivated land twenty or thirty miles from Johannesburg to re-house the population it would sooner or later evict from Sophia-town. But it didn't count on our neighborhood's formidable spirit of resistance. Sophiatown was in their blood, I'm certain, in much the same way as Jerusalem was in the blood of the founders of Israel. That spring of 1955 graffiti began to appear on the walls, threatening: 'We won't move!' Other slogans told the authorities they would have to evict people 'over our dead bodies.' But the residents' most effective defense against the tyrants of Pretoria was Father Huddleston himself, who from the vantage point of his six-foot-four white frame heaped invective on the armed po-lice keeping a heavy presence in the neighborhood in anticipa-tion of the final sweep. He actually held meetings inside his church to encourage his parishioners not to give in to intimida-tion. Two or three times a week he assembled the residents in the Odin cinema or in Freedom Square, as the open space in the middle of the neighborhood had been dubbed.

"It was there one evening that Willi and I met a small group of activists belonging to the ANC. The ban prohibiting them from all political activity for two years had just expired and they were up in arms against the government's expulsion plans. One of them was a large fellow with a slightly muffled voice. He was not much of an orator but he spoke with such passion that every-one there was spellbound. His name was Nelson Mandela. He started his talk with a cry of 'Asihambi! We are not moving!' which everyone repeated several times together. Then he clenched his fist and shouted: 'Sophiatown likhaya lam asihambi! Sophia-town is our home. We are not leaving!' While everyone present took up the chant and repeated it, the armed police rushed at Father Huddleston and evicted him from the square. 'Stick to church matters, not politics!' the officer in charge shouted at him. People booed the police who had to call for reinforcements. Mandela had started to address the demonstrators. There were many young people among them. You could feel the excitement.

The policemen nervously recorded the speaker's condemnation of the government's actions in their notebooks. Mandela recited a merciless list of charges. With each sentence the atmosphere grew more charged. Then suddenly he let himself be carried away with words that would prove to be fateful. I had never heard a black leader go so far. I took Willi's arm and gripped it as hard as I could.

"'The time for passive resistance has ended,' declared Mandela. 'Passive resistance has been a useless strategy. It will never overturn a white minority regime bent on retaining its power at any cost. Violence is the only weapon that will destroy apartheid. We, my friends, must be ready to use that weapon in the near future.'[3]

"I clung to Willi's arm. Suddenly the faces around us looked frightened. This was the first time a black leader had spoke publicly of war on the white government. A moment later a voice shouted 'Asihambi! We are not moving!' Everyone chanted the slogan in chorus. Then another ANC leader standing next to Mandela began to sing the African national anthem. Soon it was as if all Sophiatown was singing 'Nkosi Sikelel' iAfrika!' 'God bless Africa!' Then Mandela started to sing another African hymn. Willi translated the words as he went along because he was singing in Xhosa. 'There are our enemies,' went the refrain, 'let us take our weapons and attack them!' All the people repeated it in chorus. When Mandela stopped singing, he pointed to the police all around the square and called out to his audience: 'My friends, those men are lackeys of the white government. There, there are our enemies.' There was a tremendous roar of assent. Then the police entered the crowd and rushed to handcuff the speaker. The people had no time to react. The forces of order had already put Mandela and four of his companions into one of their vans. Sophiatown would never see Nelson Mandela again.

---

3. Mandela, *Long Walk to Freedom*, p. 146.

"Then came the inevitable. At five o'clock in the morning on February 9, 1955, just as the sun began to light up the rows of red roofs and the ochre tower of the church of Christ the King, over two thousand police in combat gear jumped out of trucks parked in an arc around the houses. Each unit leader held a submachine gun in one hand and an eviction paper bearing the name and address of the family who lived there in the other. They shouted in Afrikaans: *'Maak julle oop! Maak julle oop!'* 'Open up! Open up!' Through the window we saw two trucks pull up outside our house. Before we had time to open the door, a policeman struck one of the pillars of the veranda with a pick. It shook the whole house so I thought it was going to come down around our heads. The man holding the eviction order commanded us to move all our furniture and belongings outside. Imagine having to move out a lifetime's possessions in a few minutes. I looked in anguish at Willi's father and mother. They had built that house with their own hands. It was their own little castle. They had known there the happiness and freedom of Sophiatown, that corner of paradise in the heart of an Africa that did not know hatred. When Willi and his parents had loaded the contents of the house into the trucks, the police officer in charge ordered us to get into one of the vehicles.

"Then I witnessed something my eyes and ears will never forget. Out of the alleyway came Hugh Masekela leading his small band of Jazz Maniacs to send us off with his famous trumpet. 'We'll Meet Again' was played by the musicians by way of a farewell. Even the policemen's faces were stiff with emotion. I had no tears left to shed when Hugh Masekela, Dollar Brand, and their companions turned on their way to play the same farewell song outside another house. As our two trucks headed off to a destination that none of us knew, another noise filled the freshness of the dawn. It was the sound of caterpillars scraping over the ground. I knew then that in a few hours' time Sophiatown would be no more than a memory. The prime minister's bulldozers had arrived."

★

IT TOOK THE AUTHORITIES three days to move the 60,000 residents out of Sophiatown. The trucks and buses deposited the deportees and their meager possessions some thirty-five miles from the former Johannesburg suburb, on an immense uncultivated tract of land in the middle of nowhere called Meadowlands. One day it would form part of Soweto, the largest black township in South Africa. It was an agglomeration of small brick houses stacked up against each other in the middle of wild grasses. Each family was allotted one of these precarious dwellings without toilets, water, or electricity. After being razed to the ground and disinfected, Sophiatown would be rebuilt with attractive houses for sale or rent to the white managerial staff working in Johannesburg, just as its developer had intended seventy years earlier. As if to spite its former occupants one last time, the neighborhood was renamed Triomf—Triumph.

★

SOME 4 MILLION BLACKS and coloreds suffered the fate of those evicted from Sophiatown. Most were deported to the Bantustans, reserves designated for people on the basis of their presumed ethnic origins. Despite government promises to establish industries in the proximity of these ghettos, hundreds of thousands of blacks found themselves condemned to farm infertile land to avoid starvation. Some managed to take refuge in the hovels built near mines or industries that needed a cheap and abundant black workforce. But the removals were sprung on their victims haphazardly. Generally the process began with a rumor. Then a government emissary visited the leader of the targeted community, and then an eviction notice appeared in the *Government Gazette*, the administration's official newspaper. A team of social engineers would then arrive from Pretoria to prepare for the operation. To forestall any resistance, these officials proceeded to close the schools and all local businesses, divert bus routes, stop maintenance and repairs to public and private buildings, and prohibit agricultural labor.

But often, especially in formerly black rural areas recently declared white, only the droning of bulldozers and the howl of police dogs at the crack of dawn told families that they were being deported. Declared a "white area" by government order, District Six, famous throughout the Cape region, would experience the refinements of an execution in slow motion. Instead of transplanting its 60,000 inhabitants all at once and razing all its buildings to the ground at the same time as they had done in Sophiatown, the authorities decided to evict people in stages, which made the demise of this almost unique symbol of a multiracial and fraternal South Africa all the more painful.

Wednesday, February 17, 1957, was market day in District Six. Hanover Street, the main thoroughfare, was a river of people, cars, barrows, buses, and animal carts; a noisy tide of voices, cries, laughter, shouts, and horns. There were buxom matrons with bags of provisions balanced on their heads; turbaned mullahs; pretty colored girls with long shining plaits; black schoolboys in shorts; paunchy traders looking like potentates with tinted glasses and tarbooshes at rakish angles on their heads; packs of teenage boys with studded belts around their waists; elegant young girls veiled in mauve tulle sprinkled with plastic jewels and sequins; porters buckling under the weight of blocks of ice, sacks of sweet potato, and demijohns of white wine; traveling salesmen, peddlers, beggars, and even lepers shaking their begging cups. With its parade of Oriental, Semitic, African, and European visages, faces from Malaysia, India, Mozambique, Eastern and Western Europe, Hanover Street was a mosaic of features and colors.

Into this multiracial market day hubbub, the first police van arrived. Six men armed with submachine guns got out and began hammering the butts of their guns against the door to Apollon Davidson's tattoo parlor. With them was a civilian in spectacles, white shirt, and black tie, holding in his hand an official document bearing several stamps and signatures. He was the government agent, come to notify the Upper Ashley Street tattooist of his expulsion. In a week's time a truck would turn up to take him, his family, and his possessions to the Cape Flats, an area a few miles from Cape Town. Davidson was the first victim of the decision to turn District Six into a suburb reserved exclusively for whites.

This colorful neighborhood would not let its celebrated tattooist go without a proper farewell. On the day of his deportation hundreds of residents invaded Upper Ashley Street at the instigation of Zanzibari, the café owner who had built the multiracial public urinal, and Salomon Tutu the barber. The men took off their shirts to reveal their chests on which Davidson had tattooed their protest in blue ink. "Everyone against apartheid! Everyone against apartheid!" the crowd chanted as the removal truck and the police arrived. All—whites, blacks, coloreds, and Indians— shouted abuse and threats at them. The police beat them off with their batons. The situation was turning dangerous.

At this point Davidson appeared standing on a packing case, his arms reaching out to the excited crowd. He signaled that he wanted to speak and the mob fell silent. "Friends," he cried, "for twenty-seven years we have lived together in this neighborhood in peace and fellowship. Tomorrow, these streets and houses will no longer exist because of the madness of the people governing us. I would like to take away with me one last picture of peace and love. Calm down. Listen to your hearts. No one will ever really be able to separate us. Soon we shall meet again somewhere in this country and then the values of our beloved neighborhood will live again. . . ." He broke off, his voice choked. He had run out of strength. "Good-bye, my friends!" he finished in a whisper.

The emotion was so intense that the police bowed their heads. A bulldozer's arrival forced the crowd back. District Six's agony had begun. It would last for six years.

★

NEVER WOULD A SMALL-TOWN MAYOR in the Transvaal have imagined that the place that was his namesake would one day represent the misery of apartheid in the eyes of the whole world. This was the reality forty-four-year-old John Sharpe was obliged to face on March 21, 1960. Yet by comparison with other South African townships, Sharpeville was a model of success: the homes of its 21,000 inhabitants all had electricity, running water, and sewage pipes. Some even had bathrooms. But at the beginning of the 1960s unemployment rose in Sharpeville and throughout the surrounding region. The residents' desire to look elsewhere for work was thwarted by the small red books that controlled their movement. Indeed, the despised cardboard pass became the pretext for a fresh nonviolent black revolt against apartheid. In Sharpeville and three other townships in the Transvaal, as well as in Langa and Nyanga in Cape Province, and finally in Soweto, a huge coordinated campaign of "voluntary arrests" began that fateful morning of March 21.

Tens of thousands of men and women marched on the police stations in the various townships to be arrested. They had received an order from the ANC leadership to break the law by leaving their red passbooks at home. In Orlando, an area forming part of the sprawling township of Soweto, the protestors marched behind a long banner proclaiming: "Today, 308 years after whites attacked Africa's sons and daughters and stole their land, the citizens of this country are out to win back their native land." There was no aggressiveness about those marching crowds. Following their traditions, men and women sang and chanted, shifting in place from one foot to the other, sometimes bringing their knees up as high as their chins. It was the famous toyi-toyi, the ritual dance of black revolt. One day all of black South Africa would win freedom dancing in this way.

The protests' organizers knew that by the next day they would fill the country's prisons. To restore order the government would have no alternative but to abolish the confounded passbooks. But Verwoerd refused to be intimidated. Instead of sending armored cars to charge the 10,000 protestors, he sent two Mirage air force jets to fly low over their heads. He thought the roaring aircraft would terrify the protestors and instantly break up the processions. He was wrong. Taking it as a show of sympathy for their cause, the protestors waved their hats at the pilots in joyous appreciation. A second flyover even closer to their heads was equally ineffectual. Undaunted, the Sharpeville procession continued toward the local police station. Then, without provocation and without warning, police mounted on the turrets of two armed vehicles guarding the building opened fire. Some women screamed while others laughed, probably thinking the police were firing blanks. In vain several people shouted, "Stop shooting!" The officers were young men visibly panic-stricken at the sight of the mass of humanity still advancing despite the gunfire. Police reinforcements arrived and fired their weapons at random. People fell by the dozens, others staggered about, screaming. Humphrey Tyler, a reporter for *Drum* magazine, saw a little boy wrap a blanket around his head as protection from the bullets. Shoes, hats, bags, bicycles were strewn about the vast esplanade that was soon littered with the dead and injured. It was butchery. Sixty-eight people were killed and over two hundred injured. It put Sharpeville on the world maps and provoked universal horror.

Terrified at the thought of a general black uprising, whites in the Transvaal and the Cape rushed to arm themselves with rifles and revolvers. In Johannesburg, stock prices plummeted as investors panicked, while in Pretoria foreign consulates were flooded with requests for emigration visas. The reality was inescapable: with the Sharpeville massacre, genocide was in the making.

★

THE LEADERS IN PRETORIA had no intention of letting up, imposing a state of emergency, hardening repressive laws, outlawing the ANC, incarcerating thousands, and calling up security forces on leave, especially after a few extremists set fire to the pass office and black police housing in Langa near Cape Town; in Cape Town itself, outside Caledon Square police station, another tragedy was barely averted. A police chief shouted through a loudspeaker: "No one will have to show their red or green pass for a month," and at the very last minute 30,000 demonstrators withdrew from the perimeter of the building.

Mandela, Sisulu, Tambo, and all the black resistance leaders observed once again that nonviolent action failed against the tyrants in Pretoria. There would be no getting rid of the red and green passes. As Mandela himself had said to those due to be evicted from Sophiatown, violence was the only weapon that could put an end to apartheid.

Violence! A terrible transition for men of reason shaped by a long tradition of peaceful action, activists marked profoundly by India's Mahatma Gandhi who, thirteen years previously, had led a fifth of humanity to freedom without firing a single shot or setting off a single terrorist bomb. But in 1960, on the twelfth anniversary of apartheid, there was no way left but to go underground and prepare *umkhonto we sizwe,* the spear of the nation. This expression, invented by Mandela, became the code name for the new armed branch of the ANC responsible for planning and executing armed black resistance operations. Umkhonto's first decision was to clandestinely dispatch Oliver Tambo across the South African border to create support bases in neighboring countries. The second was to send Mandela to Algeria for terrorist commando training. The third was to find a place inside the country for a secret headquarters. An abandoned farm in the middle of marshland in the Rivonia region, twenty miles north of Johannesburg, was eventually chosen. A place even the government's best bloodhounds would never find, or at least so Mandela and his companions thought. Mandela found himself forced to leave behind the pretty social worker he had taken for his second wife when he went on his mission to Algeria. But Winnie Madikizela Mandela was resigned. At the wedding ceremony, her father had told her never to forget that the one to whom she had joined her destiny for better or for worse was already married—to South Africa.

The leaders of Umkhonto we Sizwe spent several months organizing their campaign of sabotage, setting up networks, and dividing the country into operational cells ready for immediate action. At first, to avoid unnecessary loss of human life, their targets were only economic and political. Would this opening series of operations suffice to make the fanatics in Pretoria change their policies, they wondered. Or would the whole country have to be dragged into civil war?

The first explosions went off on December 15–16, 1963, in post offices, administrative buildings, and rail and electrical installations in Durban, Johannesburg, and Port Elizabeth. Over the next eighteen months more than two hundred similar attacks claiming numerous lives disrupted the country. The Umkhonto activists were often outflanked by extremists who were prepared to use any form of violence. South Africa thus became the setting for acts of savagery—burning police stations, assaulting prisons, pillaging shops, and attacking white homes. Five whites, including a woman and two little girls, were found stabbed to death beside a river in the Transkei, a crime that horrified the whole white population.

Even though the ANC was not guilty of all these attacks, the master in Pretoria aimed his wrath at it. Verwoerd had reorganized his security forces from top to bottom and appointed his own minister of justice to lead them: a six-foot-two force of nature with a terrifying, steely gaze. As a former activist in a secret organization that had opposed South Africa's entry into war against Germany in 1939, fifty-two-year-old John Vorster had engaged in sabotage, blowing up ships set to transport volunteers to Europe. To crush Umkhonto's underground operatives as quickly as possible, he had called up a comrade from the war years, a secret operations intelligence expert named Hendrik van den Bergh. Between them, Vorster and Van den Bergh were sure they could put an end to any revolutionary threat from the ANC and the various black resistance movements operating in its wake.

To secure victory, Pretoria had armed itself with a new emergency law called the Sabotage Act, which authorized its security forces to detain any suspect for a period of ninety days without an arrest warrant or recourse to legal assistance. But above all the Sabotage Act authorized a death sentence for any person arrested in possession of a firearm or explosives. Sometimes mere hours would elapse between sentence and execution. On July 24, 1964, former teacher Frederick John Harris, who had blown up an engine in Johannesburg station, killing a woman and injuring twenty-three passengers, marched straight to the gallows from his sentencing, singing the famous American civil rights anthem, "We Shall Overcome."

★

AMID THE ARBITRARY ARRESTS, interrogation, torture, abduction, summary justice, and executions of the government's war on Umkhonto activists, the Rivonia hideaway remained undiscovered. No matter! Pretoria was preparing a top secret operation that promised this time to destroy black resistance, an operation worthy of Nazi Germany's Dr. Mengele. Its headquarters were located behind high metal portals and double electric fencing in a forest of eucalyptus trees some ten miles north of Pretoria. A simple sign in English announced the nature of the site: Roodeplaat Research Laboratory. A guard post and perimeter road patrolled by police dogs protected the walls surrounding a series of dark brick buildings that contained biological laboratories sealed behind doors operated by remote control. Security doors in the basements gave access to decontamination rooms with showers, as well as rooms where hundreds of dogs, cats, and young baboons were caged. At the far end of a long corridor was a huge incinerator for the animals that died in the experiments. An unbearable smell of rotten cabbage and urine pervaded this mysterious place. Masked figures in white lab suits worked at a

series of apparatus and measuring devices. Extra security restricted access to rooms reserved for the handling of dangerous
bacteria and viruses. The Roodeplaat Research Laboratory was
a death factory: it produced lethal substances capable of exterminating by the millions enemies both inside and outside the
country.

★

LATER, THIS DEMENTED ENTERPRISE gave rise to a forty-one-year-
old military cardiologist with a close-cropped beard named
Wouter Basson. In 1981, the government chose him to start up
and head Project Coast, a program ostensibly intended to provide
South Africa with chemical and biological weapons to counteract
external attack, because he was an expert in unconventional
weapons, especially those using neurotoxins, poisons that inca-
pacitate mental faculties. Nearly twenty years later, a sensational
trial would reveal to South Africans and a horrified international
community the details and scope of this enterprise. The sixty-
seven counts of indictment, fifteen hundred pages of testimony,
and two and a half years of hearings before a special tribunal sitting in Pretoria set a record surpassed only by the Nuremberg trials. Among the most notable accusations was that Basson had
suggested to his bosses the idea of manufacturing chemical
products to lower the fertility rate of people of color. Such a program would give the apartheid leaders the means to reduce the
number of blacks living in the country. In Pretoria these proposals were greeted with enthusiasm. Unlimited funds were
granted to the man who would soon secretly be known as the
South African "Dr. Strangelove."[4]

---

4. Dr. Wouter Basson, head of South Africa's chemical and biological warfare program, was acquitted of all the charges against him on the grounds of
"insufficient evidence." This verdict caused a scandal (See appendix "What
They Became," p. 245, and the bibliography, p. 259). What follows nevertheless relates all that the charges and proceedings revealed during the trial.

Wouter Basson began, it was alleged, by making the rounds of various Western countries, gathering information about biological warfare from the best sources. He shamelessly exploited the American, British, and French secret services. How could he not be welcomed everywhere with open arms when he presented himself as acting in the name of a country that, he explained, was dedicated to damming the tide of communism sweeping through Africa? True, he profited from his travels, buying himself a luxury apartment in New York, another in Brussels, and a manor house in England. But the bounty of classified information he brought back with him made his government turn a blind eye. It only remained for him to equip his laboratories and recruit a team of top chemists, scientists, toxicologists, and veterinarians prepared to work on the monstrous project.

Seeking to invent a killer bacterium capable of exterminating blacks in a way that mimicked natural causes: this would be the first charge against the doctor. Before assembling his own collection of experimental animals, he shot poisonous arrows at monkeys in the Kruger National Park so he could study the circumstances and duration of their agony. After outraged tourists protested, he had the animals captured and subjected to slow death within the confines of his laboratory. Evidence at his trial suggested that his chemists experimented with all kinds of vectors for infecting blacks with fatal substances. Knowing how much they loved beer, he added poison to cans destined for the township *shebeens*. Then he put anthrax bacilli into cigarette cartons, cyanide into chocolate bars, botulin into bottles of milk, and even ricin, one of the most virulent poisons there is, into whisky. Finally he laced packets of household detergent readily available in hardware stores in black neighborhood with mandrax, a powder with paralyzing effects. Basson and his perverted alchemists were convinced right was on their side. The day their lethal products were made available for sale in African stores, whites would have taken a decisive step toward their goal of reducing the black population of South Africa by any means possible. To speed the pace of genocide, the laboratory came up with a whole panoply of devices: clever umbrellas that fired small, disease-carrying balls; cylinders that looked like screwdrivers but released a cloud of paralyzing gas; compressed-air pistols that could be used to fire projectiles packed with anthrax, ecstasy, cocaine, or marijuana-based hallucinogens that could calm an angry crowd almost instantaneously.

As he worked on the dogs and monkeys in his laboratories, Basson became interested in chemical substances transmitted by animals to others of their species to provide information about their sex, and social and reproductive status. He established that this signal, called a pheromone, worked in very weak concentrations and sometimes at considerable distances to induce stereotypical sexual and social behavior in its recipients. Basson was convinced that the same might be true for human beings. To pacify crowds, it would only be necessary to send out chemical signals capable of inducing more peaceful behavior. The cardiologist's laboratory was also accused of planning to poison Nelson Mandela by adding thallium to the medication he took.

Basson never seemed to run out of ideas. He managed to introduce poisonous particles into the glue on envelope seals and cobra venom into bottles of deodorant. He even invented a relaxing gel that instantly inhibits the will to resist. Some years later, at the height of the apartheid tragedy, the South African air force would use this gel to paralyze 250 Namibian prisoners of war so that they would not resist when dropped out of the sky into the sea. Basson was furthermore accused of trying to find a bacterium that would poison only blacks and a contraceptive that could be administered to women of color without their knowledge. If he had been successful, the descendants of the Voortrekkers would have won the greatest of all their battles against the African tribes since they had first set out to conquer the continent: the battle of numbers.

★

ON JULY 11, 1963, A BLACK SOUTH AFRICAN police informant who had infiltrated the ANC network provided Pretoria with its greatest victory. That morning at dawn, several dozen police surrounded Lilliesleaf Farm, Umkhonto's hideaway in the Rivonia marshlands north of Johannesburg. The movement's leadership was caught with documents and a map of South Africa spread out on a table revealing to Vorster's and Van den Bergh's men the targets for the general uprising the ANC activists were preparing to unleash. Spear of the Nation was decapitated. Or almost. For that morning Nelson Mandela was not at Lilliesleaf Farm. It was a miraculous but, alas, only temporary reprieve.

After his commando training in Ethiopia, the head of the armed branch of the ANC had returned to South Africa by one of the numerous routes that linked the province of Bechuanaland to the Transvaal. Then, in a black Austin driven by a member of the organization, he reached the port of Durban under an assumed name to report to the ANC's president on his mission outside the country. The next day, still in the same car, he started out for Johannesburg, jotting down on the way, in the notebook he always carried, the locations of possible targets for future sabotage. After his hard weeks in the Algerian desert, he relished the lush beauty of the Natal countryside. How beautiful South Africa was! Crossing the border the previous evening he had marveled at the clarity of the winter night and the brilliance of the stars. He had just returned from a world where for the first time he had experienced freedom of movement to one where he was a fugitive. Still he felt profoundly happy to be back in the land of his birth. And, at the end of the road, just before the first Johannesburg suburbs, he knew that his wife Winnie and his children waited for him in a hiding place loaned to them by a friend. Mandela was carried away with happiness and impatience at the prospect of seeing them again. But a Ford V8 occupied by four white men in civilian clothing overtook the Austin. Mandela looked back through the rear window and saw two more cars full of whites in civilian clothing. The Ford had stopped a little farther on and two men got out and signaled to the driver of the Austin to pull over. Mandela knew in that instant that this was the end of his freedom. There was no hope of resisting or trying to escape. They were clearly outnumbered.

It was over. One of the whites immediately made for the window of the Austin on the passenger side. He had the drawn features and stubbly cheeks of someone who had spent all night on a police hunt. Mandela calmly gave his identity and presented his passbook. He claimed to be a wholesale grocer. The policeman smiled. He showed neither surprise nor aggression. He only said, "You're Nelson Mandela and you are under arrest."[5] He politely invited him to step out of the car and come with him to his vehicle. As he got out, Mandela managed to slip his loaded revolver and his notebook into the upholstery between the seats. Strangely, the police never discovered them.

In Pretoria the news rang from the rooftops. The arrest of the leader of the armed branch of the ANC was reported on all the country's radio stations. A rumor spread that a CIA agent had informed South African authorities of Mandela's presence in Durban and his departure for Johannesburg in the black Austin.

★

"I NOW HAD TIME TO RUMINATE on my situation," Mandela was to recount in his autobiography. "I had always known that arrest was a possibility but even freedom fighters practice denial, and in my cell that night I realized I was not prepared for the reality of capture and confinement. I was upset and agitated."[6]

A few days later Winnie was allowed to visit him. Mandela noticed that she was dressed up and appeared relaxed. She brought him a new pair of silk pajamas as an expression of love. He did not have the heart to tell her that he would never be able

5. Mandela, *Long Walk to Freedom*, p. 301.
6. Mandela, *Long Walk to Freedom*, p. 302.

to wear such luxurious clothing in jail. Time was precious, so they hastened to discuss family matters. Mandela was worried. How would she support herself and the children? He mentioned some friends who might help her and clients of his who still owed him money. He instructed her to tell the children about his imprisonment and that he would be away for a long time. He tried to comfort her. "I said we were not the first family in this situation and that those who underwent such hardships came out the stronger," he was to write.[7] He wanted to talk to her about so many things. "The officer supervising the visit turned a blind eye," he was to recall, "and we embraced and clung to each other with all the strength and pent-up emotion inside each of us, as if this were to be the final parting."[8]

In a way it almost was a final parting. It would be twenty-seven years before Nelson and Winnie Mandela embraced each other again.

★

MANDELA AND HIS NINE comrades arrested in the raid at the Rivonia farm knew they were facing death at the end of a rope. How could it be otherwise? The government's case rested on the discovery of the six-page plan of action found at the farm. Entitled "Operation *Mayibuye iAfrika*—Let Africa Return," this document laid out the broad outlines of an insurrection aiming to overthrow the state. Nothing less. The plan was for guerrilla units trained in other African countries to land at half a dozen points on the South African coast as a provisional government was proclaimed in the capital of a neighboring country. The accused were further charged with complicity in over two hundred acts of sabotage intended to spark an armed uprising. Over a period of nearly two years, under an implacable prosecutor, the

---

7. Mandela, *Long Walk to Freedom*, p. 305.
8. Mandela, *Long Walk to Freedom*, p. 305.

state gathered its evidence, entered into the record thousands of documents and photographs, and produced 173 witnesses.

Mandela was ready to die. "To be truly prepared for something," he was to say, "one must actually expect it. . . . We were all prepared, not because we were brave but because we were realistic."[9] As he climbed into the armored police van that would take him to the apartheid court, he thought of these lines from Shakespeare: "Be absolute for death: either death or life shall thereby be the sweeter." But before he faced the gallows, the black leader fully intended to use his final confrontation with white man's justice to make a fierce stand on behalf of his people. "We saw the trial as a continuation of the struggle by other means," he would say later.[10] Paradoxically, despite its racism, the apartheid regime offered its black defendants a quality of justice that did not exist in any other African country or in any other totalitarian state.

The trial of the ten Rivonia conspirators opened on October 9, 1963, four days before the United Nations General Assembly in Manhattan voted for sanctions against South Africa. The Supreme Court building in Pretoria was a fortress under siege. Hundreds of antiriot police kept the crowds of sympathizers from approaching the courthouse. Through the barred windows of the armored van that passed through a double line of guards, Nelson Mandela caught sight of the statue of Paul Kruger, the former president of the Republic of the Transvaal who had fought so tenaciously against British imperialism in the nineteenth century. On a plaque at the foot of the statue, the accused made out the message of the white people's hero: "In full confidence we lay our cause before the whole world. Whether we win or die, freedom will rise in South Africa like the sun from the morning clouds."

Mandela presented himself before his judges with a symbolic act of defiance. He was draped in a *kaross*, the leopard-skin attire

---

9. Mandela, *Long Walk to Freedom*, p. 360.
10. Mandela, *Long Walk to Freedom*, p. 346.

They came from Holland to plant lettuce on the extreme tip of Africa

On April 6, 1652, three caravels flying the Dutch flag dropped anchor off Table Mountain (*photo 1*) on the southernmost tip of Africa, near what was to become the site of the city of Cape Town. On board the *Drommedaris* were a thirty-four-year-old surgeon named Jan van Riebeeck (*photo 2*); his wife, Maria; their four-month-old child; and ninety expatriates under his command. They brought with them sacks full of lettuce and other seed. Employed by the all-powerful Dutch East India Company, Van Riebeeck and his companions were tasked with growing vegetables on this strategic stopping-off point for ships on the spice run, providing crews decimated by scurvy with much-needed vitamins. It was a mission the young Dutchman was to carry out "with his back to the rest of the continent," avoiding all contact with the indigenous people. There was no thought towards colonization, much less conquest. Van Riebeeck had no idea that by embarking on the farming expedition he would in reality be writing the first chapter in the story of a country that did not yet exist: South Africa.

2

The epic begins with a handful of whites in a territory three times the size of California

The lettuce farmers soon left their vegetable plots to build an attractive community they called Cape Town (*photo 1*). Then the most adventurous decided to go northward in search of grazing land for their herds. Faithful readers of the Bible, they were convinced they were journeying into a new promised land. Wanting to sever links with their motherland, these farmers—known as Boers—decided to change their identity. Henceforth they would be "Afrikaners." Their migration on cattle-drawn wagons was to be an epic journey fraught with every kind of danger

from wild animals and swarms of tsetse flies to native tribes determined to defend their territories. When the men were injured, the women would takeover their guns to repel attackers (*photos 2 and 3*). Protected from the relentless sun by their broad-brimmed hats and tent canopies (*photo 4*), the Afrikaners would frequently set up camp in the vastness of the Veld—the African savannah on which their herds grazed.

The black tribes rally against white imperialism

Driving their herds into the interior of austral Africa, it was not long before the Boers, soon accompanied by British colonists, encountered the native populations that occupied the lands the whites coveted. In 1846, over five hundred Xhosas were massacred by a British cavalry regiment (*photo 1*). Fortunately, many encounters between whites and blacks had less tragic consequences. Many blacks left their tribes to work on farms in the Cape Colony. They were not paid money but were remunerated with goods, which they took home with them (*photo 2*). Of the most prized possessions were guns. Of all the blacks encountered by "the people of the wagons," the most bellicose were the Zulus (*photos 3, 4, 5*), who had perfected their military skills. Armed with spears and clubs, they killed a large number of Boers and also British soldiers. One of their fiercest kings was Dingane (*photo 4*). He massacred a whole column of Boers who had come in peace to negotiate the purchase of pastureland.

Heroes to lead the people of the
New Covenant to the promised land

The migration of various groups of white people northward in what would be called the Great Trek was a heroic adventure that went on for years (*photo 1*). The leaders of these wagon trains quickly became legendary Afrikaner figures: men such as Andries Pretorius (*photo 2*), who was to give his name to the South African capital of Pretoria, and the Huguenot Piet Retief (*photo 3*), who on February 6, 1838, was killed along with sixty of his men by the Zulu king Dingane.

Pretorius (*photo 2*) would avenge this massacre by wiping out an army of 15,000 Zulus on the banks of a tributary of the Blood River. This was assisted by his innovative wagon formation into a defensive circle known as a *laager* (*photo 4*). Wagons, themselves, would also evolve to alleviate the work of the teams and make it easier to pass obstructions (*photo 6*). With a double roof against the sun and the elements, and bigger lockers to store the largest family's clothes, bedding, utensils, victuals, and weapons, they were remarkably well-adapted to the terrible adventure they had to endure. Easily dismantled (*photo 5*), the Voortrekkers' "freedom wagons" became indispensable accessories on the march to the promised land.

A savage war between Africa's two great white tribes: the Boers and the British

Led by legendary figures such as Paul Kruger (*photo 1*), Frans Joubert (*photo 2*) and M.W. Pretorius (*photo 3*), the Boers soon had to defend their republics against an enemy infinitely

more powerful than the Zulu and other native tribes: the British under Queen Victoria. The Anglo-Boer war was a terrible conflict. For the first time artillery was used in South Africa. The British unloaded cannons from their warships and mounted them on wheeled gun carriages (*photo 4*). As for the Boers, they were able to bring four Schneider siege cannons from France (*photo 5*), capable of firing forty-three-kilo shells over six miles. To lead the fight against the Boers, the British called up the best generals in their army—Field Marshal Roberts (*photo 6*) and Horatio Kitchener (*photo 7*)—

while Cecil Rhodes (*photo 8*), a prominent figure in British imperialism in South Africa, conceived and supervised the British forces' strategy in their all out war against the Boer army commandos (*photos 9 and 10*). One of the principal stakes in this fratricidal clash between the two great white communities was ownership of the gold and diamond mines. One year after the discovery of the first diamond seam in 1867, the Kimberley excavation (*photo 11*) became "the biggest manmade hole in the world."

The white nationalists take power and establish the apartheid regime

On May 28, 1948, 296 years and 21 days after the first Dutchman set foot in Africa, the 3 million white nationalists that made up the National Party won election and took power. Their leader, the former Dutch Reformed Church minister, Daniel François Malan (*photo 1*), declared on the rostrum in parliament: "At last South Africa belongs to us.

Let us pray to God that it will always be thus." Outside parliament a white crowd noisily manifested its joy and pride.

Ten years earlier Malan and his supporters had roused the Afrikaners' sense of nationalism by commemorating their ancestors' historic venture on the Great Trek (*photo 2*) with a dozen wagons. All along the commemorative journey, over eight hundred miles between Cape Town and Pretoria, hundreds of thousands of Afrikaners had amassed to proclaim their pride in belonging to the people God had chosen to spread Christian values across Africa. In order to better defend their cause the Afrikaners created a secret society, the Broederbond—League of Brothers (*photo 3*)—which promoted white nationalist ideals in every section of society and was to become the pillar of apartheid.

Blacks mobilize to defend their rights but succumb to a pitiless white dictatorship

From the very beginning of the twentieth century the black elite had tried to resist their white oppressors. On January 8, 1912, the young lawyer Pixley Seme (*photo 1*) gathered together the leaders of the principal tribes and, with the support of his fellow lawyer, the pacifist Indian resistant Mohandas Gandhi (*seated in the middle, photo 2*), formed what in time was to become the African National Congress (ANC). For three generations this militant organization would embody the nonviolent crusade of black South Africans for equal rights and freedom. A young lawyer named Nelson Mandela (*photo 3*) would become one of their most illustrious leaders. Desmond Tutu, bishop of Johannesburg and later archbishop of Cape Town, was also one of the most committed activists in the black struggle for civil rights (*photo 4*). Despite its efforts, the ANC was unable to prevent the white apartheid government from carrying out its program that forcibly removed the black populations and isolated them to reserves situated on the peripheries of the country. These deportations were conducted with extreme brutality. As depicted here in the Transvaal in 1983 (*photo 5*), families were driven out of their homes and transported along with their meager possessions in trucks to a reserve. Black workers who were granted permission to work in a white area had to live in sordid dormitories attached to their place of work (*photo 6*).

The apartheid tyrants arrange for the largest deportations in history

The racist apartheid system found implacable rulers to impose the dictates of the white minority on the black majority. Hendrik Verwoerd (*photo 1*) and John Vorster (*photo 2*) were among the most famous. With the help of an army of land surveyors and town planners (*photo 3*) the regime carved up South Africa into white areas and black areas.

Over 3 million blacks were evicted from their places of residence, forcibly loaded onto trucks (*photos 4 and 5*), and moved along with their possessions to the reserves they had been allotted. To dispel any fears that these removals gave rise to, Prime Minister Verwoerd publicly declared that black deportations were intended to "promote their national unity, protect their ethnic and political interests, and improve their living conditions."

The blacks rebel:
there are hundreds of dead and injured

Blacks burned effigies of their tormentors (*photo 1*) and organized nonviolent marches in protest against the white government, demanding, among other things, the abolition of "passes"—the internal passports used to restrict their movements. The passes enabled the authorities to control the comings and goings of 25 million South Africans of color, and to ensure the implementation of the regulations that determined where members of the different tribes must live.

In Sharpeville on March 21, 1960, the white crackdown on a nonviolent march for the abolition of passes claimed over sixty lives (*photos 2 and 3*). Several hundred others were wounded. In Moddendam (*photo 4*), as in many other townships, government bulldozers pitilessly destroyed the homes of those evicted. Once cleaned up and disinfected, these slums would become white residential areas.

They were the proof that people could coexist in peace and harmony in a multi-racial South Africa

Before the introduction of apartheid, some neighborhoods had demonstrated that it was possible for whites, blacks, and coloreds to cohabit, as in the famous District Six of Cape Town (*photos 1 and 3*), where inhabitants of all races mingled to celebrate their festivals. In Sophiatown, another neighborhood near Johannesburg remarkable for its racial integration, the legendary jazz musician Hugh Masekela (*photo 2*) and the Anglican priest Trevor Huddleston (*photo 4*) formed the most effective ramparts against racial intolerance. District Six and Sophiatown were both to be razed to the ground by apartheid bulldozers.

A legendary leader to represent the black revolt against white oppression

The black resistance leader Nelson Mandela, seen here with his wife, Winnie, after their marriage (*photo 1*), was sentenced, despite the protests of his followers (*photo 2*), to forced labor for life in Robben Island prison off the tip of South Africa. Mandela was to spend his years of detention breaking stones with his companions (*photos 3 and 4*) in the courtyard of block 3 in the top security section. He would be entitled to receive and send only

one letter every six months. Sometimes his wife would have to wait two years before she could visit him. His incarceration went on for twenty-seven years. But in prison Mandela set up a "university" to teach his fellow detainees history and give them a political education. He himself learned Afrikaans so that he could talk to his oppressors in their own language. Robben Island is now a museum visited by tens of thousands of South Africans and foreigners who want to see the most famous apartheid prison.

In the midst of the apartheid era Helen and Chris salvaged a little of South Africa's lost honor

Sanctioned and boycotted by the world's nations for its racial segregation policies, South Africa suddenly regained universal regard thanks to the exploits of two of its citizens.

In Cape Town, a thirty-two-year-old white speech therapist, Helen Lieberman (*photo 1*) transformed the wretched life of one township through her courage and dedication. Braving the prohibitions of apartheid, together with its occupants she founded an association to promote development that is now the largest humanitarian organization in the whole of South Africa.

On December 3, 1967, the surgeon Christiaan Barnard, aged forty-five (*photo 2*), performed the world's first heart transplant by grafting the heart of Denise Darvall, a twenty-four-year-old road accident victim, into the chest of Louis Washkansky, a fifty-two-year-old wholesale grocer in the terminal phase of heart disease. Hailed by the world's media (*photo 3*) as a major advancement in the medical history of humanity, the event united a country torn apart by the demons of racial hatred.

The symbolic image of
half a century of tragedy

On June, 16 1976, schoolchildren in Soweto, the largest black township in South Africa, rose up against the apartheid authorities who wanted to impose Afrikaans, the language of whites, on all schools attended by blacks. Forming immense processions, they marched to Soweto's large stadium. Hundreds of anti-riot police were posted at the various cross-roads to bar their way. Violent confrontations occurred. Stones and tear gas canisters rained down upon police and demonstrators, alike. Suddenly shots rang out and from out of the chaos there emerged a teenaged boy carrying in his arms the first victim to die in that fatal confrontation. His name was Hector Petersen. He was thirteen years old. From his refuge behind a policeman's shoulder, photographer Sam Nzima took this photo, which went all round the world, for no image better symbolized the South African tragedy than this *pietà* of three schoolchildren on a black township street. Soweto had its martyr. One day the free South Africa would give the name Hector Petersen to the crossroad where he died.

The nightmare is over: Nelson Mandela and Frederik de Klerk have led South Africa to freedom

On Sunday February 11, 1990, after twenty-seven years in jail, Nelson Mandela savored his first day as a free man (*photo 1*). It was sixteen minutes past four in the afternoon. Hand in hand, Nelson and Winnie gave the ANC salute, arms raised with fists clenched, as a sign of victory. Shortly afterwards he was to address the crowd gathered on the parvis of Cape Town's city hall. Reunited with his people, he cried: "I therefore place the remaining years of my life in your hands." Four years

later, on May 10, 1994, after difficult negotiations culminating in a general election on the basis of "one man, one vote," Nelson Mandela and Frederik de Klerk, the apartheid regime's last prime minister, sealed the reconciliation of whites and blacks (*photo 2*). Nelson Mandela became the first democratically elected president of South Africa. Frederik de Klerk (right) and Thabo Mbeki (left) were to be his government's two vice presidents. A nightmarish half-century had come to an end, but much work would remain before South Africa could find peace and prosperity.

of dignitaries of his tribe. "I had chosen traditional dress to emphasize that I was a black African walking into a white man's court," he wrote. "I was literally carrying on my back the history, culture, and heritage of my people. That day, I felt myself to be the embodiment of African nationalism, the inheritor of Africa's difficult but noble past and her uncertain future. The *kaross* was also a sign of contempt for the niceties of white justice. I well knew the authorities would feel threatened by my *kaross*, as so many whites feel threatened by the true culture of Africa."[11]

Those present rose as one when the accused entered. The rows of seats were filled with South African and international journalists, and representatives of numerous foreign governments. For the African press and for the world at large, the political trial about to begin was the most important in the history of South Africa. In the public gallery, Mandela spotted a woman with the beaded hairdo and traditional long skirt of the Xhosa. It was Winnie. She had come all the way from Transkei with the black leader's mother. Their eyes met. The accused raised their fists and shouted in unison "*Amandla!* Power!" Their fists also raised, Winnie and all those present answered "*Ngawethu!* Power is ours!"

Mandela then turned to face the man who, he believed, would end his life. On his dais of gilded wood, dressed in his red velvet robes, the Afrikaner judge, fifty-two-year-old Quartus de Wet, looked as impassive as a cathedral statue. Although he was not considered an ardent supporter of apartheid, all the blacks on trial dreaded the notorious severity of his judgments. Next to him fidgeted an elegantly dressed little bald man. Fifty-year-old Percy Yutar led the case for the prosecution. His hissing voice and theatrical rhetoric had sent more than one black man to his death. He had spent weeks and months questioning, gathering overwhelming testimony to demonstrate the guilt of Mandela

---

11. Mandela, *Long Walk to Freedom*, p. 311.

and his companions. Each day the press speculated as to how the accused would ever escape the ultimate punishment.

Nelson Mandela had taken responsibility for his own defense. In his cell, for nights on end, he had worked on the long statement he wanted to make in his people's name to the marmoreal figure representing white justice. For four long hours, not an eyelash, not a lip, not a nostril of Judge de Wet moved during the reading of the speech for the defense written by the man the court had designated "Accused No. 1." Though Mandela's voice was, as always, a little muted and deliberately devoid of eloquent effects, his many supporters in the courtroom hung on his words. Undaunted by his robed interlocutor's closed eyes, the accused began by affirming that the ideological creed of his people did not consist of crying "drive the white man into the sea," but of claiming their just share of South Africa. "My Lord," he declared, "children wander about the streets of the townships because they have no schools to go to, or no money to enable them to go to school, or no parents at home to see that they go to school, because both parents (if there be two) have to work to keep the family alive. This leads to the breakdown in moral standards, to an alarming rise in illegitimacy and to growing violence."[12] Mandela also protested strongly against the living conditions imposed on the majority of the country by a law that was in his eyes "immoral, unjust, and intolerable." The accused were bound by conscience to oppose these conditions and try to change them.

Mandela paused to take a breath and then continued: "Men, I think, are not capable of doing nothing, of saying nothing, of not reacting to injustice, of not protesting against oppression, of not striving for the good society and the good life in the ways they see it."[13] The black leader then enumerated the terrible grievances of Africans against the oppressive system imposed by the oppressors in Pretoria. In one sentence, he summed up his

---

12. Mandela, *Long Walk to Freedom*, p. 353.
13. Mandela, *Long Walk to Freedom*, p. 317.

people's principal demand: "Above all, we want equal political rights, because without them our disabilities will be permanent. I know this sounds revolutionary to the whites in this country because the majority of voters will be Africans."[14] Mandela stated that he would repeat till his dying breath that the black struggle in his country was "a struggle for the right to live."[15] It was the prevailing tyranny in the country that had made a criminal of him, not his actions. He had been declared a criminal by virtue of the ideal he sought to defend.

There was no reaction to this address from the judge, who did not take a single note and seemed absorbed in his own thoughts, waiting for the moment to reveal his decision. The black leader placed his papers on the table and concluded with words that came straight from his heart. "During my lifetime I have dedicated myself to this struggle of the African people," he exclaimed, his voice straining. "I have fought against white domination, and I have fought against black domination. I have cherished the ideal of a democratic and free society in which all persons live together in harmony and with equal opportunities. It is an ideal which I hope to live for and achieve. But if needs be, it is an ideal for which I am prepared to die."[16] At that moment the accused noted that the judge's eyes had opened but were empty of expression. Mandela could read neither compassion nor hatred in them. They were the eyes of a man without emotion. Troubled, Mandela sat down again. Though he could feel the whole room looking at him, he did not turn around. After a silence that seemed to last an eternity, he heard a woman sobbing. He recognized those cries instantly. They came from the woman who had given him life as he faced the man who, in all likelihood, would take it away.

★

---

14. Mandela, *Long Walk to Freedom*, p. 353.
15. Mandela, *Long Walk to Freedom*, p. 354.
16. Mandela, *Long Walk to Freedom*, p. 354.

ON FRIDAY JUNE 12, 1964, the accused from the Rivonia farm
and their leader entered the courtroom for the last time. Security
was tight. All roads leading to the Palace of Justice were closed to
traffic. The convoy transporting the prisoners from their place of
detention went through the streets blaring their sirens, flanked
by motorcycle police. Police checked the identity of anyone trying to get near the court. Checkpoints were set up at bus stops
and railway stations. Despite these measures, thousands of sympathizers, some waving banners and placards demanding that the
prisoners be pardoned, opened a path to the Palace of Justice.
The whole world had mobilized, too, as the time for the verdict
neared. Fifty British MPs had organized a march in London
while hundreds of supporters gathered for a prayer vigil in St.
Paul's Cathedral. The First Secretary of the Soviet Communist
Party, Leonid Brezhnev, and the U.S. representative to the United
Nations, Adlai Stevenson, sent telegrams to Prime Minister Verwoerd asking for the prisoners' release. The dockworkers' unions
in several European and Asian countries threatened to stop load-
ing merchandise destined for South Africa. The international
press published thousands of open letters calling for clemency.
Against this tide, Verwoerd had climbed onto the rostrum in the
Cape Town parliament and declared, "Protests and telegrams
from all over the world will have no influence on the normal
course of justice of a sovereign country." Then he boasted of having "tossed into the waste-basket all the telegrams from socialist
nations."[17]

As the accused entered, the packed courtroom was charged
with emotion. Mandela spotted Winnie and his mother in the
crowd and motioned to them, heartened to see them there.[18] He
imagined how strange they must feel in that room, expecting to
hear the person dearest to them condemned to death. "Though I
suspect my mother did not understand all that was going on, her

17. Mandela, *Long Walk to Freedom*, p. 364.
18. Mandela, *Long Walk to Freedom*, p. 361.

support never wavered. Winnie was equally stalwart and her strength gave me strength."[19]

A registrar called out, "The State against Nelson Mandela and others." At these words the red-robed judge nodded to the accused to rise. Mandela tried to catch his gaze but De Wet did not even look at those whom he was about to sentence. His eyes seemed fixed on some point between them. His face was very pale and he was breathing rapidly. Mandela and his companions shook their heads. It was death. Why else would this normally calm man be so nervous now? He began to speak. His voice was breathless, barely audible. "The function of this court, as is the function of the court in any other country, is to enforce law and order and to enforce the laws of the state within which it functions," he declared. "Normally, a case such as this would bring the death penalty." The judge's voice had become so inaudible that the accused had to guess at his words. "I have decided not to impose the supreme penalty." He stopped to catch his breath. Finally he declared, "But consistent with my duty that is the only leniency which I can show. The sentence in the case of all the accused will be one of life imprisonment."[20]

Mandela and his companions received this incredible news with a simple nod of the head. But the spectators who had not heard the verdict began to call out. "What was the sentence?" Relatives, friends, and supporters wanted to know. Mandela turned around, his face beaming. He looked for Winnie and his mother in the excitement of the courtroom. Someone shouted: "Life, life, life, LIFE!"

★

THAT NIGHT, JUST BEFORE LIGHTS OUT at the huge Pretoria local prison where the convicted were locked up before being transferred to Robben Island penal colony, hundreds of detainees

---

19. Mandela, *Long Walk to Freedom*, p. 361.
20. Mandela, *Long Walk to Freedom*, p. 362.

sang their thanks at the top of their voices, striking up "Nkosi Sikelel' iAfrika," the poignant hymn of the black people calling upon God to protect Africa. Then from the cells the cry of *Amandla!* went up, to which hundreds of voices responded *Ngawethu!* The call and response of those nameless prisoners shook the prison from one end to the other, as if they were giving the condemned courage for what lay ahead.

★

ROBBEN ISLAND! A gulag patrolled overhead by cormorants and migratory birds, pounded by shark-infested waters, situated on the southernmost tip of Africa, facing the majestic slopes of Table Mountain and the magnificent bay of the Cape. Here the apartheid government had set up a penal colony its opponents would never escape. The island measured from two and a half to four miles wide. It was torrid in summer and bitterly cold in winter. It had long been the place where the country's lepers and madmen were sent to die. Now it served the same purpose for a thousand ordinary offenders serving heavy sentences, and for political prisoners sentenced by apartheid tribunals. Though Robben Island had no gas chambers or crematoria, its 250 white guards had been chosen for their inhuman cruelty. Many of the political prisoners, like Nelson Mandela and his codefendants from the Rivonia trial, were serving life sentences. On the morning of August 13, 1964, they stepped from a DC3 military transport plane onto the short airstrip at one end of the island. Their first sight was a lighthouse with a red signal light, then some houses clustered around a small church with a gothic bell tower, then the leper cemetery with its worn gravestones, and finally a collection of buildings surrounded by high gray walls. At the entrance to Auschwitz concentration camp, constructed by Adolf Hitler's Nazis, so admired by Prime Minister Verwoerd, were the words *Arbeit Macht Frei*—Work sets you free. The notice hung over the entrance to the penal colony of the architects of apartheid proclaimed more soberly: *Robbeneiland*—We serve with pride— *ons dien met trots.*

The new arrivals soon discovered the reality. Guards threw them brutally into cells in section B of the maximum-security block. They were cages six feet six inches long by six feet wide, furnished only with a sisal mat on the bare ground for a bed, a toilet bucket, and a lightbulb on the ceiling that burned day and night. A skylight protected by thick bars let in a little daylight. A plate over each door indicated the occupant's name and reference number. Mandela was given the number 466-64, which meant that on that August 13, 1964, he was the 466th prisoner to arrive that year on that accursed island.

The winter was icy. The prisoners shivered. To remind them they were kaffirs whose only calling was to be servants, the guards forced them to give up their trousers. In exchange they were given coarse-woven cotton shorts. Mandela protested against this humiliation. It would be his first battle as a lifer. When he entered his cell on that first day he was overcome with despair. "I was forty-six years old," he was to say, "a political prisoner with a life sentence, and that small cramped space was to be my home for I knew not how long."[21]

★

AN ANNOUNCER'S VOICE broke in on radios everywhere across the country. "Stand by!" it ordered. "We have an important announcement." From the cafés of Cape Town to the township *shebeens* of Natal and the Transkei, from the offices of Johannesburg to the farthest villages of the highveld, wherever men and women of all races and colors were listening to the radio that Tuesday, September 6, 1966, people felt surprise, then concern. South Africa held its breath. It had to wait some ten minutes to hear the dramatic news. Prime Minister Hendrik Verwoerd had just been killed, stabbed three times during a parliamentary session in Cape Town. The perpetrator of the crime had been arrested on the spot. He was of mixed race, about forty years old, the son of a Greek immigrant and a mother born in Mozambique. Everyone

---

21. Mandela, *Long Walk to Freedom*, p. 370.

inside that venerable assembly knew, at least by sight, the tall, likable guy with the prominent nose and double chin who worked as a messenger between the various departments of parliament. No one would ever have dreamed of preventing Demitrios Tsafendas from approaching the prime minister's bench where he regularly took papers and documents. In a way Tsafendas was part of the furniture. In any case, no one saw him take a butcher's knife out of his jacket that day. Verwoerd had no opportunity to defend himself as his assassin plunged the blade into his chest three times in succession.

"The father of the nation is dead!" radio stations around the country announced a few moments later. "The Moses of the Afrikaner tribe is gone at the height of his glory," a famous journalist commented. "Apartheid's architect leaves South Africa orphaned," ran the headline in the special editions of the printed press. But what was the reason for this crime? "There is nothing to suggest a plot. This is the work of a lone killer," remarked John Vorster, the minister of justice, in a front-page headline of the Johannesburg *Star*. Verwoerd's natural successor feared above all a white racist backlash against the colored and black communities. He spread the word that the killer was in fact "a simple-minded man whose action could not have political implications of any kind." To further convince public opinion, Vorster simply had the assassin locked up in a mental asylum. Tsafendas would remain there until he died thirty-three years later, without ever revealing what motivated him to commit the greatest political crime ever committed in South Africa. Like Lee Harvey Oswald in Dallas, he would take his secret to the grave.

At the time, the blacks and coloreds were careful not to celebrate the violent end of a man who had often declared that Africans were lower than animals. They knew an even more intractable tormentor would likely succeed him and that the apartheid laws in South Africa would surely multiply. The first victims of this clampdown were the prisoners serving life sentences on Robben Island. As Mandela was to recount, "We had just put down our picks and shovels on the quarry face and were walking to the shed for lunch. As one of the general prisoners wheeled a drum of food towards us, he whispered, 'Verwoerd is dead.' That was all. The news quickly passed among us. We looked at each other in disbelief and glanced over at the guards, who seemed unaware that anything momentous had occurred. . . . As often happened on the island, we had learned significant political news before our own guards. But by the following day it was obvious that they knew for they took out their anger on us. The tension that had taken months to abate was suddenly at full force. The authorities began a crackdown against political prisoners as though we had held the knife that stabbed Verwoerd."[22]

That evening the authorities decided to deal the Robben Island prisoners a blow by flying in one of the most violent guards in the prison system. With a swastika tattooed on his wrist, Piet van Rensburg was infamous for being the terror of South African prisons. His taking over of the penal colony was the first sign of an imminent hardening of apartheid policies. Vorster would be worse than Verwoerd. Mandela and his companions had no illusions: the Calvary of the African people was just beginning.

---

22. Mandela, *Long Walk to Freedom*, p. 418.

Three

Helen and Chris:
Two Lights in the Darkness

THERE WERE NO CLOCKS or watches on Robben Island, and the prisoners in the penal colony lost all sense of time. This torture was part of a program of disintegration scientifically designed by the oppressors in Pretoria. To have any idea they had to track the bells and the guards' whistles and shouts. Every week was an exact copy of the one before, and the prisoners had to mobilize their memory to work out the day and the month. "One of the first things I did was to make a calendar on the wall of my cell," Mandela was to confide. "Losing a sense of time is an easy way to lose one's grip and even one's sanity."[1]

Of all the torments devised by the system to demoralize its political prisoners, the worst was not being forced to hammer blocks of lime for ten hours at a stretch in the blinding southern light. Nor was it being served food spattered with urine by sadistic guards; or being locked up naked in solitary confinement for sighing too loudly. The worst was being condemned to receive only one letter and one visit every six months. The authorities contrived to exacerbate this torment in a thousand ways. All correspondence, like all visiting, was expressly limited to "first degree" relatives, a restriction that the black leader considered a racist attack on the meaning of family in African life, where any ancestor or cousin, however distant, was considered part of the family. As it turned out Mandela had to wait nine months before a guard handed him his first letter from Winnie. But the censor's hand

---

1. Mandela, *Long Walk to Freedom*, p. 375.

had been so brutal that the poor man found nothing but her final greetings. All the rest had been cut out with a razor. For a man who worried constantly about the plight of the woman he loved, the health of his elderly mother he feared he would never see again, and the future of his children condemned to grow up without him, it was an inhuman ordeal. Not to mention his anguish about his comrades in the struggle left rudderless by his capture and confinement. The system made waiting for mail an experience that Mandela described as "overwhelming."[2] Yet the clearest demonstration of its determination to crush all resistance was in how arrangements were made for the rare visits. The barbarity began with the subtle tormenting of the prisoners' relatives. Continually harassed, threatened, and humiliated since her husband's life sentence, Winnie Mandela lived under surveillance in her distant home province of the Transkei. No one in her family was allowed to live with her, not even her two young children. Her existence was one long nightmare. The authorities wanted to break her ties with her husband to seal their prisoner's isolation and abandonment.

One day, however, there came a surprising respite. Two inspectors wearing the suits and ties of security police turned up at the young woman's home to inform her that she had been authorized to visit her husband the following afternoon. The journey entailed an expensive flight to Cape Town. No luggage was permitted. Winnie would have to present herself at the prison in her traveling clothes. She promptly dug out the silk and satin dress she had worn on their wedding day. After so long a wait wasn't this visit a renewal of her marriage? Then, trembling with emotion, she sprayed herself from head to toe with the patchouli perfume Nelson loved.

A real way of the cross faced her before she would set eyes on that beloved face. She was subjected to rigorous police ques-

---

2. Mandela, *Long Walk to Freedom*, p. 386.

tioning, an intensive search, and the intolerable humiliation of being treated like a "stinking kaffir" before being allowed to board the launch for Robben Island. On the island a gloomy, windowless visiting room welcomed her. Dividing the room in two were five small cubicles equipped with an opening covered with distorting glass, a microphone, a speaker on either side and a third wired to the earpiece of the guard listening in on the conversation between the prisoner and his visitor. The sinister coldness of the setting was intentional: blacks were subhuman and deserved no better.

Thirty wretched minutes, speaking in English or Afrikaans and conversation restricted to family matters. A single word in Xhosa, Mandela's tribal tongue, or any other African language, a single political reference, and the meeting would be terminated. Escorted by guards, each advanced toward the distorting glass. They saw each other like images on a poor quality black-and white television screen. Mandela tried his best to hide his turmoil. To see Winnie without being able to touch her was almost worse than not seeing her at all. It was a torture he was to endure for twenty-one years. The first seconds were bewildering. After so long a separation, it was hard to find words. Finally Winnie broke the silence. She thought Nelson looked thinner and inquired about his health. She had been told the prisoners on Robben Island were physically abused. He reassured her by thumping his chest to show how fit he was. It was his turn to be concerned. Was she still on a diet? He begged her to put on a bit of weight. At that point Nelson recognized his wife's satin dress. His lips tightened and his eyes welled with tears, but he quickly regained his self-control. The guards then heard a casual exchange of questions and answers. The children, my mother, my sisters? Your father, your mother? Suddenly an African name came up that was not part of Nelson and Winnie's immediate family. The chief guard immediately broke into the conversation. Precious minutes were lost explaining that this was a member of another branch of the family. In fact it was the code name of an ANC leader who stayed in contact with Winnie. Their conversation could resume. The news that Winnie brought him about this pseudo relative reassured Mandela. His comrades had regained confidence and were more motivated than ever. Even if it promised to be long and bitter, no one doubted that the black struggle against white oppression would ultimately triumph.

Then a voice interrupted: "Time up!" Mandela stared at the guard with surprise. Could half an hour have elapsed already? One day he was to write: "For all the years that I was in prison, I never failed to be surprised when the guard called, 'Time up!' . . . Visits always seemed to go by in the blinking of an eye."[3] He felt a powerful urge to kiss the glass to say good-bye to his wife but stopped himself. They waved a cursory farewell. The guards led them out. Besides Winnie's face, Mandela longed for a trace of her perfume but the scent of patchouli had not penetrated the hermetic seal dividing the room.

Back in his cell the black leader tried to relive every instant of that magical half hour. In his head he went over every word they had exchanged, every expression they had shared. He knew that for days, weeks, months, he would keep recollecting every second. He knew he could not see Winnie again for at least six months, but in fact he would have to wait two years to see his beloved behind the distorting glass of the prison visiting room again.

The apartheid tormenters soon understood that their only chance of breaking their principal adversary was to put pressure on his wife. Neither his mother's death nor the loss of his eldest son Thembi in a car accident in the Transkei, nor the authorities' refusal to let him attend their funerals had driven Mandela to the point of despair. During those interminable white nights spent on the freezing floor of his cell, his eyes staring up at the ceiling, he thought constantly of one person: Winnie.

The young woman had left the Transkei with their two children and taken refuge in their small house in Soweto, where

---

3. Mandela, *Long Walk to Freedom*, p. 389.

Nelson had met with his friends on Election Day. It was there that two security police inspectors came and picked her up in the early morning hours of May 12, 1969, to detain her without charge under the Terrorism Act passed two years earlier. Her arrest was part of a nationwide raid. All over the country hundreds of people, including Winnie's sister, were arrested without warrants.

Nothing tested the prisoner's inner equilibrium more than Winnie's brutal captivity. He tried to put on a brave face but inwardly he was shattered. He could not sleep. What were the police doing to his wife? How would she stand being incarcerated? Who was taking care of their daughters? Who would support them? Not being able to answer those questions was the worst torture. And the torturers wearing shirts and ties in the government offices of the Union Buildings in Pretoria knew it.

The new prime minister intensified the enforcement of apartheid laws. The moral and physical torture of men and women in police custody reached new excesses. To break their principal adversary more quickly the torturers in Pretoria resorted to a particularly odious stratagem. They began to spread rumors about his wife's purported infidelities with members of the ANC. Mandela refused to believe these slanderous lies, but in his isolation they felt like stabs to the heart. To rise above this ordeal, he decided to shift his political struggle onto ground never anticipated by the white government. Since the regime's prison administration had made the monumental error of grouping all its political prisoners in the same maximum-security wing, he was going to turn it into a temple of learning and culture. Many detainees could scarcely read or write. Many had had no education in politics or history. If the whites of the Great Trek had been able to sustain their will to survive and conquer with Bible verses, the black inmates of Robben Island would acquire on the benches of "Mandela University" the knowledge and training they would need to one day lead South Africa. Of course the expression in no way reflected reality. There were no benches or lecture rooms in grim Block 3 of Robben Island. Only a board shelf fixed at chest height to the wall of each cell. After a day in the quarry breaking up limestone, having to stand up to study a book or write an essay brought more pain than exaltation in learning. Mandela and his companions protested, resisted, fumed. But in that universe without reference points where the notion of time no longer existed, they had to wait a year before the boards were lowered by a few inches and every cell acquired a piece of furniture that would help a handful of men serving life sentences along their path of education: a stool.

★

1976. THE TWELFTH YEAR of Calvary for the inmates of Robben Island's Block 3. If they kept their sanity it was thanks to their studies and to the anticipation of news coming infrequently from their families about their comrades, their struggle, and their country. Alas, when some piece of information did reach them, it was often so old and outdated that it brought no comfort. Suddenly, however, spring appeared like a whirlwind within the walls of Robben Island. The maximum-security wing block was filled up with several dozen young prisoners who had just been given heavy sentences for terrorist acts perpetrated in various parts of the country.

Mandela understood instantly that these young men were different from all the other comrades he had seen arrive since the beginning of his incarceration. They were aggressive, they refused to obey orders, they shouted revolutionary slogans and would not conform to even the most basic rules of detention. How to make these rebels behave rationally? As a last resort the prison commandant called upon Mandela and his companions for help. The elderly leader was careful not to intervene personally because he was on these young men's side. When she had visited a few months earlier, Winnie had managed to tell him in their coded language that there was a new generation of angry blacks ready to take action. Their existence, she had said, was something to be urgently reckoned with.

The new prisoners who landed on Robben Island in that twenty-eighth year of apartheid belonged to a movement that had taken up the torch of the ANC and the Communist Party. It intended to go on openly defending the rights of black people against the oppression of the Pretoria regime. Its founders had called it black consciousness. In fact it was less of a movement than a philosophy preaching the idea that blacks must first free themselves of the sense of psychological inferiority engendered by three centuries of white domination. "Black men stand up for yourselves!" it advocated. "Let us be proud of our blackness! Let us defend the principle of a nonracial society but let us prevent the white moderates who support us from playing an active role in our struggle!"

The driving force behind this new ideology was a twenty-nine-year-old medical student at the nonwhite University of Natal. Steve Biko's fervent gaze and winning smile stirred a wind of renewal in the black people's struggle for freedom. Hundreds of thousands of young Africans joined. The letters BC, standing for black consciousness, soon appeared on walls, buses, and stations all across the country, announcing a new crusade against white oppression.

★

CERTAIN DATES CONVEY the history of a country. On June 16, 1976, as Sue Krige, a twenty-six-year-old white teacher, was explaining the history of the French Revolution to a group of pupils at a private secondary school in a Johannesburg suburb, she could never have imagined that the morning would be a turning point in her country's history, that June 16, 1976, would become as decisive for South Africa as July 14, 1789, had been for France.

It was ten o'clock when the throb of low-flying helicopters deafened Sue Krige and her pupils. They ran onto the school's veranda to watch the aircraft heading in a pack toward Soweto, the largest black township in South Africa, half a dozen miles to the west. Neither Sue nor any of her pupils guessed the reason for the helicopters. Yet their presence indicated a violent threat to the domination over South Africa exercised by the Great Trek's descendants. Dozens of heavily armed police were being flown to the battlefield of the most significant uprising ever unleashed by the country's black population. Extraordinarily, those involved were children, most not yet fifteen. Soweto was a patchwork of some forty neighborhoods of varying degrees of poverty at the edge of Johannesburg; a phantom city without boundaries or streetlights, with no electricity or running water in three-quarters of the homes; a city full of overcrowded Zulu hostels where ritual murders were carried out with bicycle spokes sharpened to a point; a city without architectural coherence in which tribes, churches, and clandestine *shebeens* converged in a confused tangle; a sometimes terrifying world that whites could not enter without an official permit and then only by day; a place where police burst out of armored cars to break down doors to houses and seize alcohol and drugs, shouting "Die, kaffirs!" Soweto was a township of 1.2 million inhabitants, not counting those living underground or outside the law, where life expectancy often did not exceed forty, where in some neighborhoods half the population was unemployed, in short, a place of every kind of misery. Nevertheless, Soweto managed to send 200,000 children into 350 scattered schools directed, managed, and monitored by officials in the ministry for native education in Pretoria according to the restrictive rules laid down by Hendrik Verwoerd, the father of apartheid. The education there systematically excluded subjects that whites considered unnecessary for blacks to fulfill their karma as subhumans. These run-down schools had few teachers and even fewer books but were packed, bursting with life and attentive to the message of hope from medical student Steve Biko and his black consciousness movement. This was the volatile terrain where in the spring of 1976 the government introduced an order that would start a revolution. Obtuse or simply arrogant, the decision to impose Afrikaans as an additional language to be studied and used in all black schools jolted teachers and pupils alike. How could a generation of young blacks already struggling to master English begin overnight to study history or geography in Afrikaans, when there were not enough teachers or textbooks in Soweto or the other townships to ensure that they would be taught? The schools were boiling with rage. Bureaucrats sent to transmit the government's instructions were greeted with stone throwing, driven away, or taken hostage. Protest meetings were held everywhere. "If the whites suddenly want to force us to talk and write their Afrikaans it's because they want to cut us off from our roots forever," declared young Sally Mpshe, a pupil at the Morris Isaacson high school. "It's primarily to unsettle us, to stop us becoming better black pupils," fifteen-year-old Steve Lebelo from Madison high school echoed. Thirteen-year-old Martha Matthews from the Kelikitso junior secondary school in Orlando suggested that "the tyrants in Pretoria want to force us to run away from school and leave South Africa." In many schools pupils reacted by boycotting lessons in Afrikaans and setting fire to books and exam papers in the detested language. Soon a consensus emerged about their formal response. Teachers and pupils would say no to speaking white Afrikaans. They would say it peacefully in a grand protest march on Wednesday June 16, 1976, from their respective schools to the large stadium in Orlando East. It would be a festive day to celebrate the struggle of the black people to take charge of their own destiny.

Alas, Wednesday, June 16, 1976, was to be above all a day of horror.

It was six in the morning when the first groups assembled outside a dozen schools. The atmosphere was good-natured, even joyful. Black consciousness activists handed out cardboard placards on which was written "DOWN WITH AFRIKAANS," "TO HELL WITH THE WHITES' BANTU EDUCATION." At seven o'clock the first group set off singing and hopping from one foot to the other in the traditional South African toyi-toyi. Other groups got under way at the same time and soon a myriad of processions bristling with banners were surging toward the rallying point. Police armed with submachine guns and rifles had been posted at the main crossroads, among them many supplemental troops of color. All carried haversacks containing tear gas canisters. The first incident occurred almost immediately at the White City junction. Gunshots rang out. Two schoolboys running to get to the head of the procession were hit. But the procession went on. At the next crossroads the police were forced back by the pressure of the crowd. Would the demonstration turn into a confrontation? A teenage boy climbed onto the hood of a car to try to prevent the worst. "Brothers and sisters!" he shouted at the top of his voice, "I beg you to stay calm, please. We have just received word that enormous police reinforcements are about to arrive. Don't provoke them! Don't attack them! We are not here to fight but to show our peaceful determination!"

No sooner had the speaker jumped down from his platform when a column of trucks packed with police with riot shields broke through. The men were deployed in six rows blocking the road. For several minutes police and demonstrators stood facing each other. Suddenly a triumphal song broke from a thousand throats: the black people's anthem. *"Morena boloka sechaba sa heso"* (Lord, bless our nation!) shouted the schoolchildren in one voice, stamping their feet impatiently. A sergeant responded by throwing a tear gas canister over the nearest heads. Another fired his submachine gun by mistake. This twofold assault caused panicked movement in the rows of demonstrators, then a surge of anger. A deluge of stones rained down on the police, who responded with gunfire. Many youngsters fell to the ground.

At this point there suddenly appeared from the chaos a vision worthy of Michelangelo's *Pietà*, in which the Christ taken down from the cross was a black child covered in blood; where the Virgin holding him was a teenager in dungarees, his face twisted with terror; where Mary Magdalene at their side was a young girl in tears with her hand held out pleading for mercy. Three figures whose pain showed the sheer horror that had just broken out. From behind a policeman's shoulder, Sam Nzima, a photographer for the Johannesburg *Star*, captured this image for eternity. In a few hours his photo would travel around the world. Nothing could have better symbolized the tragedy of South Africa than that heartrending *Pietà* in motion. The thirteen-year-old boy dying in the arms of his older brother was a student at Orlando West named Hector Pieterson. The bullet had struck him directly in the chest and he died within minutes. Already Soweto had its martyr. One day free South Africa would name the crossroads where he died after him.

★

THE RIOTING SPREAD RAPIDLY. Soon fires and bloodshed broke out all over the township. Barricades sprang up across the dusty roads. Two white employees from the ministry of Bantu education were dragged from their offices into the street and lynched. Liquor stores were looted and bottles smashed on the pavement to shouts of "Less alcohol and more schools!" The government ordered all schools closed and sent thousands of police to patrol the township. In parliament Prime Minister John Vorster declared, "The government will not allow itself to be intimidated." Afrikaans would continue to be imposed on the schools. To stop the demonstrations, he outlawed assemblies of more than three people on the public highway.

Despite its firm tone, the speech reassured only half the prime minister's supporters. White supremacists were quick to express their fears. Could the lovely unity of the descendants of the Great Trek be about to crack? The uprising claimed a tragic toll: hundreds dead, thousands wounded, dozens of administrative buildings burned. Moreover, the violence of that fateful Wednesday and the days that followed would spread to other townships throughout the country. Soweto became the epicenter of a racial revolt that could no longer be put down.

As always happens in times of trouble, the international stock market registered the panic most tangibly. As televisions and newspapers broadcast images of the violence, raw material prices collapsed. In a single session gold and diamonds lost 15 percent of their value on the London stock exchange. And foreign investment, considered vital to the welfare of the South African economy, fell by half in a matter of hours.

★

THE CLAMPDOWN WAS SAVAGE. But no threat seemed capable of stifling the resistance of the young people in Soweto. On the pediments of their schools they placed a new slogan: "Enter here to learn, leave to serve." During the fiercest clashes, as their children risked their lives in the township's streets, parents received pamphlets saying: "Be glad you have a child with such moral fiber . . . a child who prefers death to a poisonous education condemning him and his parents to perpetual subordination."

Of course stone throwing and barricades were no match for assault rifles and mass arrests. But beneath the calm that gradually returned to Soweto, reality had changed forever. The bloody confrontations of June 1976 abruptly ushered in a new generation of Africans proud to show their courage defending their cause and struggling for their rights. On the crest of this activism, several hundred young people decided to cross the border to join ANC commandos based in neighboring countries. After being trained in guerrilla techniques and terrorist activity, they crossed back. For several weeks in the spring of 1980, the Johannesburg sky was darkened by thick black smoke from the explosion of six oil tanks at a refinery over fifty miles away. But it was by sabotaging the Koeberg nuclear station near Cape Town that the township schoolchildren-turned-ANC guerrillas dealt the morale of the authorities in Pretoria their heaviest blow. Believing his people's survival was at stake, Vorster decided the terrorists must be captured. Protecting the country's nuclear installations, the pride of the regime, was vitally important. Wasn't it even rumored that South Africa had the atomic bomb? Vorster therefore mobilized all the resources of the continent's best police force.

On the evening of August 18, 1977, a police roadblock outside Grahamstown, in the Eastern Cape, intercepted public enemy number 1, the medical student Steve Biko, charismatic founder of black consciousness and inspiration of the students of Soweto. Biko, in handcuffs and ankle chains, was taken under armed escort to the secret police headquarters in Port Elizabeth. Then began his twenty-six-day ordeal at the hands of police practiced in the Nazi methods so admired by the founders of apartheid. Biko was beaten, tortured, bullied, and left naked and unconscious on the concrete floor of his cell. His torturers would stop at nothing to find out what new actions the black consciousness movement was planning. The prisoner could answer them only with a gasp. With the arch of his eyebrows cloven, his nose broken, and his skull swollen, he was a bleeding wreck. His face, usually so full of life, was a tragic mask of suffering. His breathing would stop for long moments. He was finished, on the brink of a coma. Panicked, the guards threw him naked and still chained at the ankles and wrists, without medical care, water, or food, into the back of a Land Rover and took him to the dispensary at Pretoria prison, some 740 miles away. The black leader would not survive this final way of the cross. He died on arrival.

At the inquest Pretoria's chief magistrate, Marthinus Prins, heaped a final insult on the legendary hero of the black struggle: "The cause or likely cause of Mr. Biko's death was a head injury, followed by extensive brain injury and other complications including renal failure. The head injury was probably sustained during a scuffle with the Security Police. . . . The available evidence does not prove that death was brought about by an act or omission involving an offense by any person."

His assassination shocked, anguished, and finally enraged millions of Africans, especially in the townships. There were demonstrations in his memory everywhere. Black South Africa wept openly: it had been orphaned.

★

STEVE BIKO'S BLACK SOUTH AFRICA was now truly an orphan. Mandela and all the ANC leaders were entering their thirteenth year of incarceration in Robben Island's Block 3. Only the guerrilla fighters who had taken refuge across the border could threaten the apartheid regime's iron grip, but apart from acts of sabotage and attempted assassinations their influence was still marginal. But things were not going well for the man with the double chin ruling from his flowery offices in Pretoria. A growing number of UN members were calling for an embargo on arms deliveries to his country. Many in American financial circles loudly advocated freezing investment in or divesting from South Africa. Western trade unions began boycotting maritime, air, and postal links to the nation. As if this were not enough to bring home to him the disastrous image his country presented to the world, Vorster then poured oil on the fire.

Basil d'Oliveira was an English cricket star who had brought England victory in a number of international matches. He and his team were soon to face South Africa's champions. But a problem arose when the high priests of race classification officiating in Pretoria discovered that Basil d'Oliveira, who was originally from South Africa, was of mixed race. How could South Africa's 100 percent white team play against a foreign team that included a colored player in its ranks? It simply was not possible! John Vorster considered the affair important enough to warrant his personal intervention. In a public speech in Bloemfontein, he declared solemnly that South Africa would never be able to welcome a team made up not of sporting opponents but of political opponents. His words provoked universal outcry. Overnight the country found itself ousted from all world competition, its athletes excluded from the Olympic and Commonwealth games, its stadiums shunned by foreign teams. The boycott would last ten years, an unspeakable ordeal for a people who had given the rugby world one of its legendary teams, the Springboks.

★

BUT THESE POLITICAL, ECONOMIC, and sporting pressures in no way affected the prime minister's determination to pursue the politics of segregation initiated by his predecessor. Since apartheid meant separate development, the eviction of blacks from all areas decreed to be "white" continued with increased vigor.

All resistance was forcibly crushed. The government actions in Sophiatown and District Six had shown the way. Entire communities were deported. As a woman from the Ciskei recounted, "They arrived with their dogs and guns, they threw our things into a truck, and they took us away." A journalist for the *Rand Daily Mail* reported seeing police charging at the occupants of a squatter camp near Cape Town, tearing their clothes off them, setting dogs on them, confiscating their passbooks, and clubbing anyone who tried to resist. In Modderdam near Bellville, in Crossroads, west of Cape Town, loudspeakers on police cars informed several thousand people: "The destruction of this area will begin in fifteen minutes!" Panic-stricken, they grabbed a few clothes, a bed, a table, some pieces of crockery, and fled. As promised, the neighborhood was immediately bulldozed to the ground. Violence broke out at some eviction sites. Blacks defended themselves with bottles and knives against those trying to drive them out. In Werkgenot, a white woman prevented a massacre by brandishing a crucifix at the police. In Kwaggafontein, north of Pretoria, Anglican priest David Purcell threw himself in front of a bulldozer to save a family about to be crushed in the hovel they had not had time to evacuate.

A photo in the Johannesburg *Star* captured the victims' anguish. It showed a man, a woman, a little girl, and a goat huddled together in front of a corrugated iron shack emptied of its contents. They were waiting with their few worldly goods for the government truck that would take them to the Northern Transvaal. The resignation and dignity of that wounded family prompted thousands of indignant letters to the newspaper, a flood of correspondence that showed not all white South Africans supported apartheid.

During the night of May 16, 1977, three security police cars and a truck pulled up outside 8115 Orlando West in Soweto. The house with its corrugated iron roof belonged to Nelson

Mandela. The prime minister's police had come to pick up Winnie and her daughter and deport them to Brandfort, a township in the Orange Free State over 250 miles away. In that gloomy, desolate place people spoke Sotho, a language neither of them could understand. It was an exile worse than imprisonment. When the news reached Mandela several weeks later, he broke down. In fifteen years he had seen his wife just four times, and always through the distorted glass of the visiting room. But at least when she was in Soweto he could imagine her doing familiar, everyday things. He could picture her cooking in the kitchen or reading in the living room, or waking up in the house he knew so well. That had been a comfort to him. In Soweto, even when she was under house arrest, there were friends and family nearby. In that remote township she and their daughter Zindzi would be alone. He did not know then how familiar the address—802 Black Township, Brandfort—would one day become to him. Suddenly he felt as though Winnie and he were both in prison.

John Vorster and his ministers felt no regret about the plight of their victims, whatever their status. At the end of the 1970s they were busy celebrating their monstrous achievements. Over 20 percent of South Africa's 6 million blacks had been removed to ghettos under their program of ethnic redistribution. The descendants of the people chosen by Calvin to spread Christianity in Africa had accomplished one of the most colossal deportations in the history of humanity.

★

CAPE TOWN, THAT DISTANT POINT on the globe where the fiercest and most extravagant of colonial epics began on an April day in 1652. Cape Town, where the people of a new covenant had set off for a promised land in the heart of Africa. What did that dazzling garden city, floating like a Utopia amid the scent of pines, know of the tragedy that was unfolding in the country whose attractive qualities it continued to symbolize? What did it know of the suffering Vorster and his apartheid torturers had inflicted on the black population? Despite the fact that its parliament had enacted the most terrifying arsenal of laws ever voted against freedom, in truth it knew very little. Apart from the eviction of the occupants of District Six and repeated removals from some of the local squatter camps, the city had experienced only sporadic racial confrontation. For the most part, the communities were separated peacefully, though some white businessmen complained that there were no restaurants where they could sit at the same table with their clients of color. But suddenly in this tranquil context, a deeply distressing racial confrontation was to occur.

Thirty-two-year-old Helen Lieberman was a cheerful, green-eyed blonde, married to Michael, a lawyer. The couple lived with their three children in a luxurious villa in the coastal suburb of Sea Point, a few miles from the center of town. Sea Point looked out onto the magnificent waters off Cape Town with the rock of Robben Island in the sometimes foggy distance. Helen knew there was a penal colony on the rock but did not really know who the prisoners were or why they were being confined there. If she had heard the name Nelson Mandela, like many South Africans she knew very little about him. She would certainly have difficulty recognizing him in a photo. The authorities prohibited newspapers and national magazines from publishing pictures of the black leader or any of his companions. In the same way that the French were ignorant of General de Gaulle's features during World War II, most South Africans did not know the face of the man who would one day head their country.

Of her Jewish parents, one of whom had fled pogroms in Lithuania and the other World War II, Helen recalled people who expressed themselves so rarely and in such a strong accent that she struggled to understand the little they said. It was reading a book about deaf mutes soon after she graduated that determined the direction of her life. She was awarded a grant for graduate study in speech therapy. Once she was qualified, Helen opened a speech therapy practice. And then a letter arrived that would make her reputation. The head of the department of maxillofacial surgery at Groote Schuur hospital was offering to set up for her a clinic for the retraining of children with congenital deformities of the mouth and lips. Harelips that split the upper lip to the base of the nose, cleft palates that prevented children from eating or speaking—these were the young South African woman's specialities. The fact that the invitation came from Groote Schuur filled her with pride. Groote Schuur hospital, built on the site of a "great barn" on land donated many years before by Cecil Rhodes, was the most famous establishment of its kind in the southern hemisphere, a university teaching center where patients flocked from all over Africa, Australia, Singapore, and Malaysia for the most advanced medical and surgical treatment. Groote Schuur with its thousand beds, its two thousand patients a day, its twenty-five operating rooms, its lecture halls, and its research laboratories. Everyone in Cape Town knew the enormous seven-floor institution that in its parklike setting on the slopes of Table Mountain looked like a luxury hotel from the 1930s. Driving there in her small blue Anglia took the young speech therapist only minutes. But as soon as she drove through the entrance and saw a monumental stone statue of Hygeia, goddess of health, she was faced with a choice, which was symbolic of the tragedy crushing the country to which her parents had come seeking to live in freedom. Should she take the ramp leading to the right side of the building or the one that led to the left side? To the right side was the part of the hospital for whites. The left was for blacks and coloreds. The young woman did not hesitate. It was in the left side that she was expected.

Shock, horror, revulsion. This young South African, who had never shown the least hesitation about washing the ears, eyes, mouths, or any other part of a white baby's body, was overcome by the singular smell of the treatment room she entered. "A fetid, nauseating smell that caught my throat, made me reel, forced me to run to the toilet to throw up," Helen was to say. "I was ashamed. I knew it would take me days to get used to contact with those little black patients, to accept their filthiness and not mind the stench that issued from their ears, from every pore in their body. Yes, it would be days before I could pick them up in my arms, days before I could meet their mothers' entreating gazes. But I also knew that the day would come when I would be able to do all those things and that that day would be a second birth for me."

Such suffering was beyond anything she could have imagined. The treatment room for children with deformities was a real "court of the miracles." The piteous sight of those black mothers who tried to breast-feed their babies but saw the milk spurt back out of their children's noses every time they sucked because of their cleft palates. The frightful sight of those infants choking on the tiniest amount of food. The overwhelming sight of these mothers fighting desperately to keep a flame of life going in those doomed little bodies. The worst thing for the young speech therapist was not finding so much misfortune in that hospital but seeing the doctors' and nurses' disdain for their suffering, as if the pain and distress of blacks and coloreds was less deserving of relief. A visit to the ear, nose, and throat unit reserved for whites in the other wing of the hospital confirmed her fears. Here the way in which patients were admitted, the cleanliness of the premises, and the quality of the medical care were consistent with Groote Schuur's reputation for excellence. When Helen confided her indignation, the nurse in charge of the department for blacks belittled her. "Why worry yourself, dear?" the nurse retorted. "All those screaming black babies are going to die. What does it matter? There are 25 million of them and only 4 million of us. In any case their mothers will make more. Kaffirs breed like rabbits."

"That's when a young woman came to me with a baby in her arms," Helen Lieberman was to recount. "She must have thought I was a doctor because of my white coat. I was struck by the baby's beauty and by his mother's look of entreaty. She showed me the child's mouth and I realized he had just had surgery. No

one in the department seemed able to tell me precisely what operation he had undergone. After examining him I concluded it
had been to close up the roof of his mouth. I knew that, in that
case, the most urgent thing was to see that the patient was hy-
drated. His life depended on his swallowing a few drops of water.
I dared not take the baby in my arms. The smell of him was making me feel so sick. I motioned to his mother to put him in a crib.
I learned his name was Andile. I immediately prepared a bottle
with powdered milk. Then I selected a nipple. The size of the
hole in the nipple is primordial. If the nipple is too big, the child
can choke. If it's too small, he will not be able to suck ade-
quately. Either way it seriously affects the prognosis. The poor
mother followed my every move with desperate eyes. Around me
I felt a hostile curiosity. The white nurses and black auxiliaries
must really have been wondering why a white woman was paying
so much attention to a little black child. It was a completely new
feeling for me since I had never drawn a distinction medically
speaking between a white child and a black, though I'd had few
little black patients in my practice. Their attitude was probably a
consequence of apartheid, but I found it hard to admit that a political system preaching equal, albeit separate, development for
all communities could have led to such inhuman feelings. It was
frightful. I felt a desperate need to talk to Michael about it."

Helen then glanced at her watch. It was four in the afternoon. The sun was already disappearing behind Devil's Peak at
the back of the hospital. Since Shabbat was starting, the young
Jewish woman hastily gathered up her things and gave the nurses
and little Andile's mother some last instructions. She would
come again tomorrow when Shabbat was over.

★

WHEN HELEN LIEBERMAN returned to the hospital the next day,
Andile's crib was empty. She was shocked to think he must have
died. She went throughout the department to find out whether
this was the case, but the medical staff took Saturdays off to go to
the beach. Finally Helen found an orderly. "Is Andile dead?" The

black employee glowered at her and clenched her teeth. Helen grabbed her by the arms and asked her again. The young African woman broke free. "I'm just an orderly here!" she shouted. "A black orderly! I don't know anything!" Helen tried to calm herself. She sensed that a wall separated her from the poor girl, a wall of incomprehension, bitterness, and fear, a wall between two skin colors, a wall between races. This was a new feeling for the young white woman who was nevertheless not afraid to keep questioning the angry black girl. "If he's not dead perhaps he's been sent home?" she ventured. The African girl had looked away, maintaining her wall of silence. Then suddenly she drew herself up and lashed out furiously: "Here, sister, a black does not speak to a white. Leave me alone!" With these words she pointed at the ceiling. "There are devices up there that listen to what whites and blacks say to one another in this room. For the love of God, sister, don't ask me any more questions!"

Being called "sister" gave Helen reason for renewed hope. In the end surely this young black woman would tell her whether Andile had died or had been sent home! But the wall stood. How could two people born in the same country, heirs to the same past, have allowed such a barrier to be built between them? Helen Lieberman knew the question was naive. Michael could probably give her some answers, she thought. For the moment she only needed to find out what had become of the black baby. The survival rate after cleft palate operations in frail children was very low. But perhaps the bottles with the right nipples had enabled Andile to make it over the vital hurdle of the first forty-eight hours. In the colored wards at Groote Schuur, postoperative patients were not kept for very long. Andile and his mother must have been sent home. If the baby had been discharged he was in more danger of dying than ever. It was urgent that he receive medical attention. He had undergone very serious surgery that required appropriate follow-up.

"Sister, I beg you to tell me what has happened to Andile," Helen implored again. Now it was she who used the word "sister" in hoping to overcome the young black woman's hostility.

Her heart pounded as she waited for her reaction. Long seconds passed, then suddenly there came a response.

"The doctor sent Andile and his mother home."

"When?"

"This morning."

"Do you know where they live?"

The young black woman indicated she would say no more. But Helen was determined. Two hours later, as inky darkness enveloped the sea off Cape Town, a small Anglia left Groote Schuur hospital. Huddled on the backseat, with her head wrapped in a shawl, was the orderly. Although paralyzed with the fear of being spotted in a white woman's car she had agreed to direct Helen to Langa, an immense, miserable African township some ten miles outside Cape Town, a place as brutal and inhuman as Soweto, crammed with 200,000 blacks awaiting probable deportation the day the land surveyors in their Cape Town offices decided to classify the area as white. Langa was another small piece of hell on the land purportedly given by God to the people of the Psalms. That evening, however, it was also a place of hope, because of the young white woman heading into the slums with her car lights switched off. Much as Mother Teresa had answered the need for love and justice by bringing dignity to the poor lepers of the slums of Calcutta, Helen Lieberman could perhaps salvage a little of the honor lost by white South Africans.

★

THE HONOR OF THE AFRIKANER people did not trouble John Vorster. What preoccupied the prime minister, rather, was worldwide disenchantment with his country. How could he reverse this without compromising apartheid? One morning in October 1973, an elegant thirty-eight-year-old man named Eschel Rhoodie came to him with an answer to this dilemma. Before becoming the government's information secretary, Rhoodie had been press attaché at the South African embassies in countries as diverse as Australia, the United States, and the Netherlands. Everywhere, the disastrous image of his country caused by its policy of racial segregation had shocked him. He hoped to redress the situation with a bold propaganda campaign that would stress South Africa's strategic importance to the West, its role as a bastion against communism and a haven of capitalist prosperity on a continent whose economies had tilted toward socialism or communism. The campaign would cost millions, but Rhoodie was convinced the West would close its eyes to apartheid if it could be made to take a dispassionate view of its own interests.

He at once received carte blanche from the prime minister together with the assurance of unlimited secret funds. He began his campaign with an offensive on the home front. The first step was to neutralize the influence of antigovernment South African journalists from whom foreign correspondents drew much of their unfavorable coverage. Rhoodie founded a daily tabloid newspaper, *The Citizen*, which spent a fortune on creating for the land of apartheid the kind of heavenly image the Voortrekkers had dreamed of in their wagons. The campaign was only a partial success but Rhoodie had other plans abroad. Through Operation Bowler Hat he bought the collaboration of British Conservative and Labour members of Parliament with an eye to acquiring several publications, including the influential *Investors Chronicle*. Next he went to Paris to negotiate the active support of two of the finest French news magazines, *L'Express* and *Paris Match*. Though this attempt failed, he managed to set up a series of organizations in other European countries, which, under such seductive titles as the South African Freedom Foundation, invited hundreds of VIPs from all over Europe to come and find paradise in South Africa. However, this tireless spin doctor put most of his energy into winning over the United States. After attempting to purchase the *Washington Star*, he proceeded to take over California's *Sacramento Union* and then acquired 50 percent ownership of UPITN-TV, a television news agency that he made into a champion for the South African cause.

His resourcefulness, dynamism, and, above all, his small suitcase full of green bills earned him the friendship of politicians whom he turned into unconditional supporters of his country.

Pretoria's agent never failed to thank these converts by generously oiling their electoral campaigns. Even Jimmy Carter was said to have benefited from Eschel Roodie's largesse.

But then the extravagant expenditures made by the young South African public relations king began to raise red flags in Pretoria. Some of Vorster's political opponents called for an investigation. A report meant for the prime minister detailing the use of secret funds entrusted to his protégé somehow made its way to the desk of the director of an opposition weekly, the *Sunday Express*. The affair was publicized, and a huge scandal engulfed the man who tried to sell apartheid to the West like shaving cream. On September 5, 1978, John Vorster appeared before members of parliament in Cape Town and announced his resignation, citing health problems.

Thus the page was turned on one of the darkest chapters in the history of apartheid. The man who had crushed the Soweto schoolchildren's uprising, deported the residents of Sophiatown and many other black townships, and had Steve Biko assassinated was gone from power. When Mandela heard the news, he did not conceal his satisfaction. Vorster had raised repression to new extremes.

Vorster's successor to head the country was an ardent Afrikaner nationalist of sixty-two by the name of Pieter Willem Botha, or "P.W." His mother, a heroine of the Anglo-Boer war, had seen two of her children die in a concentration camp where they had been interned by the British. As for his father, on the day the Boers signed the peace treaty with Great Britain he had broken his gun in two. P.W. Botha had abandoned his university studies at the age of twenty to espouse the Purified National Party, which he had helped to win the historic victory of 1948 at the side of Hendrik Verwoerd and Daniel François Malan, high priest of the "purified" white race. Elected to parliament by a constituency in the Cape, at thirty-six he became minister of community development in Malan's government, a post from which he would sign the death warrant for District Six, where 60,000 whites, blacks, and coloreds had been living in a racial harmony that verged on the miraculous. On becoming defense minister in 1966, P.W. Botha had endowed South Africa with an arms industry and the most powerful army on the continent, which he used to prevent any encroachment from communist activities in neighboring countries. His colorful ties, paternal air, and the white and red carnation he wore in his buttonhole reassured people. They were mistaken. P.W. Botha was an even more relentless extremist than his predecessors, but more skillful and intelligent. To complement their philosophy of total onslaught he proposed a more subtle response, a total strategy, which implied he did not share Hendrick Verwoerd's mad dream of a South Africa completely rid of blacks. Instead, P.W. Botha wished to encourage the development of a middle class of color that could counterbalance the despair of the township populations. Relaxing certain constraints of racial segregation, he announced the gradual removal of discriminatory notices from stations, public transportation, and beaches, which gave rise to people's hope for more spectacular concessions, such as the abolition of the laws prohibiting mixed marriages and sexual relations between whites and blacks, or the obligatory carrying of passes.

Was this slight softening going to change a situation that fifty years of racial exclusion had congealed? While he waited to play his new hand, P.W. Botha proclaimed that it would.

★

NO SIGNS OF CHANGE were apparent to Helen Lieberman as she ventured into the enormous township ten miles west of Cape Town that winter night, hoping to find Andile and his mother. The orderly from Groote Schuur hospital accompanying her knew that white people were prohibited from entering the ghetto. The ban was enforced by both the white police guarding its approaches and the black township's leaders who would see the sudden intrusion of a white woman as a provocation. The young speech therapist at the wheel of her little car was unaware that she was risking her life.

Nothing in her experience had prepared her for what she found in the township. First there was the overpowering smell, an acrid aroma of burning wood that rose from the braziers on which the women were cooking the evening meal; then the clamor of people packing the alleyways, pavements, and court-yards. She learned how much of life Africans spent outside rather than inside their homes. She felt people's stares. Were those looks of hostility or of surprise? She did not yet know. In the din of voices, shouts, and cries, one sound stood out from all the others: the coughing fits wracking numerous chests under the shroud of sulfur and smoke. She gripped the arm of the young black orderly. "Where's Andile?" The two women stepped past mothers delousing their children on doorsteps and others washing their little children despite the biting cold. So much poverty! So many barefoot kids in rags! And yet what sublime dignity on most of the faces! Eventually they entered a window-less room with a beaten earthen floor and a roof that was open to the sky in places where bits of corrugated iron were missing. There was no furniture and no electricity, only the dim light of a paraffin lamp. An open drain level with the door teemed with rats. Helen made out the shape of a woman squatting at the far end of the room. She recognized Andile's mother, who rose to greet her. "Andile? Where's Andile?" Helen asked anxiously. The young black mother motioned her to follow. They went into an-other room where they saw several old women with old blankets or cloth shawls around their shoulders. These were the neighbor-hood grandmothers. Each was holding a baby or small child for warmth under her blanket or shawl. Helen would learn that in African society the grandmothers look after the youngest chil-dren, in some cases by themselves. Her unexpected arrival caused general astonishment. No white woman had ever come there be-fore. The children started screaming and Helen backed away in panic, but Andile's mother stopped her. Her baby was there in the arms of an elderly blind woman. Helen saw from Andile's livid color and wrinkled skin that he was severely dehydrated and needed to be put on intravenous fluids immediately. But would these suspicious grandmothers allow him to be taken to the hospital? She tried to tell them that Andile was in danger, but no one seemed to understand. She pantomimed his dying without success. One of the old women then stood up to drive the intruder out of the room. There was a scene doubtless never imagined by the inventors of separate racial development, a black grandmother preventing a white woman from saving her grandson's life. But in South Africa people's points of reference had been obliterated by apartheid.

"That was one of the most painful discoveries of my life," Helen Lieberman would say later. "The apartheid system, which till then had never affected me personally, had not only physically divided the inhabitants of my country. It had stamped hatred in their hearts."

The hospital orderly managed to calm everyone down and Andile's grandmother at last agreed to let her grandson go in his mother's arms. Less than an hour later, he was back in his crib in the ward at Groote Schuur. All that night Helen had him on the drip he needed to stay alive. It was six in the morning when she got home. Out of his mind with worry, Michael hugged her to him, stunned by the smell of wood smoke in her hair and on her clothes. "I was in Langa," she explained. "People there cook with wood." Then she burst into tears.

Helen's sobs did not stop. In the safety of her living room, Helen continued to weep. When at last she regained her composure she stood up to take in the beauty of the sunrise. Then in a steady voice she said, "Michael, I want to leave this country. After what I've seen tonight, I'll never be able to love South Africa again . . . I'm ashamed, Michael, ashamed to be white; ashamed to be part of a system that allows crimes to be committed against humanity; ashamed to work in a hospital that sends a baby back to live in degradation just because he's black."

"Michael gently wiped the tears from my cheeks," the young woman was to recount. "He kissed me, held me close to him. I could still see the frightened faces of those grandmothers and all those children. I couldn't have responded to his caresses."

Michael tried to reassure his wife.

"Darling, you know there's poverty everywhere," he said. "Langa is not unique. Think of those gigantic slums in Bombay, India, between the airport and the city center. Think of the *favelas* in Rio, Brazil. Unfortunately there will always be people who have to live in such hell holes."

"Michael, you don't understand," she replied firmly. "The people I met tonight weren't *poor*. They were *afraid*. What I saw wasn't *hunger* but *fear*. Fear at suddenly being face-to-face with a white woman, fear of raising their eyes to her, fear of letting her look at their children, fear . . . FEAR! Michael, you and I, and all South Africans are guilty of forcing an entire people to live with fear in their bellies. That's why I don't want to stay in this country any more, Michael. Do you understand, my love?"

★

HELEN LIEBERMAN DID NOT leave South Africa. However, her meeting with Andile and her brief foray into the hostile environment of a township would change the direction of her life. Her work as a speech therapist in the ENT department at Groote Schuur soon took up most of her time and she closed her private practice. Speech therapy is a demanding discipline that includes a whole host of pathologies. Teaching children to swallow again after mouth operations, helping a cancer patient learn to speak without a larynx and training those around him to give support, restoring speech to a stroke victim . . . the tasks were endless.

Seven days after saving little Andile, Helen had another victory. This time her patient was a little girl named Mina. She'd had an operation to fix a cleft palate and could not suck the nipple of a bottle. To spoon-feed her Helen had to pick her up and hold her, a difficult thing because of the child's smell. But she had come a long way in a week. Helen picked up the baby without hesitation, sat down on a stool, and began to feed her. She was radiant. That day she really became a new person.

She decided to celebrate by taking Andile and his mother back to their township. To her surprise she was welcomed warmly, even by the grandmothers. One woman even dared to speak to her. "Mama Helen, we'd like to talk to you about the possibility of doing something together to help the people of our neighborhood."

Doing something to help! In that ghetto where 200,000 victims of racial hatred struggled for survival each day, where people measured their lives not in years but in months or weeks, a place vibrating with courage and mutual support but ravaged by tuberculosis, dysentery, alcoholism, and malnutrition; an environment so polluted that thousands did not live till forty . . . there seemed no end to what needed doing. Nurseries and a clinic for the littlest ones had to be a priority; milk had to be distributed to malnourished children and a soup kitchen set up for the older ones; fountains with drinking water needed installing; the number of latrines increased. Helen knew that there were dozens of urgent needs. "I suggest we take a poll," she replied, "to find out what people here want most." The results of the six opinion surveys came three days later and they were unanimous. They were not what the young white woman had imagined. It was not material conditions the township occupants wanted to change first. The nourishment they craved was not for their children's puny bodies but for their minds. Helen was astonished. What the people in Langa wanted most was a school, so that their children could learn to read and write.

The project was like shock therapy to a population inured to crushing circumstances. People mobilized, offering their services. Even the usually distrustful township council joined in, offering a few square yards of dusty ground between two alleyways on which to set up the school. Helen's kindness to everyone, her approach to the children, and her availability soon dispelled any lingering reluctance. Word spread: there is a white woman in Langa who loves and respects all people without consideration for color. In a place without resources, building four walls with a roof for a few schoolchildren was a bold undertaking. Helen could see only one way to achieve it: by making her little Anglia a delivery van and bringing the necessary materials from Cape Town herself. She found the building foreman she needed on the spot. Sam was twenty years old with a boxer's muscles and a luminous face. Originally from the Transkei, he had traveled across the country, walking by night and hiding by day, to try to find work in a factory in the Cape. When he did not succeed, he took refuge in Langa where he searched through the garbage brought three times a week by the municipal council trucks. With what he found he managed to feed a group of teenagers who were devoted to him for life. They all volunteered to help build the school.

A young white woman pulling up in a car full of shovels and bricks with planks and sacks of cement on the roof was a truly unusual sight. Helen was met with a round of applause, cheers, and even a show of toyi-toyi danced around her car. The work went quickly and efficiently. In less than a week the small construction was up and ready to dispense the rudiments of knowledge to some thirty children. It was a great day for the woman who had wanted to flee South Africa.

She returned home late that night, delirious with happiness, images of joy and fellowship filling her head. But the sound of the telephone ringing soon interrupted her euphoria. On the other end of the line, a voice announced, "Mama Helen, some people came and started hitting Sam with clubs. Then they tied him to one of the school pillars and poured petrol over him. 'That'll teach you, you bastard, to build a school with that white whore!' they shouted at him. And they struck a match. The poor kid, he was engulfed in flames. He was screaming. It was horrible."

"Was it whites who did it?" asked Helen, appalled.

"No, blacks. Probably blacks being paid by the white police."

The young woman quickly dressed and raced with Michael to Langa. The people of the neighborhood were standing in a circle around the charred body. Someone was leading them in prayers, which they all repeated in chorus. There was no sign of a policeman anywhere. At daybreak, Helen went with her husband to the police station at the main entrance to the township.

"A young man was burned alive last night in Langa and not one of your men has come yet to establish the facts and find those responsible!" she shouted at the duty officer.

The officer curled his lip and took a thick file off a shelf.

"Lady, all these papers are reports on your illegal activities among the kaffirs in this area," he snarled. "If you don't stop it immediately, you could end up the same way."

With these words he sank back into his chair, glaring at her, and lit a cigarette.

Helen understood. The white police would spread the word that she was an informant working for them and then pay two blacks to do away with her. No one would protest. That was the way things were in the land of apartheid.

A few days later Tutu, a young woman from the neighborhood, stopped the speech therapist as she was getting out of her car.

"Mama Helen," she begged, "don't ever come back here. People are convinced you're working for the police. They'll kill you."

★

NO NEWSPAPER REPORTED on the murder in Langa. Cape Town had other preoccupations at the end of that year 1967. Christmas was a few days away and the whole city was adorning its avenues and shopping areas with lights, Christmas trees, and snowmen. The windows on Adderley and the other shopping streets were already piled with mountains of gifts lavishly wrapped and tied with colorful ribbons. That Saturday was exceptionally mild, despite the pine-scented breeze blowing from the wooded plateau of Table Mountain. In the Cape this light wind is known as the "Cape Doctor," because the local people maintain it can cure anything that ails them. For a charming twenty-four-year-old brunette receptionist at the Standard Bank on George Street, that Saturday was an afternoon for celebration on two counts. Denise Darvall had been invited to bring her parents to tea at her fiancé's home in Milnerton, and she was going to drive them on this happy excursion in her new bright green Ford.

The Darvalls were a likable family. The descendant of a Strasbourg Huguenot, Edward, the father, was a salesman at Markham's men's clothing store. A passionate lover of climbing on the slopes of Devil's Peak and Table Mountain, of line fishing and horse racing, he seldom faced a more serious decision than whether to bet on the favorite or a rank outsider at a derby. His wife, Myrtle, a plump Englishwoman originally from Coventry, had arrived in Cape Town when she was two, at the time of the Great Depression in Europe when many unemployed flocked to South Africa and Australia in the hope of a better life. Myrtle kept her third-class ticket from the *Balmoral Castle* liner in a small frame hanging on a wall in the family sitting room. It had cost forty-four pounds. Edward and Myrtle were the proud parents of three children, two boys of eighteen and thirteen and their daughter, Denise, whose forthcoming marriage was something everyone was looking forward to. Devout Anglicans, the Darvalls were taking an active part in the preparations for Christmas in their parish of St. Barnabas. The next day, Sunday, Denise was due to rehearse her role for Christmas Eve: with her brother Keith dressed up as a shepherd, she was to be the Virgin Mary in the nativity play at midnight mass.

Proudly driven by its young owner wearing a floral taffeta dress for the occasion, the little green Ford entered Main Road in the direction of the Salt River intersection at the base of the eucalyptus trees and the tall turreted facade of Groote Schuur hospital. It was not the quickest way to Milnerton, where her fiancé and future in-laws were expecting her, but in Cape Town no one went for tea without bringing some delicacy from the famous Wrensch Town Bakery. People came from all over the city and beyond to buy cream-filled doughnuts, curd tarts, vanilla and strawberry éclairs, and caramel *koeksisters,* syrup-coated doughnuts. That Saturday, as it did every year before Christmas, the bakery was also offering chocolate cakes with little iced sugar fir trees on top.

Denise parked her Ford level with the cake shop, on the other side of the narrow median dividing the roadway. "Papa and Keith, you just stay here with the car. We'll be right back!" she called out gaily. Then she took her mother by the arm and steered her toward the shop. People were already in line so there would be a wait, especially since Gert, the colorful proprietor in his leather apron, liked to talk with everyone. He was chatting with a lady of about fifty who was a regular at the bakery. For the past few weeks, her husband had been in the cardiology unit at Groote Schuur hospital across the street. Every day on her way to visit him she came in to buy two vanilla éclairs and a curd tart, his favorites. Sadly, Ann Washkansky was not sure he would be able to enjoy his treats that day. She had just received a telephone call informing her that his condition had suddenly deteriorated. This was devastating news. For two years she had given her husband encouragement and love to help him fight the illness that was slowly destroying him.

The tragedy had begun suddenly one Sunday morning when the wholesale grocer Louis Washkansky woke up with a violent pain in his chest. For a robust workingman who never went to the doctor it was a terrible shock. The military decorations hanging on his living room wall proclaimed that Louis was a World War II hero whom death had spared on many occasions. A heavy smoker, unrepentant drinker, and tireless dancer, this fifty-two-year-old Jewish grocer was a popular figure at soirées of Cape Town's merchant class. Neither his wife nor his friends nor any of his customers would ever have imagined the ordeal that awaited him. The emergency doctor called to his bedside that Sunday was certain he was suffering from a myocardial infarction. Nevertheless, Louis refused to be taken to the hospital. After two months' rest at home, he returned to work. It was too soon; while on his way to meet a customer he had another attack, even more violent than the first. He managed to stop his car outside a restaurant and call for help. A Groote Schuur ambulance arrived just in time to save his life. He was taken to intensive care in the cardiology department. The diagnosis was not hopeful. A third of Louis's heart was not functioning. A sudden edema confirmed this assessment. The patient's legs swelled to the size of an elephant's, indicating a severe lesion in the right ventricle. For days, the medical staff tried to drain the fluid from his legs. The former ranger in the war in Italy endured these painful procedures with a stoicism that won everyone's admiration. "Don't you worry, darling," he would repeat in moments of lucidity to his wife, who never left his bedside. But his condition worsened. Bouts of breathlessness and coughing up blood, unbearable chest pain, and fainting followed in succession. He had barely recovered from a diabetic coma when a cerebral stroke paralyzed his right side. X-rays revealed an enlarged heart that, instead of resembling a small rugby ball, had become more rounded like a soccer ball. This was a sign that the cardiac muscle was losing its capacity to contract. Washkansky's face gradually took on a waxy cast. Each time Ann left her husband's side, she was afraid she would not see him again. In the rare moments when he could muster the strength to utter a few words, he tried to reassure her: "Don't worry, love, I feel like a boy of twenty," he would say, his breath becoming more and more shallow.

One morning, to her horror, Ann saw that her husband's bed was empty. Panic-stricken, she looked for a nurse. Louis had been transferred to room 374 on the fourth floor, where the operating rooms for cardiac and vascular surgery were located. She found Louis in a state of excitement.

"Darling, guess who came to see me? The chief of cardiology himself," he announced proudly. "He was with a lot of other doctors. They examined me from every angle. After listening to my chest for a long time, the chief said to me: 'Mr. Washkansky, we're going to try to replace your failing heart with a healthy one.'"

Ann thought her husband had lost his sanity. She left the room to hide her confusion. "Replace his heart with another heart?" He must be delirious. Then a man in a white coat stopped in front of her. He looked so young she thought he was an intern.

"I'm Professor Barnard," said the stranger with a warm smile. "I'm chief of cardiology at Groote Schuur."

★

CHRISTIAAN BARNARD! A name almost unknown to the general public at that time but already respected in medical circles. A forty-four-year-old surgeon with movie star looks, who never hid his opposition to the racial segregation practiced by his compatriots in Pretoria. In the year 1967 alone, more than half the patients operated on in his cardiology unit at Groote Schuur hospital were blacks, although afterward they had to be cared for in wards reserved for patients of color, as Helen Lieberman had discovered in the ENT department at the same hospital. Christiaan Barnard! A true product of the South African white elite that had succeeded in acquiring all the attributes of a nation. Barnard liked to remind people that when Jan van Riebeeck first set foot on African soil to grow his famous lettuce, the closest black settlements were five hundred miles to the north and a thousand miles to the east, the same as the distances from London to Hamburg and London to Rome. He never missed the opportunity to point out to his country's critics that when New York was still a village, Cape Town was a thriving capital, and that there were more whites in the Cape of Good Hope than in all of Canada.

He thought his pride in belonging to a people that had earned the right to live and flourish on the African continent also came from his humble origins. He had been born in Beaufort West, a village in the arid Karoo. His father worked as a traveling lingerie salesman and was a volunteer captain in the Salvation Army. The Barnards were people of such modest means that Chris attended school barefoot until he was eight years old. In the evenings he would soak his bleeding feet in a basin of water with melted wax in it. Heroic people, these Barnards were just like their Voortrekker ancestors. Barnard's mother in her long black skirt did not hesitate to threaten her children with a whip to make sure they were first in their class. It was in the village square that Chris discovered racial segregation. There were two churches in the center of Beaufort West: one for whites, the other for blacks and coloreds. Their congregants worshiped the same God and sang the same hymns, often at the same time, but under separate roofs less than fifty yards apart. All because of the color of their skin.

This discovery traumatized Chris for life. He never stopped claiming his African roots went just as deep as those of the young blacks he had grown up with, and he condemned absolutely the system devised by the ideologues in Pretoria. Once he became renowned as a leading cardiac surgeon, he could safely criticize their abominable racist policies, never imagining that one day he would restore a measure of respectability to his country in the eyes of the world, by making South Africa a beacon throughout the planet.

★

TWENTY-FIVE MILES from the bakery where Denise Darvall and Ann Washkansky were selecting their cakes that Saturday afternoon, a man was changing from a dark suit and white shirt into old khaki shorts exposing his tanned torso and muscular legs. This was Chris Barnard's unchanging Saturday afternoon ritual. He was going to work on his life's dream: turning his daughter, Deirdre, a pretty, fair-haired seventeen-year-old, into a junior world water-skiing champion. That would make the name Barnard famous everywhere! Moored outside his house overlooking the clear waters of Zeekoevlei, the "hippopotamus lake," which had once been home to those animals, was a brand-new hundred horsepower motorboat. It was named after the cardiology device that produced impulses to replace those of a failing human heart. At the controls of "Pacemaker," Barnard would tow Deirdre along as she tried out new, ever more daring arabesques. He would forget everything—his discomforts, his worries, his ambitions—and just play the role of proud father.

"Ready?"

The girl signaled that she had put on her mono-ski and was holding on tightly to the handle of the rope.

"Off we go then!"

The hundred horsepower engine sent boat and skier off like a rocket. Deirdre twirled in the silver wake of the propeller. The roar of the engine, the speed, the beauty of this graceful acrobat turning left and right in a dizzying ballet all contributed to the magic of the moment. Then suddenly the girl felt the rope slacken and the boat lurched sharply. Deirdre saw her father gesturing as if in pain. She realized he was struggling with the arthritis in his hands. It was an unpredictable illness with sudden crises—a sword of Damocles hanging over the career of a man who lived by the agility of his fingers.

Chris managed to regain control of the boat and shouted cheerily, "Sweetheart, we're going back!"

Later, his pain relieved by a powerful anti-inflammatory, the surgeon settled into an armchair to gaze at the hundreds of birds flying in every direction over the lake. Plump pelicans were diving after fish for their offspring. This enchanting setting always evoked happy memories. What a road he had traveled since his barefoot childhood in Beaufort West. His penniless student days; his first steps as a cardiologist in a Cape Town hospital for coloreds; the magical offer from his elderly professor at Cape Town University to go and study in America.

America! His face had lit up when he received the invitation, and his wife, a pretty nurse who had given him a son and a daughter, was enthusiastic. He must not pass this up. She and the children would join him later.

The young South African who had once gone to school barefoot had the luck to land at the University of Minnesota in Minneapolis, in the laboratory of one of the world's leading cardiologists, Professor Walton Lillehei. He immediately took Barnard under his wing and involved him in his research, which was about to revolutionize cardiovascular surgery with such procedures as the substitution of new aortic and mitral valve prostheses in defective hearts. Above all, he introduced him to the miraculous heart-lung machine that rerouted the blood circulation while the surgeon repaired a defective heart. Barnard familiarized himself with open-heart surgery and depopulated the university kennels perfecting his technique. One day he sacrificed forty-nine dogs in succession to perfect just one surgical move. He took on all sorts of jobs to support his family, who joined him on the magnificent campus. He mowed the lawns of the neighborhood's most luxurious homes and delivered newspapers on his bicycle. He was a night watchman. His capacity for work and his determination were universally admired. When he returned to South Africa, his American colleagues gave him the best farewell present possible: a heart-lung pump that would enable him to perform at Groote Schuur hospital the surgical feats he had so assiduously learned on the Minnesota campus.

On his return he asked his brother Marius to come and work with him, and they organized a team that he trained in the highly specialized techniques of open-heart surgery.

The first operation lasted eleven hours. It was performed on a twelve-year-old mixed-race girl with a congenital heart perforation. She had been given only months to live. Chris, who had stayed awake the previous two nights rehearsing all the surgical procedures in his head, was jubilant when the little girl left Groote Schuur. The photographers lined up two deep.

Desperate patients immediately started flocking from all over the country, and soon from all over Asia. They came from India, Singapore, and Australia. In three years, Chris and his team performed a thousand open-heart operations. Over two thousand patients were waiting for the life-saving surgery. They were white but also black, colored, and Asian. In the harsh land of apartheid the huge hospital's surgical wings were oases of tolerance. They were also tremendous laboratories preparing for the most fantastic surgical adventure of all time. Since returning from America, Barnard had been preparing to perform an operation that would put South Africa in world headlines for all the right reasons: a heart transplant. Although the surgical techniques of organ transplantation had lost all mystery for one so skilled with a scalpel, one major difficulty still hampered all specialists in his field: rejection of the implanted organ by the recipient's immune system.

That obstacle was removed by the work of a South African pathologist. Forty-four-year-old Martinus Botha knew that cellular incompatibility between two individuals was not insurmountable. A specialist in immunity, Botha had done research in some of the greatest American and European laboratories. Together with the Dutchman Jan van Rod and the Frenchman Jean Dausset, he had unraveled the secrets of the complicated mechanisms by which the human body's immune reactions could be inhibited. Of all the patients at Groote Schuur hoping for a kidney, liver, or heart transplant, he was convinced that some would tolerate an organ transplant better than others. But which ones? He would have to play Sherlock Holmes to find out.

Fortune smiled on him in the form of a forty-six-year-old white patient dying of kidney failure. She had the providential last name of Black. Since the kidney that Barnard and his team had decided to give her was that of a young man of mixed race who had died in a car accident, her surname allowed the international press to run the headline "Mrs. Black receives a black kidney" and at the same time hail "the first medical act of racial integration." From Pretoria the austere guardians of racist orthodoxy reminded the hospital staff that they did not object to operations on patients of color, but the transplanting of a heart, kidney, or any other organ from a black to a white or vice versa was strictly forbidden. They would not let it be said abroad that interracial surgical experiments were being conducted in South Africa.

★

AT THE END OF NOVEMBER, it was all hands on deck on the fourth floor of the cardiac surgery unit. A heart from a traffic accident victim seemed compatible with that of the terminal patient in room 374. Barnard and his team were immediately alerted.

Nurses rushed to tell Louis Washkansky and shave his thorax before painting it with antiseptic solution. Then they wheeled his bed into the operating room where the whole team was waiting in surgical gloves, masks, and caps. The excitement was extreme. The clinical death of the accident victim was confirmed. His family had given permission for his heart to be removed. The operation could begin. Barnard was giving his first orders when a short figure appeared, waving both arms. It was Martinus Botha, the hematology wizard. Everything had to stop. A final test had revealed an unexpected incompatibility between the donor and the grocer's heart.

Back in his room Washkansky gave vent to his anger, despite his weakness. The force of it amazed the medical staff. "That man really wants to live," commented one admiring nurse. Barnard promised him there would be another opportunity and to appease him, ordered his favorite dish, a steak medium-well done with an egg on top.

★

ANOTHER OPPORTUNITY? Did Louis Washkansky have time to wait? That Saturday, December 2, for the first time his morale hit bottom. He knew that weekends in hospitals were stretches of agonizing emptiness. Would he still be there on Monday?

That Saturday afternoon comfort was on its way to him, coming up the hospital ramp. His wife, Ann, was bringing him the vanilla éclairs and the curd tart she had bought at the Wrensch Town Bakery across the street from the hospital.

As she reached the top of the ramp Mrs. Washkansky was startled by the sound of a crash coming from the street below, level with the pedestrian crossing she had just used on leaving the bakery. She looked back and saw people rushing over to a van that had stopped on the other side of the highway. "A traffic accident," she thought as she entered the hospital. A few moments later a telephone call came through to the hospital's emergency room. An ambulance left at once, sirens blaring, and arrived minutes later at the scene of the accident. Denise Darvall would never bring the cakes from the Wrensch Town Bakery to her fiancé and prospective in-laws. Her mother, Myrtle, lay sprawled in the middle of the highway, killed instantly, while she herself lay in a pool of blood with her legs, pelvis, and skull smashed. The van had hit the two women head on. Cream from the bakery cakes was spattered all over the road.

The paramedics loaded both victims into the ambulance. Edward Darvall told his son Keith to stay with the little Ford and ran to get into the vehicle. The driver switched on his siren and sped off. It took him barely three minutes to reach Groote Schuur's emergency entrance where the injured were immediately taken to an intensive care room. A few moments later, a doctor with a stethoscope emerged from the room. Seeing Edward Darvall, he asked:

"Do you know these two women?"

"I'm the husband of one and the father of the other."

The doctor hesitated.

"I'm so very sorry but I have to confirm that your wife is dead," he said at last. "As for your daughter, her skull is fractured in places. She's in a coma. I'm afraid her chances of survival are very slight."

With this pronouncement in an emergency room corridor on that Saturday, December 2, 1967, began one of the most fantastic medical adventures of all time.

★

SINCE THE FIRST KIDNEY TRANSPLANTS had proved it is possible to overcome the risks of organ rejection, the world's top cardiac surgeons in America, Europe, Japan, and the Soviet Union had dreamed of transplanting a heart. It would be a descendant of the heroes of the Great Trek at the tip of Africa who would bring about that extraordinary undertaking.

"Professor! It seems we have another donor for Mr. Washkansky!"

Barnard hung up the phone, threw on his clothes, swallowed another anti-inflammatory pill to relieve the pain in his hands, and jumped behind the driver's seat of his Triumph 2000. It was 6:00 PM by the time he reached Groote Schuur's cardiology wing. There was no question of waiting for the elevator. He took the stairs four at a time and ran to room 283 on the third floor where he found the patient registered under the number 226-070. A pretty girl with dark hair, Barnard noted, as he examined her.

With the help of an artificial respirator, her lungs were functioning almost normally. As for her heartbeat, the electrocardiograph on the wall showed a normal eighty pulses a minute. But Barnard immediately identified causes for alarm: dilated and fixed pupils, a lack of reflexes and reaction to stimulation, and, above all, a cerebral discharge from both ears. There was no doubt: Denise Darvall's brain was clinically dead. Only the respirator and drips were keeping the young woman's heart going. Could she be the donor the grocer in room 374 had so hoped for? Initial tests suggested she could: blood type O rhesus negative, no trace of infection, heart in good condition, cellular compatibility correct.

"So we can go ahead!" exclaimed the surgeon.

"Absolutely!" responded the neurologist who had found irreversible brain damage.

"Then let's get started! Get the whole team moving!"

Locating some thirty people—surgeons, doctors, anesthetists, resuscitators, nurses, and technicians on a Saturday evening in summer was no mean feat. Some were relaxing by the sea or visiting friends, others were having dinner in a restaurant or at the cinema. Barnard had the police send squad cars to the various addresses. The first arrived around ten o'clock that evening.

As he was leaving Denise Darvall's room, the surgeon saw a bunch of violets at the foot of her bed. He was startled. "Somebody had brought these flowers. Somebody had cared enough. Somebody was clinging to a hope that this young woman would live, would wake up, and find those flowers within her reach." Suddenly the professional task he was about to perform assumed a terribly human dimension. "I wondered if she was in love, if she had a young man somewhere who would weep when he learned of her end—learned she was leaving this world with only a little glass of violets sent by somebody. Yet would he weep if he knew that some part of her had given life to someone else?"[4] Barnard carefully pulled one of the flowers from the bunch and put it in his pocket. "This violet isn't just a flower," he thought. "It represents the heart that young woman is giving me to save someone's life."

Before entering the operating room where he was going to try to save that life, Bernard had to obtain authorization from Edward Darvall, Denise's father, who was waiting in a nearby room. He could grant or withhold permission for his daughter's heart to be removed from her body and placed in someone else's. It was difficult to know what to say to a father in such circumstances. Barnard gathered his thoughts for a brief moment.

"We've done everything in our power to try and save your daughter's life," he explained soberly. "There's no more hope. But we have another patient she could save if you will give us permission to remove her heart."

At these words, several images passed through the grieving father's memory. The cake his daughter had baked for him on his fiftieth birthday that she had decorated with a heart around the words: "Daddy, we love you." The dressing gown she had bought him with the money from her first paycheck. Denise was like that, he thought. She would undoubtedly have said yes if Professor Barnard had been able to ask her directly for her heart.

"If you cannot save my daughter, at least save your patient's life," Edward Darvall said simply.

★

---

4. Christiaan Barnard and Curtis Bill Pepper, *One Life* (New York: Bantam, 1971).

ON HIS WAY TO THE OPERATING UNIT, the surgeon stopped at
Louis Washkansky's room.

"So this time, it's a good 'un, professor?"

"Absolutely, Louis. And what a wonderful act of ecumenism!
A young Anglican Christian wrests a Jewish grocer from death!"

Barnard did not mention that the operation was also going to
save the life of a ten-year-old mixed-race boy, Jonathan van Wyk,
dying of renal failure in another hospital in Cape Town. That same
night another team would give him Denise's right kidney. The
authorities in Pretoria had not forbidden this act of compassion
even though it was counter to their prevailing doctrine of strict
racial segregation. Perhaps it was a sign of a change in their mentality, at least in the field of health care. But a very cautious
change. South Africa was still the only country in the world where
blood for transfusions was identified by the color of the donor's
skin, the only country where a patient could refuse a blood trans-
fusion from a donor of a different race.

Before going into the sterile changing room, Barnard stood
under a powerful shower to cleanse body and mind. He would
wash away the doubts and the criticisms he had heard over the
previous weeks. "Transplanting a human heart? But my dear fellow, a human being isn't a dog. We have no right to experiment
on a human being!" And the remark made by a foreign colleague:
"Look here, Barnard, what you're doing is turning two operating
theaters into two laboratories and substituting human beings for
experimental animals!"

"Nonsense!" Chris said aloud in the shower. "The patient I'm
going to operate on this evening has one foot in the grave. I can
save his life. I have what I need to do it: a team and a donor's
heart. As for those who doubt the value of performing a transplant if it only results in a few days' survival, they can go to hell!
They want me to say to Louis: 'No, Mr. Washkansky, I don't want
to try this operation because I don't know how many extra days it
will give you. Even though during the extra days you do have, you
might see the sun again, walk through flowers and rediscover the
joy of being alive.'"

Then the surgeon murmured a prayer: "O God, take away my doubt, keep my hands from making any mistakes tonight!"

Midnight. The incredible ballet began. A ballet that would make history. It was to last five and a half hours.

"Ready?" asked Barnard.

"Ready," the thirty team members assembled around the bodies of Louis Washkansky and Denise Darvall answered through their masks.

The first dramatic moment came at the end of two hours when the two thoraxes were open so the hearts could be removed. Denise's heart was still beating with the help of the heart-lung machine that artificially kept her blood circulating. Barnard contemplated Washkansky's heart with particular emotion. It was a heart ravaged by fifty years of buffeting: deformed, enormous, and churning like a swollen sea, with bluish currents running through it from deep within.

Once disconnected from its blood supply that heart would be of no more use. This was the point of no return. They had only to sever what was still connecting it to its owner's body. A few cuts with the scalpel would do it. Suddenly deprived of its support, Washkansky's heart dropped with one last shudder into the pericardial cavity. With one hand Barnard delicately extricated the piece of flesh and placed it on the tray a nurse held out to him. "Have I removed his soul?" he wondered as he looked at his patient's gaping chest. His brother Marius was already handing him the heart he had just removed from the deceased girl's chest. Immersed in freezing lactic acid solution, it looked very small beside the grocer's. It showed no sign of activity but Chris knew that a spark of life slumbered there and that it would start beating again as soon as the first drops of warm oxygenated blood from the coronary arteries reached it. That heart would then come back to life and save a man Denise Darvall never knew.

The operation was nearing its most crucial phase. Barnard made some final preparations and carefully placed the young woman's heart in the grocer's chest. Although it had been deprived of oxygen for a dozen or so minutes, it should start up again. The surgeon asked for an immediate coronary drip. The moment the first drops reached it, the arch of the aorta tautened again, the cardiac muscle firmed up and the heart turned a beautiful rose color. The most beautiful sunset in the world would not have looked more glorious to him.

The muscular tissues, veins, and arteries had to be reconnected with minuscule stitches. Ready to intervene at any moment, technicians and anesthetists watched the circulation and composition of the blood. The time came for the surgeon to connect the two segments of the aorta. For a few moments, the coronary perfusion had to be interrupted. Speed was of the essence to avoid brain damage. To his horror, the diameters of the two ends of the aorta were not identical so Barnard had to do some delicate suturing with fingers clumsy from the arthritis attack of the previous day. A nurse sponged the sweat from his brow. And suddenly there were shouts cheering the miracle. Tentatively at first and then strengthening, the heart of the young woman began to beat in the grocer's chest. A glance at the monitors soon showed a steady, regular rhythm. It was done. Barnard left the operating room and slumped onto a stool. His assistants would close up the incision without him.

While the body of Denise Darvall was discreetly taken away, Louis Washkansky began his new life in the intensive care unit.

★

"IS IT ALL RIGHT WITH YOU if we wake him up?" inquired the anesthetist.

The surgeon nodded his agreement, silently praying as he did so: "Dear God, let Louis wake up."

The medical staff set about interrupting the artificial sleep. Long minutes of unbearable waiting went by. The grocer showed no sign of returning to consciousness. Unable to take it any longer, Barnard bent over him.

"Louis, can you hear me?"

No response. The surgeon felt a cold sweat run down his back.

"Louis! It's me, Professor Christiaan Barnard. Can you hear me?"

"My voice must have resonated in the depths of his brain," Chris was to recount, "because the grocer half opened his eyes. With indescribable relief and joy, I saw him smile faintly and wink at me."

★

THAT MORNING CAPE TOWN radio revealed the spectacular news in its six o'clock bulletin. "The first human heart transplant was performed last night by a team of South African doctors," it announced. "The management of the Groote Schuur hospital has not divulged the identity of either the recipient or the donor."

★

THAT FIRST HEART TRANSPLANT created a sensation around the world. Something colossal had been achieved for the good of humanity in the accursed land of apartheid. But the effects were most remarkable in South Africa itself. For the first time a country rent by diabolical racism was united in shared pride around a small team of Afrikaners who had just brought the nation honor in the eyes of the world. As for the beneficiary of the adventure, in less than a week he had affirmed his return to the land of the living.

"Sister," he declared one morning to the nurse bringing him his breakfast. "If today I'm not given a well-done steak with an egg on top, I shall do a runner!"

★

THE BRAVE GROCER NEVER DID get out of the hospital, though. On Thursday, December 21, at 6:50 AM, eighteen days after receiving a new heart, he breathed his last in the presence of the man who had taken the risk of trying to save him. To the last moment, the transplanted heart continued beating vigorously. The cause of death was double pneumonia, which destroyed his respiratory function. It was a cruel outcome. During the autopsy, Barnard examined the heart he had held in his fingers, "this heart that had started up powerfully, this heart of a lovely red color, beating miraculously."

No one was more stricken by this death than the father of the young woman who had given her heart to Louis Washkansky. Edward Darvall was devastated. "After the operation I had the feeling Denise was still living," he confided. "Now there's a void. There's nothing left of my daughter."

A few hours later, the hospital held a press conference for a thousand reporters from all over the world. One journalist summed up the general concern when he asked Barnard if this setback signaled an end to his heart transplant experiments. This wasn't experimenting, the surgeon corrected sharply. The purpose of the operation had been to save a man who was at the brink of death. If the opportunity arose to perform another such rescue, they would do it again.

So Louis Washkansky had not died in vain. The world would be talking of South Africa again. The descendants of the Great Trekkers had climbed Everest. Next time they would be able to come down from it.

Four

"God Bless Africa"

ALMOST TWENTY YEARS had passed since Nelson Mandela was shut away in Robben Island, cell 466/64, the waiting room for death, where a white judge who wouldn't meet his eyes had sent him to spend the rest of his life. One day in 1976 he had written to Winnie: "Your beautiful photo still stands about two feet above my left shoulder as I write this note. I dust it carefully every morning for to do so gives me the pleasant feeling that I am caressing you as in the old days. I even touch your nose with mine to recapture the electric current that used to flush through my blood when I did so."[1]

One small concession softened the harshness of his detention. Prisoners were now allowed to receive family photos. At the beginning of the 1970s, Winnie had sent him an album into which he carefully pasted every snapshot he received. This souvenir collection became his most prized possession. "I cherished this album: it was the one way that I could see those I loved whenever I wanted."[2] The other prisoners soon found out that the man they respectfully called Madiba, after the Xhosa king from whom he was descended, had a collection of family portraits. Soon everyone was asking him for a picture from the precious album. "Those men were desperate to have something personal in their cells," the black leader said later.[3]

---

1. Mandela, *Long Walk to Freedom*, p. 484.
2. Mandela, *Long Walk to Freedom*, p. 485.
3. Mandela, *Long Walk to Freedom*, p. 486.

Of the few pleasures that relieved this living death, nothing compared with a visit. One day Zenani, his daughter, and her husband, Prince Thumbumuzi, landed on Robben Island to present their newborn daughter to him. Because of their royal status the visitors were allowed to meet their relative outside the usual visiting room with its microphones, speakers, and distorting windows. It was a magical moment. As soon as Zenani saw her father she handed her baby to her husband and threw herself into his arms. "I had not held my now grown-up daughter since she was about her own daughter's age. It was a dizzying experience, as though time had sped forward in a science fiction novel! . . . I then embraced my new son and he handed me my tiny granddaughter." Nelson Mandela held the newborn child "so vulnerable and soft" with his calloused hands that for so many years had held only shovels and picks. "I don't think a man was ever happier to hold a baby than I was that day,"[4] he would write. This extraordinary visit also had an official purpose. According to custom Mandela must choose the child's first name. He did not hesitate for one moment. His granddaughter would be called Zaziwe—Hope. "The name had a special meaning for me, for during all my years in prison hope never left me—and now it never would. I was convinced that this child would be a part of a new generation of South Africans for whom apartheid would be a distant memory—that was my dream."[5]

★

A DREAM THAT MIGHT COME TRUE sooner than he anticipated.

The effects of the UN embargo on military purchases, the disastrous consequences of international sanctions and the boycott on South African goods, economic recession, drought, racial violence—the future of white South Africa looked dim indeed at

---

4. Mandela, *Long Walk to Freedom*, p. 482.
5. Mandela, *Long Walk to Freedom*, p. 482.

the beginning of the 1980s. No one was more aware of this than President P.W. Botha, whose ambition was to turn the country into an economic giant and silence its neighbors by making them dependent on its trade. Having discarded some of the most conspicuous aspects of apartheid, he was now offering his compatriots a quasi-revolutionary slogan: "Adapt or die." He himself set the example by reforming the temple that for seventy-four years had embodied white rule in the country. The Corinthian-columned parliament building in Cape Town would thenceforth accommodate two supplementary chambers composed of mixed-race and Indian members, who, like whites, would have seats in proportion to their numbers in the country. A significant initiative even if the newcomers would not enjoy all of the prerogatives accorded to their white colleagues.

This modification to parliament was to be the cornerstone of a new constitution that would show the world that change was possible under the racist apartheid dictatorship. Unwittingly Botha had just set off a bomb, first, among blacks, infuriated by a reform from which they were totally excluded. Botha made no secret of his reasons for this exclusion. According to white ideology, blacks were not South Africans. They were nationals of the various "homelands" or reserves to which their ethnic origins destined them. The government was spending vast sums there to promote the development of "democratic" institutions and pave the way for political independence. As for blacks living within the boundaries of South Africa, in the townships of Soweto or Langa for example, in white eyes they were still not South Africans. They were foreigners, as the gold rush Uitlanders driven away by Paul Kruger had been foreigners, a line of reasoning that blacks totally rejected. At the beginning of the 1980s, a new voice of defiance was ringing out from podiums and on the radio. Eventually it reached all the way to Oslo, Norway. On October 18, 1984, a fifty-three-year-old Anglican bishop, a black man, born to a schoolteacher father and an illiterate mother in a poor village in the Transvaal, received the Nobel Peace Prize for his work in solidarity with the victims of Pretoria's dictatorship. His name was Desmond Tutu.

This impish little man, with his tightly curling gray hair and mischievous smile, made the world see the human face of the tragedy of apartheid. Broadcast over the African and Western radio and television channels, his speech on receiving the prestigious award moved the international community as much as the South African crowds. "This award is for you—Mothers, who sit near railway stations trying to eke out an existence, selling potatoes, selling mealies, selling pigs' trotters," the prelate declared. "This award is for you—Fathers, sitting in a single-sex hostel, separated from your children for eleven months of the year. . . . This award is for you—three and a half million of our people who have been uprooted and dumped as if they were rubbish. The world says we recognize you, we recognize that you are people who love peace. This award is for you—dear children who, despite receiving a poisonous gruel designed to make you believe that you are inferior, have said 'there is something that God put into us which will not be manipulated by man, which tells us that we are your children.' This award is for you—and I am proud to accept it on your behalf as you spurn a travesty of an education. This award is for you, who down the ages have said we seek to change this evil system peacefully. . . . I have the great honor to accept it on your behalf. It is our prize. It is not Desmond Tutu's prize."[6]

The bishop quickly threw himself into an all-out campaign. He urged whites to "reject this new constitution conceived by the prime minister without the participation of the true leaders of South Africa." He involved other denominations in his crusade. Methodists rejected the new charter because it was "alien to the spirit of reconciliation preached by the Gospel of Jesus Christ and could only lead to further violence." His Roman

---

6. Quoted in Shirley du Boulay, *Tutu: Archbishop Without Frontiers* (London: Hodder & Stoughton, 1988), p. 15.

Catholic colleague in Durban wrote a pastoral letter condemning a reform that failed "to take into account the interests of two-thirds of the population." For its part and serving its own agenda, the Dutch Reformed Church, historically a supporter of Afrikaner extremism, disassociated itself from the head of government on the basis that "sharing power with Muslims and Hindus could only undermine Christian values."

But the Nobel Peace laureate's campaign failed. Whites adopted the new constitution. Coloreds and Indians, but not blacks, would from then on have the right to be heard on the parliamentary rostrum. But was this the beginning of real integration or merely a stratagem to mollify international opinion? Blacks could not contain their anger. In Sharpeville, where sixty-nine people had been massacred twenty-four years before, rioters who suspected the deputy mayor of conniving with the white administration slit his throat and set fire to cars, burning their occupants to cinders. In Durban, an ANC commando seized the British consulate and took the staff hostage. In Uitenhage near Port Elizabeth, the police used machine guns to block the route to a procession of four thousand blacks threatening to attack white neighborhoods, leaving twenty dead and hundreds wounded. Despite desperate appeals from Bishop Tutu, antiwhite violence knew no bounds. In the province of the Eastern Cape, civil servants and their children were beaten to death, then doused in petrol and burned. In Pretoria a bomb hidden in a car parked outside a café exploded and killed twenty and injured over two hundred. The attack so stunned people that the defense minister launched massive reprisals against the ANC camps in Mozambique, leaving dozens dead on the ground. As in Soweto during the great uprising of 1976, schoolchildren spearheaded the fight. In the Transvaal tens of thousands boycotted schools and joined the striking workers' protest marches.

Caught off guard by the movement's size, the government called in the army. Armored cars rolled seven thousand troops into the township of Sebokeng to do a house-to-house search of

its 20,000 shacks. The violence spread to Natal and parts of the
Cape peninsula. Some theoretically independent reserves joined
in the general fury as well, but not always for the same reasons.
In KwaZulu there was intratribal warfare. In Ciskei a coup d'état
stirred up by separatist factions was quashed by the army. In the
extreme complexity of Africa the motives for confrontation were
so numerous that only radical measures could restore a semblance
of stability. At midnight on July 20, 1985, the head of government declared a state of emergency in thirty-six of the country's
magisterial districts. This measure gave P.W. Botha exceptional
powers. In a matter of days his police arrested 14,000 sympathiz-
ing with the black cause. All gatherings other than funeral processions were banned. This state of emergency would leave nearly
1,000 dead and 20,000 injured. But outcries from abroad did not
penetrate the jacaranda trees outside the apartheid leader's office, any more than the desperate warnings of the Nobel Peace
laureate in the purple cassock.

The government had decided to rid itself of this thorn in its
side by making use of techniques developed by Wouter Basson,
as evidence presented at his later trial suggested. One morning
Bishop Tutu found a baboon fetus hanging from the branch of a
palm tree in front of his residence. He suspected it was a bad
omen. He was not mistaken. In one of his laboratories at the secret Roodeplaat center, Dr. Basson, who was also the head of
state's personal cardiologist, had devised a radical means of liqui-
dating an adversary from a distance—impregnating his underwear
with the lethal chemical paraoxone, which had the advantage of
being odorless and colorless. In the case of Bishop Desmond
Tutu, the contaminated underclothes would be slipped into his
suitcase the night before he left for one of his trips abroad. The
stratagem would be tested on another black target. As general secretary of the South African Council of Churches, thirty-nine-year-
old Reverend Frank Chikane often traveled outside the country.
In April 1989, he had to go to Namibia. Here was the opportunity
Basson had been waiting for. A few hours before the priest left,

Chris, Gert, and Manie, the scientist's three hatchet men, managed to get into Chickane's home and place a pair of underpants and some undershirts poisoned with paraoxone in his suitcase. No sooner had he reached his destination than the unfortunate cleric fell ill with nausea, respiratory problems, violent abdominal and muscular pains, trembling, and vomiting. He was hospitalized at death's door without anyone being able to identify the cause of his illness and then was immediately sent back to Johannesburg. Some ten days later, the symptoms having disappeared, the priest decided to leave again, this time for the United States where his wife was staying. When he got off the plane he lost consciousness and then sank into a deep coma. The doctors at the University of Wisconsin Hospital were bewildered. They ran all the tests they knew but could not diagnose the patient's illness. Fearing a possible assassination attempt, they called in the FBI. The agents asked themselves what common denominator there might be between the two bouts of illness in Namibia and the United States. None, except for the presence in both places of a suitcase containing his personal effects. His baggage, including his underwear, were immediately scrutinized. A suspect substance was found, which proved to be the lethal paraoxone intended to kill Reverend Chikane and then Archbishop Tutu. The American investigation did not succeed in tracing the attempted murder back to its originator, but when Reverend Chikane returned to South Africa safe and sound, those in power realized they would have to find some other way to make Archbishop Tutu disappear.

★

THOSE WERE CRUEL TIMES and Wouter Basson was but one agent of white oppression among others. Before being hanged for the murder of a white farmer, a former security officer named Butana Nofomela revealed that the state police had uncovered commando units all across South Africa murdering anyone considered a threat to state security. Years later the Truth and Reconciliation Commission initiated and presided over by Archbishop

Tutu was to describe the atrocity of those executions for the victims' horrified relatives and millions of incredulous South Africans. The assassinations were intended to eliminate all regime opponents regardless of their color or political affiliation. Often the squads acted under cover of small, ultra right-wing parties modeled after the Nazis. One of the most active, the Afrikaner Resistance Movement, had as its emblem a red and white flag with a spiderlike three sevens in the middle inspired by the swastika. It was led by a fanatical forty-four-year-old orator named Eugene Terre'Blanche. Convinced that any concession to the black majority jeopardized the white's lifestyle and privileges, Terre' Blanche and his supporters demanded the immediate deportation of all blacks to their reserves, the expulsion of South African Jews, and the return of all Indians to India. They trained in camps with weapons they intended to use one day to take back control of the sacred nation of their ancestors. Under a sea of banners flying their ersatz swastika, over 100,000 of them followed a wagon train to Pretoria's Church Square to celebrate the 150th anniversary of the Great Trek. Because a number of their supporters were in the security police, they could act with impunity, for example, seizing the World Trade Center in Johannesburg to expel political opponents, or bombing public buildings where they suspected meetings were being held to promote reconciliation between the different communities. Racial hatred spawned other more or less clandestine terrorist groups that resorted to similar assassination squads. The corpses of hundreds of victims disappeared forever or would be found years later, horribly mutilated in appalling mass graves.

Foreign pressure eventually forced P.W. Botha to lift the state of emergency on March 28, 1986. He reinstated it four months later, however, as the country descended into chaos. "For he shatters the doors of bronze and cuts in two the bars of iron." Van Riebeeck had read the words of Isaiah to the caravans setting out to conquer the continent. Four centuries later those bronze doors were still there, now imprisoning the "chosen people" behind a wall of hatred and fear. Fortunately, a few glimmers of hope still shone in that bleak racist night.

★

DISREGARDING THE DANGER and the warnings, Helen Lieberman returned to Langa after Sam's murder by the apartheid police's hired killers. Little by little she became a familiar presence in the township. Slowly, cautiously, without ever imposing, she involved herself in the local culture, especially that of the women whom she admired more with each passing day. "Women are the pillars of South African society," she would say. "They are the ones who hold the survival of the black people in their hands." Helen was struck by their dynamism, their intelligence, their ingenuity. When they met, she waited for them to take the initiative. "Mama Helen, let's do this, let's do that . . ." They barraged her with suggestions that made her feel their eagerness for a better life. She was in a constant state of wonder. "Bearing in mind the tyranny, the repression, the disdain, the dangers, the fears, it was a true miracle that a white person was accepted so swiftly and completely," the young woman was to say. In the beginning Helen sought primarily to bring them the benefits of her medical experience. Soon all the newborns in the neighborhood ended up in her arms to be washed, cleaned of parasites, examined, and treated. She identified the children who were partially sighted or blind and took them to a white specialist whom she paid out of her own pocket. To help the deaf to hear and the mute to speak, she learned to sing in Xhosa and opened a speech therapy workshop. The first word she coaxed from hitherto silent throats was the most beautiful in any language: Mama. "The more familiar I became with African traditions, the prouder I became to be part of black community life. Here no one is ever abandoned. No plate ever remains empty when the one next to it is full. Food here is always something sacred to be shared."

Food! Soon Helen's small car became a sort of Santa Claus sleigh. Before heading for Langa she would do the rounds of the

Cape Town supermarkets and fill up her Anglia with staples that were past their sell-by date and would otherwise be thrown out. Meat or fish of dubious freshness, dairy products, fruit, and vegetables that could not be sold—they were all nourishment for the famished pariahs of a country that prided itself on producing the world's largest diamond and more gold than all of the American West. At Woolworths, at Pick'n Pay, in the shops in Goodwood, Maitland, and Sea Point, anywhere comfortable whites came with their colored or black servants to fill their shopping baskets, the figure of the young blonde white woman was a reminder that racial hatred was not inevitable. But Helen did not escape criticism and sometimes abuse for what she did. Her car was smeared with excrement and her tires punctured. A sense of solidarity and sharing with the population of color was rare among the "chosen people." "One by one we began to lose all our friends," she later admitted. "It was hard for Michael. No one could understand why I went and spent my days in that 'frightening black suburb,' or what I was doing there. I sensed people were acutely uneasy around me. I didn't dare speak about it because there were too many things in my heart I would have wanted to explain. At one dinner a friend was complaining about her cook who had arrived late that morning and hadn't stopped yawning all day. I wanted to ask her if she knew at what hour that unfortunate woman had to get up to catch one of the rare buses blacks could use to get to her house on time. If she knew that the poor woman only had three hours sleep a night because in the evening, when she got back to her slum, she had to cook for her children, look after her parents, help out a neighbor in need. . . .

"The lack of understanding around me did not matter. My battlefield was not the manicured avenues of Sea Point but the sordid alleyways of a South Africa whites had martyred. And my choice brought me so much in return! How wonderful it was to see little Andile grow up and speak out like any other child of his age; to see his mother taking care of other children in need; to visit the little school currently attended by some sixty children. In tribute to the young man burned alive by the prime minister's killers on the evening of its inauguration, the local people had inscribed his name on its facade: Sam's School."

Over the years, Helen's visits to the township grew so frequent that her husband became very concerned for her. A second school was created, a nursery and a clinic were opened, many of the shacks were rehabilitated with windows, doors, concrete floors, and watertight roofs. Medical teams specially trained by Helen monitored the neighborhood, checking for anyone who was sick or incapacitated and carrying out vaccination campaigns. In five years, the infant mortality rate dropped from nine to two per thousand; the number of people with tuberculosis from several thousand to less than a hundred; victims of dysentery from a few dozen to a few isolated cases. Helen credited the township women for this success. There were seven times as many of them as men, as most of the men spent eleven months of the year exiled in the grim bachelor hostels of distant factories in the Transvaal or Natal.

Was Helen Lieberman a South African Mother Teresa? Certainly, but with a difference. South Africa was not India, respectful of a saint entering its slums to preach love and compassion. The townships were crucibles of violence always about to explode. People stabbed, decapitated, and burned one another over a thousand tribal, clan, and ethnic rivalries. A white woman in such a setting, seeking only to serve, help, and attack injustice, what daring! Helen was convinced that one day she would pay for her audacity with her life.

"Suddenly on the road to Langa," she was to recount, "I found myself blocked in my car by thousands of schoolchildren in uniform. Just like in Soweto in 1976 they were advancing, dancing from one foot to the other, chanting slogans, and waving banners condemning the government. Other marchers coming from the squatter camps on either side of the main road had joined them a little further up. An angry ocean was about to engulf me. I couldn't move in any direction. From the banners I realized all those young people were on their way to Cape Town to protest outside parliament against the exam registration fees that the authorities had just doubled. They already felt so penalized by the disaster of the Bantu educational system. This was an unbearable provocation. They were unstoppable. Hundreds of them would be killed when they reached the first police blockade. And there I was, the only white woman on that road with the sun beating down. I decided to stay in my car, lock the doors, and roll up the windows. Soon I was suffocating. I could hear the shouting getting closer. When the demonstrators spotted my car and saw that a white woman was hiding in it, they would charge. It would only take them a minute to throw a torch into the engine. They would block the doors and dance a victory toyi-toyi as they watched me grill. Strangely, I wasn't afraid. I told myself that in a sense it would be a glorious good-bye to Africa, a farewell to the child martyrs of the atrocious regime to which I belonged. Yes, at that moment I felt sure I was going to die. Then out of nowhere a teenage boy with his cap on backwards appeared. With his thin, stubbly cheeks, fierce scowl, two gold earrings, and a checked shirt and torn jeans, he looked like one of these young hooligans who deal drugs around the shebeens in Langa. I thought to myself that I would rather burn in my car than have to confront that character. He tapped on the window.

'Mama Helen, what are you doing here?'

I jumped.

'How do you know my name?'

'You're my mother, Mama Helen!'

'Your mother?'

'Yes, you saved my life when my parents were killed in a taxi accident,' he explained. 'I was six years old. A family took me in. You told that family they must feed me every day. For years you brought them food so I wouldn't starve to death.'

'What's your name?'

'Vusi.'

I didn't recognize the name. The angry shouts were getting nearer.

'Vusi, what should I do?' I asked, suddenly panic-stricken. 'What's going to happen to me?'

'Nothing's going to happen to you, Mama Helen,' the boy replied firmly. 'This is my territory and no one's going to touch you. I control this area and all the demonstrators know it.' He sat down on the hood of my car and lit a cigarette. Then he re- peated: 'I'm the boss here, Mama Helen!'

'What if they try to kill you too?'

'Then I'll die for you.'

I couldn't believe my ears.

Suddenly my car was surrounded by protesters. But Vusi held his arms out to keep them back and was shielding me with his body. And they all stayed back. It was incredible. Then one of the young people turned to his comrades and shouted an order. They began singing a rousing song I recognized, the African anthem, a poignant appeal from the blacks to God to bless Africa. When the voices were quiet again, Vusi jumped on the hood and ad- dressed the crowd. He spoke in Xhosa but I could tell he was ex- plaining who I was and what I had been doing over the years to help the people of Langa. As is often the case in Africa, the con- frontation turned into a joyous celebration. Young people broke away from the procession to come and touch my hand, and bow their heads in respect. I was so overcome I couldn't hold back the tears. That day I realized I am a mother to the children of Langa."

★

THE SHELVES IN THE POLICE STATION at the entrance to the town- ship were piled to the ceiling with reports of Helen Lieberman's activities and movements. Each day spies brought fresh informa- tion. Her continuously expanding community development activ- ities and the massive support she had among the local people were disturbing to those in high places. What could be done to put an end to these subversive activities? Have Helen Lieberman assassinated? Take her husband and children hostage to force her to give up? Neither option would solve the problem because the hundreds of social workers trained by her would continue what she had started. But then, without realizing it, she played into her enemy's hands.

On June 24, 1989, on an icy afternoon in the southern winter, she met with the 250 "mamas" who helped run her development work through nurseries and preschools in a vast community hall rising above the gray of the corrugated roofs. The purpose of the meeting was to assess activities in progress and identify new priorities for early childhood development. As always, Helen was amazed at the readiness of African women to make themselves available, their will to organize for the well-being of all, their capacity to resist intimidation and threats. In three hours of constructive exchanges new links formed between the township people and their benefactor. Afterward the women returned to the poverty of their alleyways but with hearts full of hope. It was at this point that a terrifying blast rocked the building. The community hall was left a smoking rubble, its seats charred, the roof shredded, and the stage from which Helen had just been speaking was torn to pieces. A powerful bomb planted in the building had just exploded. The act of terrorism had no doubt intended to kill Helen and everyone else at the meeting, but by some miracle the detonating device had gone off ten minutes late. No one was hurt.

When they recovered from their fright, Helen and her team saw an immediate lesson to be learned from the attack. Their organization must be made official as soon as possible, its activities structured and official leaders appointed. South Africa and the world must know that in a remote township on the Cape Peninsula a citizen organization was making a stand against oppression. A few days later, with the news spreading by word of mouth, Helen called the largest meeting in the township's history on Langa's soccer field. More than three thousand people, the "mamas" in particular, came from all over the township. Despite the recent attack energy and enthusiasm prevailed. The large scarves the women wore on their heads were white, the African color of hope. Around their children's necks they had put strings of beads that sparkled in the winter sunshine. The few men present wore red T-shirts that proclaimed: "Mama Helen, we love you." Helen had dressed African-style with an ample moiré velvet shawl such as local women wore for weddings. She would deliver her message using a megaphone. Beside her, his cap on backward, was Vusi, who had become her bodyguard, interpreter, and project coordinator. Vusi had given up dealing drugs to work alongside the woman he called his mother. Together Helen and Vusi hoisted themselves onto the roof of the small Ford that they had driven into the center of the field. Wild applause greeted them followed by singing and toi-toiing. Helen raised her arm to ask for silence. It took several minutes. Finally her voice rang out: "Brothers and Sisters of Langa! Thank-you for coming to this historic occasion," she exclaimed and passed the megaphone to Vusi who translated her words into Xhosa. "I asked you here because I have an important proposition to put to you. We must respond to the bomb attack of the other day, which was meant to wipe out everything we have achieved in our township," she explained. "That monstrous act made me aware of how fragile we are. Without official legitimacy what we have built together could disappear in a single second!" Helen paused so that Vusi could translate. As he did, she studied the faces of the audience, attentive, respectful, stamped with seriousness but also curiosity. "For these people the stakes are very real," she thought admiringly.

"Brothers and sisters, I therefore propose that together we set up a foundation that will reflect our shared commitment and will form a kind of umbrella under which we shall be able to pursue our activities."

This word "umbrella" struck a chord of recognition. There was a burst of applause. Women shouted agreement, toyi-toyied, waved their scarves. A roar of triumph filled the stadium. Suddenly a voice asked, "Mama Helen, what shall we call our foundation?"

Another woman broke in. "Mama Helen, all of us here are the future of South Africa. We should call our foundation Ikamva Labantu, The Future of Our Nation." The crowd shouted its joyful approval.

The next day when she arrived in Langa, Helen was intercepted by a group of euphoric women. The oldest one presented her with a cardboard roll tied up with a ribbon. It was accompanied by a traditional beaded necklace—a great honor for her.

"Permit us to give you this, Mama Helen. It is an expression of our dearest desire."

Helen untied the ribbon and carefully unrolled the improvised parchment with the neckpiece. A large sheet of white paper had been glued to the supporting cardboard. On it some words had been carefully handwritten. Tears filled Helen's eyes as she read the message of her sisters of color: "Dr. Helen, we, the women of Langa, appoint you President of Ikamva Labantu."[7]

★

DESPITE SOMETIMES CRIPPLING RHEUMATIC pain, Christiaan Barnard remained a beacon of hope in the darkness of apartheid. He sought and tried every conceivable treatment for his incapacitating disease. Thinking that the alternating temperatures might do him good, he spent hours plunging his hands into bowls of first hot and then cold water. He wore copper bracelets, smeared

---

7. Ikamva Labantu, The Future of Our Nation, is now the largest private humanitarian aid organization in South Africa. Among its innumerable projects are over a thousand nurseries, three hundred primary schools, art and sport centers, rehabilitation workshops for adults and children, homes for the elderly, rehabilitation centers for the blind, homes for the destitute, rural development programs, training and handicraft centers, dispensaries for the treatment of AIDS sufferers, and so on. In all, over a million underprivileged people receive help annually from the organization founded by Helen Lieberman. In 1998 President Mandela came in person to pay tribute to her on behalf of the nation. To contribute to the work of this remarkable NGO, please visit www.ikamva.com.

his painful hands with oil of rosemary, peanut oil, the juice of green tomatoes, and raspberry, parsley, and celery infusions. He practiced transcendental meditation, tried acupuncture, and followed the precepts of scientology. He took vitamin pills for dogs, concoctions of guava leaf and Malaysian seaweed, and drank blood from umbilical cords. He rubbed his fingers with a paste made from stinging nettles. He stuffed his pockets with potatoes and with chestnuts from India. He tried everything, but in the end it was his courage alone that enabled him to surmount his pain and continue the medical adventure that had begun when he performed history's first heart transplant. The death of the grocer Louis Washkansky, his first transplant patient, did not discourage him. In the midst of South Africa's racial chaos, Barnard would strike a blow at his compatriots' racist ideology. The second patient whose heart he would replace was a bald dentist with a thin mustache who came from a Cape Town suburb. Fifty-eight-year-old Philip Blaiberg suffered from cardiovascular degeneration and had been given only a few weeks to live. As with any organ transplant the operation depended on the availability of a compatible donor. But how many days could the unfortunate dentist wait?

That Sunday was a day of celebration on the beach at False Bay. The thirteen children of the Haupt family were enjoying a picnic with their parents. After the meal, the boys began to play ball on the sand with some boys from another family. One of the Haupt sons was a solid young man of twenty-four, as muscular as a rugby player. Clive was a worker at a large textile company in Cape Town. In the heat of the match his sudden disappearance went unnoticed. His brothers soon found him stretched out on the sand at the other end of the beach. He looked as if he was asleep. In fact, Clive had just suffered a cerebral hemorrhage. Clinically, he was already dead. An ambulance took him to Groote Schuur hospital. Professor Barnard's team was immediately notified of the arrival of this robust, apparently fit young man. The first blood and tissue tests indicated perfect compatibility with Blaiberg, the dentist. The ideal donor! But there was one in-surmountable catch: Clive Haupt was not white. He was of mixed race.

The surgeon rushed to the dentist's room to make sure that he would not object to receiving the heart of a colored person. For his part, the donor's father readily authorized the removal of his son's heart to help a sick white man. "It's what Clive would have wanted," he stated. Barnard did not hesitate to defy official prohibitions. In a bold radio interview on the day of the operation he attacked the apartheid laws head-on: "The Haupts as 'non-whites' have no right to sit on park benches 'reserved for whites,' nor to use the same trains or buses," he declared. "They were turned out of the house where they were born and where their family lived for years because today it has been declared a 'white' area. They are prohibited from using most of the country's restaurants, hotels, and splendid holiday resorts. If Clive Haupt had met the daughter of the man who will live again thanks to him, he would not have been allowed to fall in love with her, much less marry or make love to her. And yet when I asked his father for his son's heart for Philip Blaiberg, he did not answer me: 'My son's heart is reserved for nonwhites.' He agreed without hesitation, hatred, or bitterness toward the whites who have humiliated him and deprived him of his most fundamental rights for so long."

This speech caused a sensation. A colored heart in a white chest! It was enough to make the guardians of racist orthodoxy apoplectic. But Barnard persisted with no regrets. "We have taken the heart of a colored man and put it in the chest of a white Jew whom we have treated with a serum that came from Germany," he announced to the journalists crowding each other outside Groote Schuur hospital the day after the successful operation.

A colored heart in a white chest! Was a rainbow nation begin-ning to dawn in the land of the "chosen people"?

★

WINNIE, WINNIE, WINNIE . . . Winnie, always and forever. Refusing to believe the malicious rumors of marital infidelity his guards repeated continuously, the prisoner in cell 466-64 obsessed over the suffering the government was inflicting on his beloved wife. He was tormented by his powerlessness to protect the woman who was paying so dearly for having joined her destiny to his. At times he questioned whether any cause would have justified abandoning a young and inexperienced wife in the hell of a pitiless desert. But he knew how strong Winnie was. Each time he was given permission to write to her, he sent her deeply moving messages that must have brought a lump to the throat of even the most hardened censors. "Your love and support, the raw warmth of your body, the charming children you have given the family, the many friends you have won, the hope of enjoying that love and warmth again, is what life and happiness mean to me," he wrote to her one day in February 1985. "The love and warmth that exude from you behind those unkind grey monotonous and cruel walls simply overwhelms me," she answered him. "Especially when I think of those who in the name of the struggle have been deprived of that love."[8]

Although informed about the constant harassment she experienced, Mandela had no idea the government was systematically terrorizing his wife. By breaking Winnie, the torturers in Pretoria hoped to destroy the black leader's capacity to resist once and for all. They escalated their acts of intimidation. One day killers in civilian clothes burst into the small house in Orlando and threatened to strangle her; on another day, explosive devices shattered her windows; on yet another, her dog Pluto was poisoned to death. Not only did they exile the woman to the farthest reaches of the country, but they also used the new terrorism law enacted in 1967 against her, which permitted the imprisonment of any

---

8. Winnie Mandela, *Part of My Soul Went with Him*, ed. Anne Benjamin and Mary Benson (London: Penguin, 1985).

suspects without charge and for an indefinite period of time. Thus in May 1969, Winnie was sent to the gruesome prison in Pretoria where she was held in solitary confinement under appalling conditions for ninety-one days. No fewer than ninety-nine charges were brought against her, from raising her fist in the ANC salute to keeping in touch with the organization's underground leaders. She was also blamed for getting food and clothing to a group of women who had been in solitary confinement for several years.

Security Branch police broke down the door of her house in the middle of the night. They spent hours going through everything from books down to the smallest scrap of paper. They stripped cupboards, ransacked clothing, turned over the carpets, snatched the children from their beds to inspect the blankets, sheets, mattresses, and frames. No container of sugar or soup escaped their scrutiny. At dawn, their nightmarish excavations concluded with Winnie's arrest, as her children clung to her howling at the white police: "Don't take our mummy!"

Winnie was locked in a cell on death row, a cage four and a half feet wide in which she could neither stand up nor lie down at full stretch. "Those first few days are the worst in anyone's life," she was to say of her incarceration, "that uncertainty, that insecurity; there is such a sense of hopelessness, the feeling that this is now the end."[9] The apartheid police seemed to think of everything: "The whole thing is calculated to destroy you not only morally but also physically." There was no one to talk to. The fear of being there for months or years, naked because all her clothes had been taken from her, was terrible. When her period came, Winnie asked for water and a towel. A white guard barked at her to "go and use your big fat kaffir hands" to wipe away the blood running down her thighs. Yet it was the solitude that Winnie found most unbearable. She tried to distract herself by scratching the paint off the walls with her nails. One day she brought

---

9. Winnie Mandela, *Part of My Soul*.

down a piece of plaster under which she read in big letters: "Mrs. Mandela is a sellout." After several weeks she found two living things to relieve her isolation: a couple of ants. She played with them on her fingertips for days on end. When the guards returned her clothes, it was only to subject her to a particularly cruel search each morning and night. They tore the seams and slashed her pockets. Next they inspected her hair a lock at a time, then unceremoniously felt all over her body including her private parts, the supreme humiliation, which made them grin. "If I didn't have children," Winnie was to say, "and if it wasn't for the fact that I would be playing into the authorities' hands, I might have taken my life. But one would be doing this for people who had no conscience at all."[10]

These were minor cruelties next to the interrogations. For five days and nights straight, she was chained in the office of an inspector who was infamous among South African blacks. His name was Ludwig Swanepoel. "Falling into the hands of that sadistic white man was like descending into hell," she was to say. "Even before forcing you to reveal activities that justified your imprisonment he did his utmost to break you psychologically. He began by saying: 'Mrs. Mandela, what kind of woman holds meetings up till four o'clock in the morning with other people's husbands? We have questioned the men. They have all confirmed their presence in your husband's bedroom.'" During another interrogation, the policeman tried sweet-talking her: "Mrs. Mandela, we have succeeded in telling people that you want to work for us," he said. "Do you want to work for us, so that we can release you?"

All she would have to do, Swanepoel explained to his prisoner, was make a radio appeal to the ANC forces across the border, enjoining them to lay down their arms and come and talk to the government. Winnie would then be taken by helicopter to Robben Island with top ranking police officers to hold discussions

_____

10. Winnie Mandela, *Part of My Soul*.

with her husband, who would be taken immediately to some comfortable cottage on the mainland. "The arrogance of those white men made me sick," Winnie Mandela would say. "How could they imagine I would betray the principles of a cause I'd given my life to?" One evening, a security officer decided to give the prisoner a present. "The Security Police are a special breed," Winnie was to explain. "In order to belong you have to have this particular hatred of the black man. Otherwise how would you torture people to death for ideological differences? How would you point a machine gun at a seven-year-old child and blast his brains out?"

That evening the officer flung open the door to her cell and threw a book at her feet, shouting, "There you are, you filthy kaffir. There is the Bible; ask your God to release you from jail." The gift seemed all the more ironic because the young black woman knew the respect whites had for the God of the Bible who had "chosen" them, as they never stopped boasting, to rule in his name over the destiny of Africa. That little book became as precious a companion to her as it had once been to the Voortrekkers. She read it four times in succession, until then never having thought it possible to read the Bible from beginning to end. When her interminable Way of the Cross behind the bars in Pretoria's prison finally ended, and she was released, she gave a poignant account of her prison experience. "The physical identification with your beliefs is far more satisfying than articulating them on a platform. My soul has been more purified by prison than anything else," she admitted. "I am not saying it is best to be in prison. But under the circumstances, where it is a question of what prison is better, the prison outside or inside—the whole country is a prison for the black man—and when you are inside, you know why you are there, and the people who put you there also know."[11]

★

---

11. Winnie Mandela, *Part of My Soul*.

FOR TWENTY-ONE YEARS he had not touched her hand or run his fingers over her face. For twenty-one years he had not seen her big dark eyes and sensual mouth except through the distorting glass; had not breathed the heady scent of patchouli; or heard her voice except through a speaker system. And then suddenly a miracle. Warden James Gregory informed Mandela that he would be able to hold his wife in his arms. The authorities had just given permission for political detainees to receive what they chastely called "contact visits" from their families.

"Before either of us knew it, we were in the same room and in each other's arms. I kissed and held my wife for the first time in all those many years. It was a moment I had dreamt about a thousand times. It was as if I were still dreaming. I held her to me for what seemed like an eternity. We were still and silent except for the sound of our hearts."[12]

The guard could not believe his eyes. The prisoner had lifted Winnie off the ground. She was crying and kissing him, her arms wrapped round his neck, pressing herself against him as hard as she could, laughing and sobbing. "Nelson and Winnie were so taken with being able to touch one another that they had forgotten I was there. Inside the room there was no sound, yet the emotion was overwhelming."[13]

Eighty minutes of unadulterated happiness. "To have been able to caress her at last, feel her, hold her . . ." murmured the prisoner with tears in his eyes when he was back in his cell. Those enchanted moments were followed by a new banishment for his unfortunate wife. The government still considered Winnie a danger to the state. The torturers in Pretoria persisted in thinking they could get at Mandela through her. She was once again exiled to Brandfort, where she had already spent long months. Her first letter from that forsaken corner of the Orange Free

---

12. Mandela, *Long Walk to Freedom*, p. 505.
13. James Gregory, *Good-Bye Bafana: Nelson Mandela, My Prisoner, My Friend* (London: Headline, 1996), pp. 300–301.

204 A RAINBOW IN THE NIGHT

State was full of rage. The house allotted to her was a hovel with broken windows at the edge of the town, dirty, with no conveniences, owned by a white man who demanded that she pay rent and utility bills. The shack was a state prison, she protested, let the state pay for it! She made use of her exile to help the poorest people in the village by setting up a day care nursery, a medical center, and a soup kitchen. She was helped by white sympathizers won over by the energy, tenacity, and generosity that the government could not subdue.

One day, she decided that her exile had lasted long enough and returned to Soweto. The situation was tense. Prime Minister Botha was mired in constitutional reforms that most people no longer believed in. People were dying every day in the ghettos. In 1986 Winnie was proclaimed Mother of the Nation. She owed this honor to her incendiary words and her ardor, which inspired the young ANC militants to fight against apartheid. At the height of the township revolt she encouraged her supporters to assassinate blacks collaborating with the white administration. In Kagiso on April 13, 1986, she addressed an enormous crowd. "The time for speeches and debate has come to an end," she cried. "The year 1986 is going to see the liberation of the oppressed masses of this country. . . . Together, hand in hand with our sticks and our matches, with our necklaces, we shall liberate this country," she promised, to thunderous applause.[14] Her reference to "necklaces" raised an outcry. A necklace was a particularly barbaric form of execution that involved putting a tire filled with petrol around the victim's shoulders and then setting it on fire. Hundreds died from this torture in the townships. The government was quick to exploit these excesses against Winnie, a task made all the easier as Winnie grew increasingly reckless. The press constantly updated the list of her alleged lovers. Shady

---

14. *Illustrated History of South Africa: The Real Story* (Cape Town: Reader's Digest, 1995).

characters took advantage of her generosity and encouraged her caprices. A squad of bodyguards surrounded her, young orphans from Soweto whom she gathered into the fold of what she called the Mandela United Football Club. They became a vengeful gang that terrorized the township streets, killing all those who opposed their law. When they murdered a fourteen-year-old black boy suspected of being an informer for the white police they went too far.

★

ROBBEN ISLAND! That rock had become the symbol of racial cruelty in the eyes of the world. Each day brought new international pressure on the South African prime minister to close the penal colony. From Tokyo to New York, the press carried moving reports on the interminable torment of the prisoner in cell 466-64 and his companions. P.W. Botha had to respond. But how? Pardoning the inflexible black leader who had steered the ANC's armed rebellion from his cell was impossible. The 4 million whites haunted by the *swart gevaar*—black peril—would revolt. They would take up their rifles and, like their Great Trek ancestors who massacred the Zulus at Blood River, they would sow death in the townships and homelands. Perhaps simply changing the place of Mandela's detention would be enough to defuse world indignation. That was the solution P.W. Botha chose at the beginning of April 1982.

The prisoner received a surprise visit from the general in charge of Robben Island. This was highly unusual, since the prison's commanding officer never visited a detainee in his cell. "I want you to pack up your things," he announced. "We are transferring you."[15] Mandela was worried and uneasy. What did it mean? Neither his comrades nor he had been informed of any

---

15. Mandela, *Long Walk to Freedom*, p. 497.

possible departure. They had spent nearly twenty years on the island and now they suddenly had to move.

A few minutes later, with their meager possessions, Nelson
Mandela, Walter Sisulu, and their two closest ANC companions
boarded a ferry for Cape Town. Mandela watched the island re-
cede in the golden evening light, wondering whether he would
ever see it again. "A man can get used to anything," he would later
write. "And I had grown used to Robben Island. I had lived there
for almost two decades and while it was never home—my home
was in Johannesburg—it had become a place where I felt comfortable. I have always found change difficult, and leaving Robben Island, however grim it had been at times, was no exception.
I had no idea what to look forward to."[16]

The prisoners were taken to Pollsmoor maximum security fa-
cility a few miles southeast of Cape Town on one of the world's
most beautiful highways between the Atlantic Ocean and hundreds of acres of vineyards. Rising from the vegetation deep in
the heart of this delightful countryside was a complex of concrete buildings surrounded by high protective walls and a string
of watchtowers. Here South Africa imprisoned its most dangerous common-law prisoners. And here the apartheid regime had
prepared a comfortable detention space for its four most famous
political prisoners. Beds with fresh sheets and blankets, furniture with storage capacity; separate toilets, two wash basins, and
two showers; a large open terrace with a view of the sky and tubs
of soil for gardening; meals three times a day with meat and vegetables, a feast after twenty years of cornmeal gruel; the delivery
of newspapers and magazines, including *Time* and the *Guardian
Weekly*, banned on Robben Island—suddenly they found themselves in a five-star hotel.

But it was having use of a small transistor radio that brought
the four prisoners their biggest shock. During the afternoon of
January 31, 1985, they suddenly heard over the radio the state

---

16. Mandela, *Long Walk to Freedom,* p. 497.

president's imperious voice addressing parliament. "The South African government is willing to free Mr. Mandela on condition that he unconditionally rejects violence as a political instrument," declared P.W. Botha. The prisoners heard the murmur of astonishment that ran through the assembly in response to this announcement. They were dumbfounded. Then the president's voice continued and threw a public challenge: "It is therefore not the South African government which now stands in the way of Mr. Mandela's freedom," claimed P.W. Botha. "It is he himself."

Warden James Gregory, who had followed Mandela from Robben Island to Pollsmoor, saw the elderly prisoner leap to his feet. His muted voice, usually so restrained, released a torrent of imprecations against the white leader. Had Mr. Botha not already on several occasions secretly led him to understand that he would be willing to release him on condition he return to his village in the Transkei and draw no more attention to himself? Mandela had felt insulted and never replied. And now the apartheid leader was renewing his offer, but only with the whole nation as witness. The prisoner could not hide his fury. How could the government imagine for a moment that he would barter his freedom to go and tend sheep in his native land? It was a shameful maneuver but its intent was clear: Pretoria sought by every means possible to create a rift between the legendary ANC leader and the movement's clandestine forces fighting in the field. He would respond publicly but through a voice other than his own.

He would speak through the voice of a young woman who stood for the new generation of Africans whose birth he had vowed to see when he hugged his granddaughter Hope in the Robben Island visitors' room. His youngest daughter, twenty-five-year-old Zindzi, would read his answer to the insulting bargain offered by apartheid's mouthpiece in Soweto's Jabulani Stadium, packed to overflowing that February 10, 1985, to celebrate the awarding of the Nobel Peace Prize to that other icon of the black people's crusade against white oppression, Bishop Desmond Tutu.

She was beautiful, stirring, and compelling. She had her father's stately forehead, her mother's voluptuous mouth and magnetic gaze, and the slender neck of the Thembu princesses of her ancestral Xhosa country. When she appeared on the rostrum in a white T-shirt with a logo proclaiming the imminent death of apartheid, the entire stadium rose to its feet. She answered the ovations with the ANC salute, an outstretched arm with clenched fist. At that moment the black people's invincible destiny was incarnated in that proud young woman there to speak on behalf of the mythical leader who was her father. She was conscious of the importance of her task. It was the first time the historic leader of the ANC had been able to address the African people since white justice had cut him off from the world of the living. Many in the packed stadium probably had only a vague idea of Mandela's importance in the black people's struggle for freedom. With prolonged absence, ties slackened and heroes lost their following. How many people now did not even know what the illustrious prisoner looked like? Since he could not be there in person, his daughter Zindzi's presence was the best gift he could offer his supporters. The young woman approached the battery of microphones that would carry her words across the stadium, the country, and much of the world. Calmly she unfolded the sheets of paper containing her father's response to P.W. Botha's speech.

"My father sends his warmest greetings to Bishop Desmond Tutu," she read with sincerity, "who has made it clear to the world that the Nobel Peace Prize belongs to you who are the people of this country. We salute him."

Cries of enthusiasm and admiring whistles and applause drowned out Zindzi's words. Then she read her father's recollection of the countless attempts by his comrades and himself over the last thirty years to persuade the white government to sit down with them and find solutions to the country's problems. But their offers were ignored, and "it was only when all other forms of resistance were no longer open to us, that we turned to armed struggle," Mandela recalled. The audience drank in the messenger's words in almost reverent silence. "'Let Botha renounce violence,' my father says to you. 'Let him say he will dismantle apartheid. Let him unban the people's organization, the African National Congress. Let him free all who have been imprisoned, banished, or exiled for their opposition to apartheid. Let him guarantee free political activity so that people may decide who will govern them.'"

Again the crowd's ovations forced the young woman to stop. She herself seemed increasingly gripped with emotion. Several times she raised her arm and fist. Then her voice rang out again through the loudspeakers:

"My father says to you: 'I cherish my own freedom dearly, but I care even more for your freedom. Too many have died since I went to prison. Too many have suffered for the love of freedom. I owe it to their widows, to their orphans, to their mothers, and to their fathers who have grieved and wept for them. . . .'"

Her gaze took in the entire assembly, as if to emphasize what her father was about to say. Zindzi went on, "'I am not less life-loving than you are,'" she read, "'But I cannot sell my birthright, nor am I prepared to sell the birthright of the people to be free. What freedom am I being offered while the organization of the people remains banned? What freedom am I being offered when I may be arrested on a pass offense? . . . What freedom am I being offered when I must ask permission to live in an urban area? What freedom am I being offered when my very South African citizenship is not respected?'"[17] The crowd seemed to be holding its breath as it reflected on these poignant questions. Zindzi was winning them over. But she knew that the most important words were still to come. She continued, making her father's every word stand out: "Only free men can negotiate. Prisoners cannot enter into contracts . . . I cannot and will not give any undertaking at a time when I, and you, the people, are not free. Your freedom and mine cannot be separated. I will return!"

---

17. Mandela, *Long Walk to Freedom,* p. 511.

The young woman stopped speaking. Silence fell over everyone. "Only free men can negotiate!" The message took time to sink in. And then, without any prompting, the crowd stood up and began to sing as if trembling with the same sudden urge: "*Nkosi Sikelel' iAfrica!* God bless Africa!" The anthem of black South Africa was immediately followed by cheering and applause.

In the prison at the other end of the country where he was following the broadcast, Nelson Mandela wiped away tears of pride and joy. How happy he was! Thanks to Zindzi, the South Africa of tomorrow had launched its call for the liberation of all Africans. May God bless Africa and may his message be heard!

★

PRESIDENT BOTHA HAD listened closely to the Pollsmoor prisoner's speech. He was beside himself. "Mandela's inflexible and uncompromising rhetoric shows his refusal to enter into the peaceful solution we are offering," he fumed in a television interview soon after. But did Botha really think that after all those years Mandela and his companions would abandon their struggle? "How he deludes himself!" one privileged observer, the warden James Gregory, wrote in his journal. While a new generation of combatants represented by Zindzi was growing up, these men were not about to renounce their deeply held principles. "I knew," he noted, "because I could see for myself that they were not tiring of their time in prison. If anything, they were stronger, more determined now than ever. The years had only hardened their resolve. They had by now been in jail for a generation."[18] Such men would accept nothing from the government but unconditional freedom.

Ignoring the obvious, the man in Pretoria allowed South Africa to slowly sink into a state of anarchy. When numerous countries appealed to him to abolish apartheid and negotiate, he

---

18. Gregory, *Good-Bye Bafana*, p. 307.

confiscated the passports of white students who planned to cross the border and talk "young person to young person" with members of the ANC Youth League in neighboring countries. He barred dignitaries of the Dutch Reformed Church, still a pillar of the regime, from leaving the country to meet with churchmen hostile to apartheid. As if they sensed the impending end of their domination, the descendants of the Great Trek's most fanatical pioneers showed an obsessive racism that verged at times on madness. Botha encouraged them, announcing on television that white South Africa must "mobilize against the forces of darkness that threaten to destroy the land of our fathers."

The forces of darkness! All across the planet Nelson Mandela stood for the shining hope of a racially reconciled South Africa. Many cities in England already had streets named after him. American, Scottish, and Austrian universities awarded him their highest distinctions. Pope John Paul II publicly expressed support and admiration for him. In Germany, France, and Scandinavia top leaders called for his unconditional release and an end to the "shame of apartheid." To help him "knock out" his opponents, Mike Tyson sent him the boxing gloves he wore when he won his world championship title—a gift that touched the heart of the former amateur boxer who had spent the Sundays of his youth in the boxing rings on the outskirts of Johannesburg.

Surreal! The president dared to justify the incarceration of Mandela and his companions by comparing it to that of Rudolf Hess and the Nazi war criminals sentenced at Nuremberg. But then a wind of panic shook the corridors of white tyranny. Mandela was said to be dying from advanced prostate cancer. The possibility that the oldest political prisoner in the world might die in an apartheid prison terrified the men in power. The whole Afrikaner community would be held responsible. That tragedy must be prevented at all costs, and the elite Volks Hospital in Cape Town, strictly reserved for white patients, would see to it. At noon on November 3, 1985, two prominent South African urologists, assisted by two eminent professors from Edinburgh and Zurich, proceeded to remove the little gland on which, it seemed, the future of South Africa depended. The operation was successful. Thanks to the vigilant care of white staff charmed by his great simplicity, Mandela recovered like a young man. The government had just skirted disaster.

Two years later, however, there was another alarm. Mandela suddenly collapsed with breathing difficulties. This time he was taken to a celebrated clinic in Cape Town frequented by wealthy whites. The announcement of another health problem elicited renewed concern. The media besieged the hospital; supporters, white and black, held communal prayer meetings in many churches. On the financial markets, the price of gold followed the black leader's temperature fluctuations. The two liters of brownish liquid that were drained from his lungs revealed that Mandela was suffering from tuberculosis. Not a surprising diagnosis considering his twenty-five years in the often freezing dampness of his prisons. It would be a long recovery, but he had so many visitors that he saw his illness as a blessing.

Among those privileged to sit regularly at his bedside was an eminent member of P.W. Botha's government. At fifty-six, justice minister Kobie Coetsee belonged to a new generation of Afrikaner politicians who had not attended the Nazi political rallies, a generation who wanted to give South Africa's whites a different ideal than apartheid. He was the first representative of the white government to meet the black leader. "Ah, Mr. Coetsee, how nice to see you! At last!" Mandela exclaimed joyously. Then, thinking what a waste all those lost years had been, he added sadly: "I'm sorry we did not meet together sooner!"

★

CHANGING FROM HIS HOSPITAL PAJAMAS into a tailored suit, putting on a shirt, tie, and shoes—these were not challenging tasks in themselves. But after so many years in prison, the ANC leader no longer knew how to knot a tie or lace up his shoes. Thus the most important meeting in South Africa's history since Paul

Kruger met with Queen Victoria's prime minister began with sartorial fumbles. But what did that matter when history was on the move! On February 5, 1989, the South African head of government received a visitor with unlaced shoes and a crooked tie in his elegant Dutch Tuynhuys-style residence in suburban Cape Town. P.W. Botha had finally succumbed to the liberal arguments of his justice minister. The man nicknamed Die Groot Krokodil (the Great Crocodile) was about to have tea with his greatest enemy.

For Mandela, this was supping with the devil. "The door then opened," he was to recount,[19] "and I walked in expecting the worst. From the opposite side of his grand office, P.W. Botha walked towards me. He had planned his march perfectly, for we met exactly halfway. He had his hand out and was smiling broadly, and in fact, from that very first moment, he completely disarmed me. He was unfailingly courteous, deferential and friendly." A photographer then entered the office to take a shot that, in a few moments, would amaze the world: the historic handshake of the two most implacable adversaries in South Africa.

"At that moment I told myself that the fratricidal war between whites and blacks that had torn our country apart for so long was over," Kobie Coetsee, who witnessed the scene, said later. Alas the young minister was mistaken. After half an hour of polite exchanges, Mandela again asked for the unconditional and immediate release of all political prisoners, including himself, whereupon the Crocodile stood up and snapped. "That's out of the question, Mr. Mandela! Those men are still enemies of the people God has chosen to reign over Africa."

Fortunately for South Africa, a stroke forced the author of this biting reply to retire from government seven months later.

★

19. Mandela, *Long Walk to Freedom*, p. 539.

HIS SUCCESSOR WAS JUST as bald but twenty years younger. Frederik Willem "F. W." de Klerk was fifty-three years old and built like a rugby player, with an open face and regular features despite a slightly crooked nose, the result of a hockey accident. He had been a baby at his mother's breast when Verwoerd and his companions brought back from their travels in the Third Reich the Nazi myth of white supremacy that would shape the ideology of apartheid. But de Klerk had been born into the Afrikaner establishment and imbued with its racial values, first by his grandfather, an eminent pastor in the Calvinist Church that, like the Dutch Reformed Church, gave dogmatic and religious justification and support for racial separation, and then by his father, who for fifteen years had served in the apartheid government as a dedicated minister. After a pampered childhood, F. W. de Klerk excelled in his law studies and rejected a career in politics to practice law. This choice, which held for ten years, greatly pleased Marike, the pretty brunette teacher's daughter whom he had married at the age of twenty-three and with whom he adopted three children. A passionate big game hunter in the bush, which had been the Voortrekkers' source of food for their African conquest, a great lover of golf, and an outstanding lawyer, de Klerk stood aloof from the agitation surrounding the leaders in Pretoria. Until the day came when politics got him, too.

Overnight, he left his law practice to stand in a parliamentary by-election for the National Party, the party of the apartheid militants. He was elected. Six years later President John Vorster invited him for a drink in his office, in fact to suggest that he join his government. De Klerk had just turned forty-two and was one of the youngest ministers in the history of the Republic of South Africa. He would hold in succession the positions of minister of telecommunications, sport, energy, internal affairs, and education. But it was his meteoric rise within the National Party that enabled him to carve out for himself a decisive role in the direction of his country's affairs. With the fortuitous disappearance of the Great Crocodile, he was suddenly promoted to head of the party, then head of state.

In both roles he faced immediate crisis. South Africa in the early summer of 1989 was on the brink of civil war. Out of a survival instinct—as much for himself as for his country—de Klerk initiated an emergency process of transformation. He received the full support of the Broederbond, the influential League of Brothers that, fifty years earlier, had launched South Africa on the way of apartheid. He also had the backing of the business community that was beginning to find international economic sanctions intolerable. Finally and above all, he was riding on the great changes that had occurred in the wider world. The fall of the Berlin Wall and the dismantling of the Soviet empire had dispelled Afrikaners' obsessive fear of communism. The climate was ripe for real upheaval.

As the noon hour approached on February 2, 1990, the new president of South Africa prepared to deliver a speech that would reverse the course of his country's history. The building was crammed. Hundreds of South African journalists and special correspondents from all over the world crowded the galleries while a forest of television cameras stood ready to broadcast the event. From the humblest fishing villages to the imposing skyscrapers of Johannesburg, from the sordid bachelor hostels of Soweto to Durban's Indian bazaars, from the Zulu sanctuaries of Natal to the farms of the veld, everywhere people of different color and walks of life were waiting nervously in front of television screens that morning. Across the borders, in the ANC camps in Zambia, Mozambique, Zimbabwe, and even farther away in Europe, America, and Asia, where the tragedy of South Africa aroused ever greater concern, millions of others waited to hear what the new head of state would say to save South Africa from civil war.

His voice was calm, confident, convincing. Persuaded that "only an agreement between all representatives of the population" could achieve a lasting peace, de Klerk courageously announced, "The time for negotiation has arrived." He promised that soon everyone in the country would enjoy equal rights. The 25 million South Africans of color still crushed by the tyranny of apartheid were waiting above all for evidence of a fundamental break with the racist policies of the past. De Klerk was quick to answer their hopes. "I am in a position to reveal that we have come to some momentous decisions," he declared. The journalists looked at each other in amazement while millions of listeners and television viewers held their breath. "I am announcing the lifting of all restrictions on the hitherto banned organizations of the African National Congress, the Pan Africanist Congress, and the South African Communist Party," he proclaimed. "All persons currently imprisoned for belonging to these organizations will be identified and released immediately." Lest anyone doubt his word, de Klerk reminded people that he had already (in the previous August) ordered the release of eight of the principal political prisoners sentenced at the Rivonia trial.

The head of state paused and prepared to utter the name of the legendary figure who had embodied the black struggle against white oppression. That a former champion of that very oppression should evoke his name in the house where so many barbarous laws had been passed restricting people's freedom was not the least paradox of that astounding day. In solemn, almost reverential tones Frederik Willem de Klerk let it be known that his government had "taken the irrevocable decision unconditionally to free—Mr. Nelson Mandela."

★

IT WAS 4:30 IN THE MORNING of Sunday, February 11, 1990. A clear summer's day broke over the hills of Cape Town. After ten thousand days and ten thousand nights without freedom the oldest political prisoner on the planet was about to cast off the chains that were supposed to shackle him until his dying breath. He started the last day of his life sentence as he had every morning for the last twenty-seven years, with a workout. The day promised to be hectic right up to his official release set for exactly 3:00 PM. There was little likelihood of it happening on schedule, however. First because Winnie, though she knew that her husband would never leave his place of detention without her hand in his, was late arriving from Johannesburg. And then because of a sudden order from Pretoria to disarm all prison personnel. The British secret service MI5 had warned the government that several of the guards had been bribed to shoot the black leader as he left. Mandela laughed off the threat. At the request of the hundreds of journalists who had camped outside all night, he would leave the prison gates accompanied by his wife.

Suddenly catching sight of the tall, slightly stooped figure with a swarm of helicopters over his head, one photographer expressed the excitement of all: "Look, Look! There's Mandela, taking his first steps as a free man!" The cameras relayed close-ups of a smiling face that virtually no one recognized because for over a quarter of a century South Africa had prohibited publishing his photo. Here in flesh and blood was the man whom so many years in prison had made a living legend, who after a lifetime of dedication to the struggle for his people's rights had come to this last crossroads, this decisive and long awaited moment when he would enter history. He raised his fist in salute and a great roar went up. He had not been able to make that gesture for twenty-seven years, he thought to himself with a surge of joy and strength. It was sixteen minutes past four. At the age of seventy-one, he felt as though his life had just begun again. His ten thousand days of imprisonment were finally over.

At Cape Town's city hall he was to give a speech to mark his reunion with South Africa. The road to that cradle of white colonialism ran through lush countryside, flourishing vineyards, and well-tended farms. A number of white families had come to see the motorcade go by. Mandela could hardly believe his eyes; many were raising their fists in salute. Seeing this gesture of solidarity with the ANC in a conservative white area galvanized him. He had the car stop and got out to thank them. "The South Africa I was returning to was very different from the one I had left," he would say with emotion.

The grand parade in front of city hall teemed with an impatient crowd that had been waiting for his arrival for hours. The car bringing the elderly leader tried to open a path through the tide of humanity. Some people rapped on the windows and roof, others jumped on the hood and rocked the vehicle. Mandela squeezed Winnie's hand affectionately. "The crowd may well suffocate you with their love," joked the driver.

At last he reached the balcony to find an endless sea of men, women, and children of all races, colors, and origins, shouting, waving flags and banners, applauding, singing, and hopping from one foot to the other. He raised his fist and the crowd responded with an enormous cheer. Mandela was overwhelmed. "Those cheers fired me anew with the spirit of the struggle," he was to say.

"*Amandla!*" he called out in his husky voice.

"*Ngawethu!*"[20] responded the crowd.

"*iAfrika!*"

"*Mayibuye!*"[21]

When the excitement at last died down, he took a sheet of paper out of his pocket and reached for the microphone.

"Friends, comrades, and fellow South Africans. I greet you all in the name of peace, democracy, and freedom for all!" he declared. "I stand here before you not as a prophet but as a humble servant of you, the people. Your tireless and heroic sacrifices have made it possible for me to be here today. I therefore place the remaining years of my life in your hands."[22] But, he warned, "the sight of freedom looming on the horizon should encourage us to redouble our efforts." The climate conducive to a negotiated settlement, ending the need for the armed struggle, was in sight but had yet to be achieved.

The next day, his first press conference brought the black leader face-to-face with world opinion. It was a magnificent occasion for him to show the historic stature he had earned.

"What about the whites?" asked one journalist. "What role do they have in your vision of the new South Africa?"

---

20. *Amandla ngawethu!* The power, it is ours!
21. *iAfrika mayibuye!* Africa, may it return!
22. Mandela, *Long Walk to Freedom*, p. 555.

"That of essential participants," he responded unhesitatingly.

He explained that above all he did not want to destroy the country before freeing it. Driving the whites away would bring the nation to ruin. On the contrary, whites must feel safe. "We appreciate the contribution that they have made towards the development of this country," he affirmed. "We must do everything we can to persuade our white compatriots that a new, nonracial South Africa would be a better place for all."

A few hours later he flew in a helicopter over Soweto, a city he called the "Mother City of black urban South Africa" and the only home Mandela had ever known as a man before he went to prison. He scanned the overpopulated slums, the tin shanties, and the dirt roads teeming with people. He was amazed at how much Soweto had grown. Some areas looked prosperous with rather attractive little houses, but on the whole, the city looked even poorer to him than when he had lived there with his family in the small house at 8115 Orlando West. He looked for its roof in vain.

The helicopter was now circling over the ocean of different races filling the stands of Soweto's large stadium. How many were there for this first meeting of the black people with their icon? 150,000? 200,000? Mandela was worried. So many people were clinging to the roofs of the stands and to the streetlights, spilling from the aisles, staircases, and benches. The aircraft landed beside a stage that had been erected midfield and decorated with flags. As the tall figure in a navy blue suit and tie appeared, a storm of cheering and applause broke out. Mandela saluted them at length with his fist outstretched. Then he took the microphone and told them of his intense joy at being back among the Soweto community to which he was so proud to belong. At the same time, however, he could not conceal his sadness at seeing that his people still suffered from a lack of housing, from schools in crisis, from unemployment, and from crime. He opened his arms as if to embrace the whole stadium. Then slowly, solemnly, he declared that South Africa was now irrevocably on the road to a nonracial and united democracy, based on the sacred principle of one person, one vote. "It was the dream I cherished when I entered prison at the age of forty-four," he proclaimed.[23] It was the dream he had kept before him during the lonely years in prison, the dream he would work toward during the remaining years of his life, the dream for which he was still prepared to die.

★

THE CHANCE TO FULFILL a personal dream awaited Mandela that evening. As he entered the small house at 8115 Orlando West with Winnie, he suddenly felt that he had really left prison. Through all those years of incarceration that address had occupied the center of his imaginary world, "the place marked with an X in my mental geography."[24] In his mind it was the place of intimate reunion with his wife after twenty-seven years of separation. But when the moment of his release came, fate denied him both his dear little house and his beloved wife; 8115 Orlando West was no longer the refuge where he would recover the life he had as a young man, to do the things he had once done with his loved ones near him, the things he had missed most in prison and had promised himself he would enjoy once he was free. 8115 Orlando West could no longer be the family home he had dreamed of. It had become a shrine inhabited by crowds of devotees who filled it day and night with a deafening din of singing, shrieks of joy, drum-rolling and trumpeting. For the man who had once lived here was no longer a man like any other. He had become a myth. Mandela learned that the wife he had loved so much in this modest dwelling had built herself a luxurious residence a few streets away, where she lived in grand style surrounded by sycophants. The discovery shattered him. His associates pressed him to distance himself from the woman whose

---

23. Mandela, *Long Walk to Freedom*, p. 560.
24. Mandela, *Long Walk to Freedom*, p. 561.

increasingly scandalous reputation threatened to affect his image and political work. Winnie had even been involved in a murder accusation. Tensions had surfaced between them during the months prior to his release, but he had continued to believe steadfastly in the power of their love. Their moving emergence from the prison hand in hand; their enthusiastic salutes, side by side, fists raised; the joy radiating from their faces before the crowds in Cape Town and Soweto had been intended to express this conviction. Whatever rift had opened between them, Mandela remained convinced that they would be able to retie the threads of their love, frayed by long separation. He was mistaken. Winnie did not share his first night as a free man in the house he loved. She had another date elsewhere that night.

★

NELSON MANDELA FACED this adversity with a generosity that earned him the admiration of all. He took full responsibility for Winnie's indiscretions. He reproached himself for leaving her alone "in the hell of a pitiless desert." He was convinced he would carry his remorse to his dying day and was determined to remain at her side throughout the ordeals ahead of her. Just then the court in Johannesburg decided to try her for complicity in the murder of a young black killed by one of her bodyguards. The case dated back several months but the government was bringing it up again, determined to discredit the woman who had caused so much trouble during the ANC leader's years in prison. Mandela did not miss a single court session. He was so convinced of her innocence that he had prepared a declaration he planned to read to the court when she was acquitted. On May 14, 1991, however, the court found Winnie Mandela guilty and sentenced her to six years in prison. When the sentence was read, it was a broken man who slipped his sheet of paper into the bottom of his pocket. Winnie was entitled to an immediate appeal, and bail was set at three hundred rand, approximately one hundred dollars; and so she left the courtroom a free woman.

However, Winnie's complicity in murder was the last straw for Mandela. In April 1992 the couple whom South African blacks called "Father" and "Mother" met before an array of journalists, photographers, microphones, and television cameras to announce their separation. It was an opportunity for the black leader to pay a touching tribute to the woman he had loved so much. "During the two decades I spent on Robben Island she was an indispensable pillar of support and comfort," he said of Winnie. "She endured the persecutions heaped upon her by the government with exemplary fortitude and never wavered from her commitment to the freedom struggle. Her tenacity reinforced my personal respect, love, and growing affection." He took her hand, triggering a fireworks display of camera flashes. He went on: "I shall personally never regret the life Comrade Nomzamo and I tried to share together. Circumstances beyond our control, however, dictated it should be otherwise. . . . I embrace her with all the love and affection I have nursed for her inside and outside prison from the moment I first met her. Ladies and gentlemen, I hope you will appreciate the pain I have gone through."[25]

All eyes then turned to Winnie. What would she say? She raised her husband's hand to her lips and kissed it. Then softly she murmured, "Good-bye and good luck, my love."

★

FOR TWO CENTURIES the splendid manor house hidden in the shrubbery of the Groote Schuur estate had been the residence of the British governors of the Cape Province. Now in May 1990, its sitting rooms paneled with precious woods were receiving the protagonists who would decide the future of South Africa. Around Nelson Mandela and his faithful companion, Walter Sisulu, huddled the principal leaders of the ANC and the antiapartheid resistance. Their host, President F. W. de Klerk, was ac-

---

25. Mandela, *Long Walk to Freedom*, p. 591.

companied by numerous members of his government. The meeting was historic: it marked the end of the master-slave relationship that had characterized relations between whites and blacks in South Africa for nearly four centuries. "We had come to the meeting not as suppliants or petitioners," Mandela was to say, "but as fellow South Africans who merited an equal place at the table."[26] Despite forecasts of gloom, the conference began in an atmosphere of cordiality. It was extraordinary to see the apartheid leaders shaking hands with the enemy they had demonized for decades. As Thabo Mbeki, who one day would be president of South Africa, would say, "Each side had discovered that the other did not have horns." The purpose of these preliminary talks was to draw up a list of the various subjects of disagreement between whites and blacks that would become the focus of specific negotiations. There were enough of them, heaven knew: the official abolition of apartheid, the lifting of the state of emergency, the return of exiles, the release of political prisoners, the withdrawal of troops from the townships, the end of the ANC's armed struggle, the removal of international sanctions, the means of putting an end to violence, and above all else, the creation of a new political system to govern the South Africa of tomorrow: these were just a sampling of the innumerable issues. During the three days of discussions, generously lubricated with the estate's superior wine, each side got to know the other and agreed on an agenda for a peace conference.

But in politics as in life, there is no birth without pain. Hardly had the conferees parted when a series of massacres once more drenched the country in blood. The instigators of this new tragedy were mostly blacks belonging to a legendarily warlike tribe. Zulu hostility had haunted the collective memory of whites ever since 1838, when unarmed Boers who had come to negotiate the purchase of land from the Zulu sovereign were killed; a few days later the Zulus then massacred a thousand Voortrekkers,

---

26. Mandela, *Long Walk to Freedom*, p. 592.

including five hundred women and children. The Afrikaners had memorialized the place of that brutal killing, known as Weenen, *"The valley of tears."* Hundreds of British soldiers had subsequently perished in a war with the Zulus, after which the fierce warriors seemed to settle down.

The Zulus had laid down their spears in farmland in the northeast of the country. There, one century later, a chief of royal blood, Mangosuthu Buthelezi, gathered them into a powerful nation under the aegis of Inkatha, a popular nationalist movement named after the sacred ring that was the Zulu people's emblem of unity. Buthelezi had a reputation as a clever pragmatist. He appeared docile toward the Pretoria government while condemning apartheid and claimed to be a friend of Mandela while denouncing the ANC's armed struggle, an ambiguous position that he believed would guarantee him an influential role at the negotiating table. His dream was to walk away with an independent state for his 5 million Zulus. To achieve it, he thought it would be best to make his voice heard first—in Zulu fashion, of course.

The campaign of violence that followed in 1990 exceeded in horror anything that South Africa had experienced at the hands of the freedom fighters. Zulu commandos invaded villages reputed to support the ANC, decapitated many inhabitants, forced thousands to flee, and set fire to farms and houses. In the townships near factories and mines, Zulu workers emerged from their miserable hostels and slit the throats of workers from other tribes or burned them alive with flaming "necklace" tires. Killers boarded trains to sow terror. Between Soweto and Johannesburg, between Jeppe and Benrose several dozen passengers had their throats cut and hundreds were wounded. On July 22, 1990, hordes of Zulus in buses streamed into the township of Sebokeng. They were escorted by police cars belonging to the white government, confirming Mandela's fears that Buthelezi and de Klerk were probably in collusion. Their alliance would after all give the Afrikaner head of government the support of 5 million Zulus to tip the outcome of the negotiations in his favor. For the

Zulus, allegiance to Pretoria would increase their chances of having an independent state. Now they were in the streets of Sebokeng wreaking carnage under the impassive eyes of the white police. They decapitated dozens of inhabitants with their spears and cut off the breasts of many women. Mandela rushed to the area and then hurried to Durban to address a hundred thousand Zulus gathered in the King's Park soccer field. "Throw your assegais and machetes into the sea!" he begged them. "Put down your knobkerries! We are all brothers. Let us shake hands and make peace!"

But the voice of the Father of the Nation failed to resonate as the slaughter continued. Mandela's fears intensified when he learned that a white militia made up of police renegades and officers belonging to extreme right-wing parties were joining in the massacres alongside the Zulus. He protested vehemently against this treachery, but all he received from Pretoria was a surprising decree authorizing the Zulus to carry their traditional weapons, whether spears or knobkerries, at all meetings.

Convinced that this campaign of terror would deal a fatal blow to the peace process, Mandela made a secret visit to F. W. de Klerk. The man he met one-on-one seemed very different from the man who had taken part in the initial negotiations held in Cape Town's colonial residence. He realized that for all his protestations of goodwill de Klerk was not the emancipator he had hoped to count on. He was a prudent pragmatist who was willing to introduce reforms as long as he stayed in control. The ANC leader renewed his pleas for a British-style majority parliamentary system in which the winner would exercise power. But he realized that de Klerk was not prepared to negotiate the end of rule by the white minority unless that minority had the right to veto decisions made by the black majority. "In short you want a new form of apartheid under a different guise!" Mandela exclaimed before adding, at the end of his patience, "in any case, how dare you talk of negotiations when you are letting our people be massacred!"

That same evening, in a brief statement relating his disappointing encounter with the head of government, the black leader announced his decision to suspend peace talks with de Klerk.

★

PEACE! DESPITE THE WIND OF CHANGE that had been blowing from the heights of Pretoria since F. W. de Klerk's assumption of power, apartheid continued across the country. On the Cape peninsula, for example, the forced removal of black and colored people, begun fourteen years earlier with the destruction of District Six, was still going on. The squatter camps that sheltered thousands of black families prohibited from living in Cape Town or any of the region's towns that had been declared white were the government bulldozers' most consistent targets. The largest of these camps was situated a few miles from the township of Langa where Helen Lieberman went to work every day. Because of its position at the intersection of two roads, it was called Crossroads. Tin shacks were heaped together, most without doors or windows and almost always without running water, electricity, and sanitation. Several thousand poor people were living in these wretched conditions, forced to defy the Illegal Squatting Act, the terrible law that gave the authorities the right to destroy any construction without prior notice if the occupant failed to produce a deed of ownership. A surreal requirement in a country where no citizen of color had the right to own one single square yard of land outside a few authorized townships and homelands.

At dawn one morning as she was on her way to Langa, Helen came upon a large-scale eviction operation under way at Crossroads. To speed the squatters' departure the police had set fire to the slum. Surprised in their sleep, most of the occupants fled screaming, taking nothing with them. Others managed to save a few clothes and other belongings from the blaze. Terrified children ran about the flames. Helen rushed to help the injured; the fire was taking a heavy toll. Suddenly in the turmoil Helen recognized the fiftyish man with a scarred face who delivered her milk every morning in the Sea Point area. His name was Cuma. Thanks to her, he had obtained the pass that allowed him to work for six hours a day in a white area. The poor man was distraught. His shack was burning and his wife and children had disappeared.

Helen tried to talk the police into letting her go and look for the milkman's family. Unaccustomed to a white woman intervening on behalf of blacks, the police hesitated. At that moment the officer from the nearby Langa police station appeared on the scene with several men. He had known Helen for years. After threatening her many times over the years, he had been converted to the merits of her work and since then he and the men at his station had protected her.

"Let her go," he ordered. "That woman does a lot of good."

Scouring the ruins of the camp, Helen eventually found Cuma's family taking refuge in the cemetery. She took the woman and children to her black friend, having made up her mind to rescue all four of them. That evening as soon as it was dark she would come back and then drive them to her home in Sea Point, where she would secretly house them in her garage. In that way the milkman and his family, unlike their neighbors, would not be deported to a camp in the Transvaal.

At the appointed hour Helen came back with some friends and several vehicles. Some thirty survivors of the fire would make it into the cars discreetly parked outside the ruins of the slum. It was a high-risk rescue operation. To smuggle thirty blacks into the middle of a white city and keep them hidden there contravened the most sacred principles of racial segregation. Helen and her husband could be denounced for the slightest infraction. They risked years of imprisonment for "betraying their race."

Helen had taken Michael's three BMWs out of the garage and converted the large space into a reception center hastily equipped with mattresses, cupboards stocked with food and clothing, cooking utensils, and a stove. She had even thought to set up a television to make their confinement more bearable, especially for the young ones. But it was an ordinary wall mirror that stirred the curiosity and then the enthusiasm of the refugees. "When they had all found somewhere to sleep, I wished them a good night and slipped away," Helen was to recount. "After a while I went and looked through the garage window to make sure everything was all right. I shall never forget the sight of all those blacks congregated in front of the mirror, suddenly seeing their image for the first time. Children were hopping from one foot to the other, pulling face in front of the glass. Mesmerized by the images the magic piece of glass was reflecting back at them, young women were running their hands over their faces, stroking their foreheads, cheeks, and necks. Others suddenly became touchingly flirtatious, smoothing their hair and adjusting their scarves. Yet others just laughed as they looked at themselves. I was deeply moved: an oppressed people, a people forced for so long to live like animals, a crushed people, . . . suddenly discovering its face, the face of men, women, and children created by the hand of God."

Helen hid her protégés for four weeks, the time it took for her companions in Ikamva Labantu, the development organization she had founded in the township of Langa, to find them a safe and certain refuge. This rescue operation was one of her finest successes.

★

1990 TO 1994. It would take South Africa four long years to emerge from the hell of apartheid and forge its future: four years of negotiating, deal making, and haggling that began with the release of Mandela but that were thwarted by fierce local antagonisms. "Four years of Russian mountains," as Archbishop Desmond Tutu was to remark humorously.[27] Although the principal participants—Nelson Mandela and F. W. de Klerk—finally man-

---

27. Corinne Moutout, *Défi sud-africain—De l'apartheid à la démocratie: Un miracle fragile,* Série monde HS no. 99 (Paris: Éditions Autrement, 1997).

aged to agree on a plan for nonracial national elections on the basis of one citizen, one vote, and on a vision of a democratic state based on a parliamentary constitution, the same was not true of the numerous factions tearing the country apart. De Klerk was attacked on one side by white extremists who accused him of selling out South Africa to the demands of the blacks, and pressured on the other side by his black negotiating partners who demanded that apartheid be swept once and for all into the dustbin of history. In March 1992, de Klerk decided to make a decisive move. If it failed he would resign. He called for an all-whites referendum to determine whether they would accept the end of apartheid and the continuation of negotiations. On March 17, 1992, over 88 percent of all white voters went to the polls. The yes vote won with an overwhelming 68.73 percent support. F. W. de Klerk had dealt a fatal blow to the extreme white right and strengthened his position in relation to his black negotiating partners. "This is the most crucial time in our history," he declared.

True, in parts of the country there was still bloodshed. In a last-ditch attempt to fly his ersatz swastika over an independent and sovereign Volksraad, the right-wing extremist Eugene Terre'Blanche tried to spark a civil war by arranging the murder of one of the most popular figures in the antiapartheid movement, communist Chris Hani, friend and confidant of Mandela. The Zulus for their part were determined to win themselves an autonomous state and continued to slaughter entire villages. Their militias even invaded the center of Johannesburg, leaving its streets and squares strewn with atrociously mutilated bodies. But the march of progress could no longer be stopped.

On June 3, 1993, negotiators from the two sides reached a historic decision 341 years, one month, and nineteen days after Jan van Riebeeck landed on the Cape to point his wagons of white Voortrekkers toward the heart of austral Africa: they set April 27, 1994, as the date for the first South African general election. There would be 20 million voters and 10,000 polling stations. For blacks and coloreds it would be a magical day, the first time they would go to the polls to choose the leaders of their country.

★

NATURALLY, THE PRIME MOVER of the feverish electoral campaign throughout South Africa was the former Robben Island prisoner. For years in the solitude of his cell or the blinding light of the prison's stone quarry, Mandela had imagined, prepared for, and idealized the moment when all South Africans would be free to decide their destiny and that of their children. As the time approached for that long-awaited freedom he took pains to keep things from getting out of hand. He had the ANC draw up a document entitled *A Better Life for All,* informing every voter what the advent of democracy would mean. "Life will not change dramatically," warned Mandela, "except that you will have increased your self-esteem and become a citizen in your own land. You must have patience."[28]

The man who had endured relentless punishment from whites for twenty-seven years also had something to say to his persecutors, displaying a magnanimity, a greatness of soul, and an intelligence that would guarantee him a place apart in the pantheon of politicians. To be sure, when he addressed whites he did not mince words about the horrors of apartheid. But it was a message of realism for the future he wanted to convey to them. "We do not want you to leave the country," he insisted on numerous occasions. "We need you. You are South Africans, just like us, and this is your land, too."[29] He wanted to be a prophet of reconciliation. "We must forget the past and concentrate on building a better future for everyone." To guarantee that future, he had secret meetings with the nation's principal economic leaders and assured them that the new South Africa would respect the liberal model in place.

---

28. Mandela, *Long Walk to Freedom,* p. 605.
29. Mandela, *Long Walk to Freedom,* p. 606.

It was in a television debate with F. W. de Klerk ten days before the election that the black leader would show the full nobility of his nature. He knew he was a good debater. On Robben Island he had had plenty of opportunities to hone his skills with his comrades while they chipped at the limestone blocks in the quarry. But on the eve of this crucial encounter with the white people's chief representative, he suddenly felt uneasy. So he arranged for a rehearsal with a well-known journalist playing the role of his adversary. This test run was not encouraging. His campaign advisers took him to task for speaking too slowly and not being aggressive enough. Mandela's interminable incarceration had aftereffects that sometimes caught up with him, as did his cancer operation and, above all, his painful separation from Winnie. Though he wore them lightly, his seventy-six years had slowed him down, left him with a stoop, and written furrows across his handsome face. But none of it mattered on the day of his debate with de Klerk; he showed his claws and pounced on his opponent like a beast upon his prey. He started out by accusing de Klerk and his party of inciting racial hatred, lying about ANC intentions, and sowing discord. De Klerk, unfazed, energetically defended himself. Near the end of the debate, however, Mandela suddenly felt that he had been too hard on the man who, the day after the elections, would share responsibility with him for leading a government of national unity. He made amends honorably: "The exchanges between Mr. de Klerk and me should not obscure one important fact," he declared. "I think we are a shining example to the entire world of people drawn from different racial groups who have a common loyalty, a common love, to their common country. Sir, you are one of those I rely upon. We are going to face the problems of this country together." With these words he stood and reached over to take the white leader's hand. "I am proud to hold your hand for us to go forward."[30] The

---

30. Mandela, *Long Walk to Freedom,* p. 609.

head of government could not conceal his emotion. As in the previous year in Oslo, when they had jointly received the Nobel Prize for Peace, the two men warmly embraced.

★

NEVER HAD A PEOPLE endured so many obstacles on the path to making their voices heard. How many people, after being starved of democracy, would show up at ballot boxes on April 27, 1994? Twenty, twenty-one million, perhaps more? The exact geographical distribution of the population, the vast majority of whom had never set foot in a polling station, was unknown. Apart from the infamous little green or red passbooks that they were obliged to carry, black South Africans had no identity papers. Many were illiterate. It would take prodigious effort to get them to the ballot boxes that signified so much: from inscribing their finger with indelible ink to prevent them from voting more than once, to finding and bringing to the boxes those whom centuries of underdevelopment had exiled to remote areas deprived of all means of communication.

Fortunately the violence had almost ceased. The Zulu chief Buthelezi had eventually given in to the pleas of Nelson Mandela and F. W. de Klerk, and his followers agreed to take part in the election. To organize operations on the ground, Pretoria had transformed its 200,000 guardians of apartheid into an army of electoral agents. Distributing 30 million ballots to 10,000 offices, many of them huts along the dusty roadsides of the Karoo and the Kalahari, was an achievement only a few white fanatics living in the Cape refused to acknowledge. Instead, they looked in their Bibles for consolation and asked Isaiah if Yahweh was still leading them to the land he had promised his chosen people. Others turned to the book of Revelation, as their ancestors in the wagons had done, to find out whether they were still a "new people walking to a new heaven and new earth." In the absence of immediate reassurance, all those who feared that a black government was the beginning of the end of the world decided to take precautions. They rushed to the food and candle stores and emptied the shelves.

★

IT WAS THE DAWN of the world's first morning that broke over South Africa on April 27, 1994. The Africa of the white heroes and the black heroes of four centuries of tumultuous history. The Africa of Jan van Riebeeck, of Paul Kruger, Cecil Rhodes, Andries Pretorius, Oliver Tambo, Daniel François Malan, Hendrik Verwoerd, Helen Lieberman, Steve Biko, Chris Barnard, Nelson Mandela; the Africa of the Dutch East India Company lettuce planters, the Voortrekkers, King Shaka's Zulus, the Khoikhoi cattle traders, the Xhosa diamond diggers, the brave ANC combatants, the slave laborers in the gold mines, the inventors of apartheid, and the Robben Island convicts; the multiracial, multifaith Africa that God and man had created in one of the most beautiful places on earth, so that its people could perform the sacred act of making their voices heard through the ballot.

From first light they came by the millions to live the most unforgettable day of their lives. Endless processions covered the whole country, snaking their way to the polling stations—whites, blacks, coloreds, and Asians mixing together under the unrelenting sun of the Transvaal, Natal, and the Orange Free State, or in the torrential rain of the Cape peninsula. People waited in line together. Doctors, lawyers, laborers, farmworkers, domestics and the ladies who employed them, all formed single lines moving slowly toward the booths. It was the first time they had rubbed elbows. They swapped newspapers, shared sandwiches and umbrellas. In the crowd in Sharpeville, the township in the Transvaal so horribly afflicted by apartheid, an old woman of ninety-three named Miriam Mqomboti gratefully proclaimed her happiness. "I came from the Transkei when I was eighteen," she said. "I never thought I would see this day."

Outside the polling station in Gugulethu, a township on the outskirts of Cape Town, a little man in a purple cassock stood waiting in line. Archbishop Desmond Tutu wanted to vote with the rest of his people. As he put a ballot slip into the box, they all heard him utter a triumphant "Yippee!" "I felt completely light-headed," he was to say. "It was like falling in love. The sky seemed bluer and more beautiful. I saw people in a different light. They were beautiful, transfigured."[31] But fear suddenly gripped the Nobel laureate. He was afraid someone would come and shake him, bring him back to a different reality, to the nightmare that apartheid had been for him and millions of his compatriots. He heard a man next to him say to his wife, "Darling, don't wake me up. I like this dream too much!"

When he came out of the polling station, Archbishop Tutu saw people dancing, singing, and shouting for joy. "You would have thought it was a festival," he said later. Finally they felt like they existed—all those who had borne the burden and the violence of repression, all those humble people whom apartheid had made into anonymous faceless, voiceless nonentities in their own country, all those people who every day had been trampled lower than the earth.

★

A POLLING STATION AT THE OTHER end of the country was the place where Nelson Mandela chose to seal the triumph of his long freedom struggle. Ohlange School in Inanda, a small town in Natal, just north of Durban, had been built next to the grave of his greatest inspiration in the battle against white oppression. Reverend John Dube had been one of the founders of the African National Congress in 1912 before becoming its first president. Mandela had long drawn inspiration from this pioneer of the black nonviolent struggle for civil rights. By casting his vote that April day close to the place where Dube lay buried, he felt as if he were completing the cycle of history begun eighty-two years before by one of the principal driving forces of his life.

---

31. Desmond Mpilo Tutu, *No Future Without Forgiveness* (New York: Doubleday, 1999), p. 12.

As he entered the classroom, he thought, too, of other heroes who had sacrificed themselves so that his people might at last make their voices heard. He thought of the companions he had lost: Oliver Tambo, Chris Hani, Steve Biko, and many others. He was not entering the polling station alone. They were all there with him. When he got to the ballot box, he was surprised to find someone dear to him waiting with outstretched arms: Zaziwe, the little girl he had christened "Hope" sixteen years before in Robben Island's gloomy visitors' room, because for him she embodied the dream of a new generation of South Africans to whom apartheid would soon be no more than a distant nightmare. Zaziwe-Hope was now an attractive teenager with her mother's determined expression. She had come to pay homage to her grandfather on this solemn occasion on behalf of the young Africans for whom he had struggled so long. Moved to tears, the old man hugged her close. What happiness to perform this final act of his struggle with this bright symbol of a new South Africa near him. Carefully he marked a cross next to the three letters ANC on his ballot. Then, respectfully, he dropped the slip of paper into the simple wooden ballot box. It was half past twelve on April 27, 1994. Everyone in the line heard him explode with happiness.

"I have cast the first vote of my life!" he announced jubilantly.

★

OF THE 10,000 POLLING STATIONS scattered across the immense country, none symbolized what that glorious day stood for better than Sam's School, the tin hut in Langa township named after the young black burned alive by apartheid thugs. It had been repainted white and decorated with palm branches to welcome its voters in style. Vusi, the former drug dealer Helen Lieberman converted to working in the development organization, commanded the entrance with drum rolls that shook the neighborhood. Behind the ballot box stood a big fellow of about twenty in jeans and a pink shirt. He welcomed the voters, registered their names, and handed out the ballots. Everyone in Langa knew

him. He was one of the organizers of the Ikamva Labantu association. His name was Andile. One night, nineteen years earlier,
Helen Lieberman had saved his life by taking him from his
grandmother's arms and bringing him back to Groote Schuur
hospital for the lifesaving intravenous fluids he needed.

All at once Vusi's drum beats went wild. Mama Helen had
just arrived accompanied by Cuma, the milkman. Andile and the
neighborhood's residents immediately scrambled to form a line
of honor outside the school. It was here, among the people
whose poverty she had fought so hard to redress, that the woman
who had founded Ikamva Labantu—The Future of Our Nation—
had chosen to cast her vote for the new South Africa. A white
woman among blacks. One people. A rainbow nation.

EPILOGUE

AMANDLA NGAWETHU! POWER TO THE PEOPLE! The famous slogan was no longer a call for hope. It had become reality. With 62.65 percent of the vote, Nelson Mandela's ANC party won 252 of the 400 seats in the rainbow nation's first Democratic Assembly. F. W. de Klerk and his party of white supremacists received only 20.4 percent of the vote and eighty-two parliamentary seats. As for the Zulu-dominated Inkatha Freedom Party, 10 percent of the vote gave them forty-three members to make their presence felt in the splendid Corinthian-columned parliament in Cape Town.

Four days after the results were announced, on May 2, 1994, the last president of the apartheid era stood before radio microphones and television cameras to acknowledge his defeat and congratulate the winner. In a voice that was firm and resonant but charged with emotion, F. W. de Klerk declared his readiness to collaborate with Nelson Mandela in the first national unity government of the new South Africa. But he also had a warning for the black leader. He had walked a long way and reached the mountaintop, de Klerk said. But he could not stop and gaze at the landscape because beyond that mountain was another, and after that, yet another. His journey would never be over. Then with the same compelling gaze that had disarmed Mandela when they first met, the white leader fixed on the cameras directed at him. His 5 million white compatriots and a huge number of blacks had to be following this rendezvous with history with bated breath and constricted throats. Three and a half centuries after the first white man landed on the tip of Africa, a descendant of Calvin's followers was about to rally his race to the victorious black cause.

F. W. de Klerk did it with grace, saying that he would shake Mandela's hand like a brother in a spirit of sincere cooperation.

Apocalyptic predictions made on the eve of the elections were proven wrong. South Africa took its first steps as a free, politically united nation. After so many years of subjugation to the dogma of segregation it said no to division. "F. W. de Klerk's words were so beautiful that I had to pinch myself to believe them," said Archbishop Desmond Tutu.

Eight days later, on May 10, before assembled heads of state from all over the world, Nelson Mandela was invested as the first democratically elected president of a united South Africa. The ceremony took place in the magnificent sandstone amphitheater of the Union Buildings in Pretoria, for five decades the seat of white supremacy. His daughter Zenani was with him. First to step onto the podium, F. W. de Klerk and Thabo Mbeki were sworn in as deputy presidents. Mandela then had the floor. His speech sent a wave of emotion through the audience. "Today, all of us do, by our presence here, confer glory and hope to newborn liberty," declared the former Robben Island prisoner. "Out of the experience of an extraordinary human disaster that lasted too long, must be born a society of which all humanity will be proud. . . . We, who were outlaws not so long ago, have today been given the rare privilege to be host to the nations of the world on our own soil. We thank all our distinguished international guests for having come to take possession with the people of our country of what is, after all, a common victory for justice, for peace, for human dignity."[1]

After pledging to liberate all South Africans from the bondage of poverty, deprivation, sexism, and all other forms of discrimination, he called on his audience to bear witness: "Never, never, and never again shall it be that this beautiful land will again experience the oppression of one by another." Telling them

---

1. Mandela, *Long Walk to Freedom*.

that the sun would never set on so glorious a human achievement, he concluded with arms outstretched to the mass of deeply moved faces, "Let freedom reign. God bless Africa!"

★

GOD BLESS AFRICA! No invocation could have been more timely in that luminous austral autumn. After being "overwhelmed with a sense of history" during his inauguration, the first black president had to come back down to earth and face the realities hidden among the mountains to which F. W. de Klerk had referred. The first and probably the most alarming was the terrifying degree of crime threatening the safety of everyone—blacks as well as whites. In that first year of democracy, homicides, armed assault, rape, and burglary almost doubled. From the border with Zimbabwe to the shores of the Cape a murder was committed every half hour, a rape every three minutes, and a burglary every two minutes. This perilous situation was largely the result of years of diversion of police resources. Throughout the apartheid era, the forces of law and order had made their antiterrorist campaign a greater priority than arresting common criminals. Spending the night chasing couples suspected of breaking the law against interracial sexual relations had been more important than tracking down real criminals.

Under the second mountain lurked the devastating unemployment affecting 40 percent of the black population. Mandela had been right to appeal to those who elected him to "have patience." Three million homes, 20,000 schools, 3,000 hospitals, 187,000 miles of electric cables and almost as many pipes for drinking water were needed. Members of the first black South African government who had spent most of their life in prison or exile would have difficulty tackling these priorities. The culture of civil disobedience in which the black population had been steeped during the apartheid era would not make their task any easier. It had been a long time since millions of South Africans had paid their taxes, rent, or electricity bills.

The biggest challenge, however, was not an economic one but a moral one. "All South Africans must now unite," Mandela had stated on the evening of the election. He himself set the example with a magnanimity that won him the world's admiration. The day after his election, he had gone to Orania to see the widow of Hendrik Verwoerd, his distant predecessor who had conceived South African racial segregation along the lines of Nazi ideology. As a gesture of reconciliation, he then invited the widows of all the other apartheid heads of government to come for tea at the presidential residence with the wives of all the political prisoners from block 3 on Robben Island. Better yet, he had invited to his inauguration ceremony two representatives of the apartheid legal system who had condemned him to end his days in prison: the prosecutor Percy Yutar, whose hissing voice and theatrical rhetoric had sent so many blacks to their deaths, and Judge Quartus de Wet, who had averted his gaze as he pronounced his terrible sentence of life imprisonment. Noble and generous as they were, these gestures could not quell the desire for vengeance felt by many who had suffered racial oppression. Urgently seeking a way to prevent the country from turning into a bloodbath, he turned to one of the most emblematic survivors of white terror. Instead of instituting judicial proceedings to judge the guilty as the Nuremberg trials had done for the Nazi war criminals, Archbishop Desmond Tutu came up with an extraordinary suggestion: create a commission that would grant a pardon to all those willing to reveal the crimes they had committed in the name of apartheid. This revolutionary gamble was to be called the Truth and Reconciliation Commission. It was an idea that Nelson Mandela accepted enthusiastically.

Over seven thousand agreed to cooperate and register their request for amnesty. Among them were two former ministers in P.W. Botha's government and numerous senior police officers. The hearings went on for four years. Twenty-four hundred victims came to testify in front of their tormenters on behalf of people close to them who had disappeared. Their testimony showed how a people claiming to have been chosen by God to spread Christianity in Africa had sunk to committing savage acts of barbarism. Some confessions were so unbearable that they traumatized those charged with recording them. The task was particularly demanding for the interpreters because they had to translate the victims' accounts as well as those of the guilty parties, and express them in the first person. Thanks to this grueling process, light was shed on countless crimes, which enabled numerous families to trace those who had disappeared and start to come to terms with what had happened. By the time this unique experience, broadcast every day on television, came to an end, no South African, and no white person in particular, could claim that they did not know how apartheid had broken and destroyed millions of lives. Just as Archbishop Tutu had hoped, however, public acknowledgment of racist crimes brought with it the seeds of reconciliation. The specter of another racial war vanished from the South African landscape.

By exchanging Truth for Reconciliation, South Africa miraculously emerged from apartheid without the predicted bloodbath. An exemplary peaceful transition took the country from repression and injustice to democracy, freedom, and equality, an unparalleled achievement in the history of human conflict and an exceptional lesson in humanity for the whole planet. Now the country of Jan van Riebeeck and Nelson Mandela needed to develop a system of values that would make it a nation of brothers, proud of its diversity. The former occupant of Robben Island's cell 466-64 would be at the helm, trying to work a second miracle and keep his promise to build a rainbow nation capable of bringing forth a biblical "new earth."

Appendixes

WHAT
THEY BECAME

Nelson Mandela did not seek a second presidential mandate, and in 1999 he withdrew from political life. To go on fighting for the values dear to his heart, he set up the Nelson Mandela Foundation, which is now committed, among other targets, to combating AIDS, a disease rife in South Africa. His son Makgatho died of it at the age of fifty-four.

Nelson Mandela now lives in Johannesburg with his third wife, Graça Machel, widow of the former president of Mozambique.

At the age of ninety-one (on July 18, 2009), the elderly black leader remains one of the world's most admired figures.

Winnie Mandela, despite her problems with the law, became deputy minister of arts, culture, science, and technology in the first postapartheid government. She was forced to resign following allegations of corruption but retained her popularity with the radical base of the ANC.

In December 1997, she was obliged to withdraw her candidacy for the vice presidency of the ANC after fresh revelations about her involvement in the murder of the young boy suspected by members of her Mandela United Football Team of being a police informant.

On April 24, 2003, the woman known to her followers as "mother of the nation" was found guilty by the South African court on forty-three counts of fraudulent bank loans and theft. She was sentenced to five years imprisonment, with the recommendation that she serve eight months. On appeal the High Court overturned the conviction for theft in July 2004 but upheld the one for fraud, for which she was given a suspended sentence of three years and six months in prison.

Winnie Mandela continues to be involved in the political life of South Africa.

Frederik de Klerk retired from the deputy presidency of the first postapartheid government on June 30, 1996. In September of the following year he handed over the leadership of the National Party and withdrew from political life to live on his farm near Paarl with his new wife, Elita.

On December 3, 2001, Marike, his first wife, was murdered at her Cape Town home, making her a symbol of the crime epidemic afflicting the country.

In 2005 Frederik de Klerk emerged from retirement to publicly denounce the ANC's betrayal of its promises to respect the country's minorities.

In June 2006 the Nobel laureate underwent surgery for cancer.

Archbishop Desmond Tutu. After four years of inquiries and thousands of hearings, the Truth and Reconciliation Commission presided over by Archbishop Desmond Tutu submitted its conclusions in 1997. They provoked enormous interest in the world at large.

In 1999 the archbishop founded the Desmond Tutu Peace Foundation to nurture peace by promoting ethical human development based on the values of reconciliation.

In 2007 he became one of the founding members of The Elders, a group of world leaders who use their wisdom, impartial leadership, and integrity to tackle some of the most serious problems confronting the international community.

Archbishop Desmond Tutu is an ardent campaigner for the creation of a Palestinian state alongside Israel.

Helen Lieberman, a former speech therapist from Cape Town's fashionable Sea Point area, is still serving the disinherited of

South Africa. She is constantly invited to give talks in numerous countries where her work finds committed support.

Helen Lieberman is one of the people for whom the author of this book feels intense admiration, both because of what she achieved under the apartheid regime and because of what she is continuing to do through the Ikamva Labantu organization she founded in the late 1960s. In this connection, see Katharine Rhodes Henderson, *God's Troublemakers: How Women of Faith Are Changing the World*, and www.ikamva.com.

Christiaan Barnard, M.D., did much to redeem the lost honor of apartheid Afrikaners by performing the world's first heart transplant. He continued his spectacular operations until arthritis prevented him from holding a scalpel. His second heart transplant patient, the dentist Philip Blaiberg, survived for nineteen months. Two of Christiaan Barnard's other patients survived for twelve and twenty-three years respectively.

Barnard married three times and had six children, and died at the age of seventy-eight. The recipient of some one hundred international distinctions, who numbered among his friends Princess Diana and Princess Grace, actresses Sophia Loren and Gina Lollobrigida, Mohammed Ali and Pope Paul VI, Barnard ended his prodigious career as proprietor of one of Cape Town's best-known restaurants. In 2001 his ashes were scattered in a rose garden in the small town of Beaufort West where he grew up. His tombstone bears a simple inscription, "I have returned home," in English and Afrikaans.

Wouter Basson, M.D., was accused of devising poisoned umbrellas, thallium-laced beer, mercury-laced chocolates, and other unconventional weapons to be used against blacks. He refused to appear before the Truth and Reconciliation Commission. Still free when the apartheid era came to an end, he was finally arrested in 1997 in the course of a drug sting. It was as a free defendant that he appeared before a tribunal for the longest and most expensive trial in postapartheid South Africa, involving two and a half years of hearings, sixty-seven charges, inquiries in twenty-seven countries, 153 prosecution witnesses, and eleven hundred pages of reasons adduced. The court, presided over by a white judge whose career on the bench had begun in the apartheid era, finally acquitted Basson on the grounds of "insufficient evidence," a verdict that provoked national indignation.

Wouter Basson is now living in Pretoria, where he has resumed his former profession as a cardiologist.

THIS WAS APARTHEID

THE FOLLOWING EXCERPTS are taken from Leslie Rubin, *This Is Apartheid* (London: Gollancz, 1959). Rubin wrote this pamphlet as she represented the Africans of the Cape Province (excluding the Transkei) in the Senate. Shown below are a few samples of the seventeen hundred laws and measures instituted by apartheid legislators to guarantee the racial separation of white, black, and colored people living in South Africa.

I. To Establish Total Racial Segregation
Between Whites and Blacks

1. It is unlawful for a white person and a non-white person to sit down to a cup of tea together in a tea room in a town anywhere in South Africa, unless they have obtained a special permit to do so.

2. Unless he has obtained a special permit, an African professor delivering a lecture at a White Club, which has invited him to do so, commits a criminal offence.

3. If an Indian (or a Coloured or an African) sits on a bench in a public park, the bench being set apart for the exclusive use of white persons, by way of protest against the apartheid laws, he commits a criminal offence and is liable to a fine not exceeding three hundred pounds, or to imprisonment for a period not exceeding three years, or to a whipping not exceeding ten strokes, or to both such fine and such imprisonment, or to both such fine and such whipping, or to both such imprisonment and such whipping.

4. If a speaker, while addressing a meeting, says something which causes a Coloured (or African or Indian) member of his audience to use a counter in the post office reserved for the

exclusive use of white persons, by way of protest against the apartheid laws, such speaker commits a criminal offence and is liable to a fine not exceeding five hundred pounds or to imprisonment for a period not exceeding five years or to a whipping not exceeding ten strokes or to both such fine and such imprisonment, or to both such fine and such whipping or to both such imprisonment and such whipping; and in the case of a second or subsequent conviction, the Court may not impose only a fine but is obliged to sentence him to imprisonment or to a whipping.

5. If there is only one waiting-room on a railway station, it is lawful for the station master to reserve that waiting-room for the exclusive use of white persons, and any non-white person wilfully entering it commits a criminal offence and is liable to a fine not exceeding fifty pounds or to imprisonment for a period not exceeding three months or to both such fine and such imprisonment.

II. To Restrict the Black Population of South Africa by Every Possible Means

1. No African is entitled as of right to acquire freehold title to land anywhere in South Africa, nor is it the intention of the present Government ever to grant such right to the African, even in his own Reserves.

2. No African, lawfully residing in a town by virtue of a permit issued to him, is entitled, as of right, to have his wife and children residing with him.

3. If an African was born in a town, has lived there continuously for fourteen years, and has, during that period, worked continuously for one employer for nine years, neither his wife, his unmarried daughter or his son aged eighteen (although each is completely dependent upon him) is entitled, as of right, to live with him for more than seventy-two hours.

4. An African who has, since birth, resided continuously in a town is not entitled, as of right, to have living with him in that town for more than seventy-two hours, a married daughter, a son who has reached the age of eighteen, a niece, a nephew or a grandchild.

5. It is unlawful for an African worker to take part in a strike. If he does so he is liable, on conviction, to a fine not exceeding five hundred pounds, imprisonment for a period not exceeding three years, or both such fine and imprisonment.

III. To Institute a Police State with Complete Power
over the Black Community

1. A Group Areas inspector may, for the purpose of ascertaining whether a non-white person is occupying premises in a white group area, without previous notice, enter such premises at any time during the day or night, and put questions to any person found by him on such premises.

2. The Minister of Native Affairs may, unless the local authority objects, by notice in the Gazette, prohibit a social gathering in a private home in a town, at which an African is present, if, in his opinion, such gathering is undesirable having regard to the locality in which the house is situated. Any African attending such a gathering is guilty of an offence and liable to a fine not exceeding ten pounds or to imprisonment not exceeding two months or to both such fine and such imprisonment.

3. Any policeman may at any time call upon an African who has attained the age of sixteen years to produce his reference book. If a reference book has been issued to him but he fails to produce it because it is not in his possession at the time, he commits a criminal offence and is liable to a fine not exceeding ten pounds or imprisonment for a period not exceeding one month.

4. In a township established for occupation by Africans in 1957, any policeman may, whenever he wishes, for any reason whatsoever, to inspect the dwelling occupied by a resident of the township, enter that dwelling at any time of the day or night.

5. Any policeman is entitled without warrant, to enter and search "at any reasonable time of the day or night" premises in a town on which he has reason to suspect that an African boy eighteen years of age is committing the criminal offence of residing with his father without having the necessary permission to do so.

6. The Governor-General (in special circumstances, the Minister of Justice) may, if he is of the opinion that the safety of the public is seriously threatened and that the ordinary law of the land is inadequate, by proclamation, empower any police constable to arrest any person and imprison him without a trial.

IV. To Extend Prohibitions into Every Sphere of Life, including Churches, Schools, and Hospitals

1. The Minister of Native Affairs may, provided that the urban local authority concurs, by notice in the Gazette, prohibit the attendance of Africans at a Church service in a town, if it is, in his opinion, undesirable that Africans should be present in the Church in the numbers in which they ordinarily attend that service.

2. Any person who conducts a hospital which was established in a town after 1937, and, without having obtained the permission of the Minister of Native Affairs, except in the event of an emergency, admits an African to it, commits a criminal offence.

3. The Minister of Native Affairs may, at any time, and without being required to give any reason for doing so, withdraw any subsidy previously granted by him to a school maintained by an African tribe or community.

V. To Control the Racial Integrity of the Population

1. Twenty-five years after a person has been classified in the population register as a white person, and has been issued with an identity card showing that classification, any other person may object to such classification on the ground that such person is generally accepted as a coloured person. The objection must be referred to a board whose decision is final and binding, but if the objection has been sustained, the aggrieved person is entitled to appeal against the decision to the Supreme Court.

VI. To Include Whites in the Apartheid Prohibitions

1. A white person living in a town who employs an African to do any carpentry, bricklaying, electrical fitting or other skilled

work in his home, commits a criminal offence unless special exemption has been granted by the Minister of Labour; so also does any African who performs such skilled work in a town elsewhere than in an Area set aside for occupation by Africans. Each is liable to a fine not exceeding one hundred pounds, or to imprisonment for a period not exceeding one year, or to both such fine and such imprisonment.

VII. To Prevent the Mixing of White and Black Blood

1. Any unmarried man who "in appearance obviously is or who by general acceptance and repute is a white person" and who attempts to have carnal intercourse with a woman who is not "obviously in appearance or by general acceptance and repute a white person," is guilty of an offence and liable on conviction to imprisonment with compulsory labour for a period not exceeding seven years, unless he can prove to the satisfaction of the court that he had reasonable cause to believe, at the time when the alleged offence was committed, that she was "obviously in appearance or by general acceptance and repute a white person."

A BRIEF CHRONOLOGY

1652	On April 6, the Dutchman Jan van Riebeeck lands in the Cape to plant lettuce.
1658	The first slaves are purchased.
1688	The first Huguenots arrive.
1795	First British occupation begins.
1820	Five thousand British colonists arrive.
1834	Slavery is abolished on December 1.
1835	The Great Trek begins.
1838	Boer leader Piet Retief and his companions are killed by Zulu warriors.
1838	Andries Pretorius crushes the Zulus at the battle of Blood River.
1839	The independent Boer republic of Natalia is founded.
1846	The Boers abandon Natal after the British annex it and resume the Great Trek.
1852–1854	London recognizes the independence of first the Transvaal and then the Orange Free State.
1867	Diamonds are discovered in the Transvaal.
1899–1902	The British and the Boers fight a war.
1902	The British and the Boers sign a peace treaty on May 31 at Vereeniging.
1904	Boer leader Paul Kruger dies in exile.
1910	The Union of South Africa is born on May 31.
1912	The South African Native National Congress (SANNC) is created. In 1923 it becomes the African National Congress (ANC).
1948	White extremist Nationalists win an electoral victory in May. Malan becomes prime minister.

1949	Apartheid policies are implemented.
1960	The Sharpeville massacre takes place on March 21.
1961	Nelson Mandela opts for armed struggle.
1961	ANC conducts a campaign of attacks in December.
1964	Mandela is condemned to a life of hard labor on Robben Island.
1966	Prime Minister Hendrik Verwoerd is assassinated on September 6. John Vorster succeeds him.
1976	The Soweto schoolchildren's peaceful demonstration is violently crushed on June 16.
1978	P.W. Botha becomes prime minister.
1985	Blacks fight among themselves for control of the townships.
1989	Frederik W. de Klerk becomes president of the state.
1990	De Klerk unbans the ANC, the Communist Party and all other black anti-apartheid organizations on February 2.
1990	Nelson Mandela is released from prison on February 11.
1994	The first multiracial general elections take place on April 27. The ANC party wins, and apartheid is abolished.
1994	Nelson Mandela becomes South Africa's first black president on May 10.

GLOSSARY

Afrikaans: language, derived from Dutch, developed in the period of early colonial settlement.

Afrikaners: descendants of the first Dutch colonists who landed on the Cape of Good Hope on April 6, 1652, as well as later settlers.

African National Congress (ANC): nationalist movement to further black civil rights. The South African Native National Congress, founded in 1912, became the ANC in 1923 and established itself as the principal party in the black struggle against apartheid.

Apartheid: Afrikaans word meaning "separation."

Boer: "farmer" in Dutch and Afrikaans, used to describe some or all Afrikaners.

Broederbond: secret society that promoted the interests of the white Afrikaner nation.

Free burgher: employees of the Dutch East India Company authorized to work the land on their own behalf.

Inkatha: political movement that originally promoted and defended Zulu tribal values.

Kommando: Boer military unit, usually mounted on horseback.

Laager: defensive circular formation of the wagons that transported the Voortrekkers.

Pass: passport required for blacks to move about within South Africa.

Purified National Party: extreme right-wing white party founded by Daniel François Malan, creator of apartheid.

Soweto: abbreviation of South Western Township, the largest black city in South Africa.

Township: ghetto established on the outskirts of white towns and
        cities to house their population of color.

Trekboer: nomadic farmers.

Uitlander: non-Afrikaner foreigner living in the Boer republics.

Umkhonto we sizwe: Spear of the Nation, the armed wing of the
        ANC, whose leader was Nelson Mandela.

Veld: South African savannah.

Voortrekker: participant in the Great Trek, which penetrated the
        heart of southern Africa between 1834 and 1846.

Xhosa: one of the principal South African tribes. Nelson Man-
        dela is descended from a Xhosa royal family.

Zulu: another large South African tribe.

BIBLIOGRAPHY

WHEN I WROTE *A Rainbow in the Night,* I did not set out to compile an exhaustive historical work. Rather I wanted to recount, as accurately as possible, a fabulous human epic. Much of the information contained in this book is the product of extensive personal research and has not previously been published. I would like to point out, however, that to make the account more vivid, I have chosen to dramatize several episodes and characters and, in a few rare instances, have taken some liberty with the chronology of events.

All the quotations attributed to Nelson Mandela as well as the short extracts from his letters are taken from his remarkable autobiography first published under the title *Long Walk to Freedom* by Little, Brown in 1994 and then in paperback by Abacus in 1995. This is essential reading for anyone seeking to understand the black South African struggle for civil rights and liberty.

The quotations attributed to Mandela's warden are taken from the book *Good-Bye Bafana: Nelson Mandela, My Prisoner, My Friend,* by James Gregory.

The quotations attributed to Winnie Mandela come from her moving account *Part of My Soul.*

The quotations attributed to the Anglican Archbishop Desmond Tutu have been taken from his book *No Future Without Forgiveness* and from Shirley du Boulay, *Tutu: Archbishop Without Frontiers.*

As indicated in the text, Dr. Wouter Basson, the man in charge of South Africa's chemical and biological warfare program, was acquitted by the Johannesburg court on the grounds of "insufficient proof." (See also "What They Became.") All the crimes imputed to Dr. Basson related in this book derive from the charges brought against him at his trial, as well as from three works detailing crimes attributed to him: Tristan Mendès France, *Dr La Mort: Enquête sur un bioterrorisme d'Etat en Afrique du Sud*; Marlène Burger and Chandré Gould, *Secrets and Lies: Wouter Basson and South Africa's Chemical and Biological Warfare Programme*; and Martin Meredith, *Coming to Terms: South Africa's Search for Truth*.

TO ANYONE WANTING TO KNOW more about the history of South Africa and particularly about Nelson Mandela, I recommend several worthwhile reference books.

James Gregory with Bob Graham, *Good-Bye Bafana: Nelson Mandela, My Prisoner, My Friend* (London: Headline, 1996).

Jean Guiloineau, *Nelson Mandela,* Petite bibliothèque Payot 190 (Paris: Payot & Rivages, 1994).

Georges Lory, *Afrique du Sud: Riche Dure Déchirée,* Serie Monde HS no. 15 (Paris: Editions Autrement, 1992).

Bernard Lugan, *Histoire de l'Afrique du Sud: De l'Antiquité à nos jours,* Vérités et Légendes series (Paris: Librairie académique Perrin, 1995).

Nelson Mandela, *Mandela: An Illustrated Autobiography* (London: Little, Brown, 1994).

Martin Meredith, *Nelson Mandela: A Biography* (London: Penguin, 1997).

Corinne Moutout, *Défi sud-africain: De l'apartheid à la démocratie: Un miracle fragile,* Série Monde HS no. 99 (Paris: Editions Autrement, 1997).

Robert Ross, *A Concise History of South Africa* (Cambridge: Cambridge University Press, 2000).

Allister Sparks, *The Mind of South Africa: The Story of the Rise and Fall of Apartheid* (London: Mandarin, 1991). This work is vital to an understanding of the origins and implementation of apartheid.

To those wishing to enhance their knowledge of the characters whose important roles I mention in my account, I recommend the following works:

On Frederik de Klerk:
Frederik de Klerk, *The Last Trek—A New Beginning: The Autobiography of F. W. de Klerk* (London: Macmillan, 1998).

On Dr. Christiaan Barnard:
Christiaan Barnard with Chris Brewer, *Une seconde vie: Autobiographie*, trans. Michel Ganstel (Paris: l'Archipel, 1993).
Christiaan Barnard and Curtis Bill Pepper, *One Life* (New York: Bantam, 1971).
Chris Logan, *Celebrity Surgeon: Christiaan Barnard—A Life* (Jeppestown, SA: Jonathan Ball, 2003).

On various subjects related to the history of South Africa, I draw attention to the following:
Elsabé Brink et al., *Soweto, 16 June 1976: It All Started with a Dog* . . . (Cape Town: Kwela, 2001).
Cloete Breytenbach, *The Spirit of District Six* (Cape Town: Human & Rousseau, 1997).
Josette Cole, *Crossroads: The Politics of Reform and Repression, 1976–1986* (Johannesburg: Ravan, 1987).
Eugene de Kock as told to Jeremy Gordin, *A Long Night's Damage: Working for the Apartheid State* (Saxonwold, SA: Contra, 1998).
Michael Dutfield, *A Marriage of Inconvenience: The Persecution of Ruth and Secretse Kharma* (London: Unwin Paperback, 1990).
Noor Ebrahim, *Noor's Story: My Life in District Six* (District Six Museum, 2001).
Carol Hermer, *The Diary of Maria Tholo* (Johannesburg: Ravan, 2001).

Illustrated History of South Africa: The Real Story, 3rd ed. (Cape Town: Reader's Digest, 1995).

Ben Maclennan, *Apartheid: The Lighter Side* (Cape Town: Cameleon/Carrefour, 1994).

Robin Malan, *Steve Biko: The Essential* (Cape Town: David Philip; Bellville: Mayibuye, 1997).

Mark Mathabane, *Kaffir Boy, An Autobiography: The True Story of a Black Youth's Coming of Age in Apartheid South Africa* (New York: Touchstone, 1998).

Charlene Smith, *Robben Island* (Cape Town: Struik, 1997).

Henk van Woerden, *A Mouthful of Glass: The Man Who Killed the Father of Apartheid,* trans. Dan Jacobson (London: Granta, 2001).

Monica Wilson and Archie Mafeje, *Langa: A Study of Social Groups in an African Township* (Cape Town: Oxford University Press, 1973).

ALL THAT IS
NOT GIVEN IS LOST

(INDIAN PROVERB)

THE AUTHOR OF THIS BOOK shares all his royalties with a humanitarian action that serves impoverished populations—mainly in slums of Calcutta and rural areas of Bengal in India, but also in Africa and South America.

Created in 1982 by the author and his wife, who is also named Dominique, their nonprofit Action Aid for the Lepers' Children of Calcutta has already cured one million tuberculosis patients; rescued, treated, and educated some 20,000 children suffering from leprosy and/or physical and mental handicaps; built over one hundred schools and shelter homes; dug six hundred tube wells for drinking water; distributed over 3 million dollars in microcredits; launched four hospital boats which bring help to the isolated islands of the Ganges delta; and initiated a variety of other programs for education, health, and economic development, all of which are administered through the grassroots work of locally based nonconfessional and nonpolitical NGOs. (Web sites: www.cityofjoyaid.org, www.udayan.org, www.abcindia.org, www.shisindia.org.)

On May 5, 2008, in gratitude for his philanthropic engagement, Dominique Lapierre was awarded India's highest civil decoration, the Padma Bhushan, or the Ornament of the Lotus, by the president of India.

Dominique and Dominique Lapierre administer their charitable organization with no overhead expenses. All the funds from the author's royalties and readers' contributions are sent directly *and in their entirety* to the people and projects that most need

them. The total budget for the fourteen NGOs they are supporting represent an annual amount of around 3 million dollars.

★

- Treating and educating one child suffering from leprosy
  or with physical or mental disabilities costs between $50
  and $60 a month = $600 and $720 a year.

- Sinking one tube well for drinking water costs from $250
  up to $2,500 in the Sunderbans and Ganges delta.

- Treating 10 patients with tuberculosis costs $1,850.

- Running one hospital-boat to serve several hundreds of
  thousands of isolated people for one year costs between
  $50,000 and $80,000.

★

By saving a child,
by giving her or him the possibility
to learn how to read, write and count,
by giving her or him a professional skill,
it is the world of tomorrow that we contribute to save.

★

Those moved to help can send their contributions to *taxpayer
exempted trusts*. Every donation counts—the most modest as well
as the most sizeable—and it will be used in its entirety for a priority. Thank you.

★

American citizens can send their donations to:

CITY OF JOY AID, INC.
Taxpayer Identification Number: 54-1566941
Care of Marie B. Allizon
7419 Lisle Avenue
Falls Church, VA 22043
USA
Phone: +1 (703) 847-6147
E-mail: marie@4dshift.com

UK citizens can send their donations to:

DOMINIQUE LAPIERRE CITY OF JOY AID, ENGLAND
Care of Kathryn Spink-Coo
Coachman's Cottage, Horsham Road, South Holmwood,
    Dorking, Surrey RH5 4LZ, UK
Phone/Fax: +44 1306 889 297
E-mail: kathryn_spink@btinternet.com
For bank transfers, these are the bank account details:
Bank: HSBC
418 Ewell Road, Surbiton, Surrey, KT6 7HJ, UK
Account Number: 61302914
Sort Code: 40-44-19
Swift Code: MIDLGB2159T
IBAN: GB16MIDL40441961302914

Indian citizens can send their donations from outside India *to*:

DOMINIQUE LAPIERRE CITY OF JOY FOUNDATION
Care of Mr. Francis Wacziarg and Mrs. Priti Jain
A-58 Nizamuddin East, New Delhi-110 013, India
Phone: +91 11 40 775 177
Fax: +91 11 40 775 151
For bank transfers, these are the bank account details:
Bank: BNP PARIBAS
1st Floor, East Tower (Sood Towers), Barakhamba Road,
    New Delhi-110 001, India
Account Number: FCRA A/c No. 0906506011002557
Swift Code: BNPAINBBDEL
IBAN: FR7630004008970006648210526

Citizens of other countries can send their donations to:

ACTION POUR LES ENFANTS DES LÉPREUX DE CALCUTTA (ACTION AID FOR LEPERS' CHILDREN OF CALCUTTA)
Care of Dominique and Dominique Lapierre
Val de Rian, F-83350 Ramatuelle, France
Fax: +33 (0)4 94 97 38 05
E-mail: D.Lapierre@wanadoo.fr
For bank transfers, these are the bank account details:
Bank: BNP PARIBAS
51 Ave Kléber, F-75116 Paris, France
Bank Code: 30004
Agency Code: 00892
BIC: BNPAFRPPPKL
Rib: 30004 00892 00001393127 21
Account Number: 00001393127
IBAN: FR76 3000 4008 9200 0013 9312 721

Saving one child is saving the world.

——MOTHER TERESA

IMAGE CREDITS

Page 9:   Ph. 1: Gatsha Buthelezi, South African Library, Cape Town; Ph. 2: Photo 12.com/Gandhiserve; Ph. 3: I.D.A.F./Sipa Press; Ph. 4: Stuart Conway/ Sipa Press; Ph. 5: *The Star*, Johannesburg; Ph. 6: Africana Museum, Johannesburg

Page 10: Ph. 1: PF/Agip/Rue des Archives; Ph. 2: *The Star*, Johannesburg; Ph. 3: Collection Particulière; Ph. 4: Jurgen Schadeberg; Ph. 5: UWC Robben Island Museum Mayibuye Archives

Page 11: Ph. 1: Benny Gool/Oryx Media Productions; Ph. 2: UWC Robben Island Museum Mayibuye Archives; Ph. 3: Jurgen Schadeberg; Ph. 4: Derek Carelse

Page 12: Ph. 1: Cloete Breytenbach; Ph. 2: South African Library, Cape Town; Ph. 3: Cloete Breytenbach; Ph. 4: Jurgen Schadeberg

Page 13: Ph. 1: Ullstein Bild/Roger Viollet; Ph. 2–4: UWC Robben Island Museum Mayibuye Archives

Page 14: Ph. 1 Collection Particulière; Ph. 2: *Evening Standard*/ Getty Images; Ph. 3: *The Cape Times*, Cape Town

Page 15: Sam Nzima

Page 16: Ph. 1: The Images Works/Roger Viollet; Ph. 2: *The Argus*, Cape Town

ACKNOWLEDGMENTS

FIRST AND FOREMOST I would like to express my immense gratitude to my wife, Dominique, who has shared every moment of my long and difficult research and has been an indispensable collaborator in the preparation of this work.

My ardent and brilliant agent, Jessica Papin; my talented British translator, Kathryn Spink; and my generous editor, Bob Pigeon, also deserve my utmost gratitude for their enthusiastic faith in the story that this book has attempted to recount. To their names I wish to associate those of my longtime friend Dan Green and of John Radziewicz, Lissa Warren, Renee Caputo, Joan Benham, and Paul Wise for their dedicated contribution to this American Da Capo edition. For the other editions, my thanks go to Leonello Brandolini and Antoine Caro in France; Luca and Mattia Formenton in Italy; Jesus Badenes and Berta Noy in Spain; Juan Mera in Portugal; Eduard Richter in Holland; Shekhar Malhotra in India; and JoongAng Books in Korea.

A Rainbow in the Night is the fruit of a long research in South Africa. Among the many South Africans from all backgrounds who agreed to share their experiences, memories, and archives with us, I would like to thank first of all Helen Lieberman for patiently reconstructing her South African humanitarian venture for me in the course of our numerous meetings in Cape Town, Ramatuelle, and New York. Similarly I would like to thank Deidre Barnard, John Carlin, Fr. Desmond Curran, Joanne and Stephen Dallamore, Jean-Pierre de Fierkowski, Fr. Jacques Amyot d'Inville, Dene Friedman, Tutu Gcemene, Tara and Jessica Getty, Melvyn and Sharon Gutkin, Pr. Jonker, Lynne Katz, Graham and Mary Kluk, Michele and Philip Krawitz, Fr. Emmanuel Lafont, Michael Lieberman, Aletta Lindvelt, Nobuntu

Nkanyuza, Malepa Mapitso, Mkhalema Mottantho, Piet Retief, Fr. Basil van Rensburg, Errol and Juliette Sackstein, Angel Tordesillas, Gill Washkansky.

My gratitude is also due to all those who gave so much of their time to enable me to gather the documentation for this book, but wish to remain anonymous.

Warm thanks also go to my nephew Xavier Moro, with whom I had had the pleasure of writing *Five Past Midnight in Bhopal*, and to his wife, Sita, for the meticulous research they undertook in South Africa in order to document certain episodes in this book.

I would also like to thank Gaston Dayanand for the light he shed for me on Calvin and for his valuable biblical references; Nicola Russell-Cross for transcribing the recordings of my conversations with Helen Lieberman; and Patricia Panton for her descriptions of life in South Africa under apartheid.

Finally, my heartfelt gratitude goes to my daughter Alexandra Lapierre, herself the author of several historical epics; and to Rina and Takis Anoussis, François Brousse, John and Paul Schorr, Xander van Meerwijk, Francis Wacziarg, Harriet and Larry Weiss who were the faithful companions of so many of my travel adventures.

My profound gratitude also goes to Marie B. Allizon who runs with such great dedication our U.S. humanitarian foundation City of Joy Aid, Inc., and to all those supporting my philanthropic work in India, Africa, and South America. They are too numerous to be mentioned here, but I would like them to know that their generosity is my inspiration.

INDEX